THE LOST LENNON
INTERVIEWS

THE LOST LENNON

INTERVIEWS

by Geoffrey and Brenda Giuliano

ADAMS MEDIA CORPORATION
Holbrook, Massachusetts

DEDICATION

*To Michael McClaine for giving me the chance to
finally ply my trade as an actor, and for having the faith
to underwrite our grand experiment.*

All photographs, unless otherwise noted,
are from the collection of Khemani Photographics.

Published by Adams Media Corporation
260 Center Street, Holbrook, MA 02343

ISBN: 1-55850-638-1

Printed in the United States of America.

J   I   H   G   F   E   D   C   B

Library of Congress Cataloging-in-Publication Data
Giuliano, Geoffrey.
The lost Lennon interviews / Geoffrey and Brenda Giuliano.
p.   cm.
Discography: p.
Includes index.
ISBN 1-55850-638-1 (pbk.)
1. Lennon, John, 1940–   Interviews. 2. Rock musicians—England—Interviews.
I. Giuliano, Brenda. II. Title.
ML420.L38G58   1996
782.42166'092—dc20   96–28055
CIP
MN

This publication is designed to provide accurate and authoritative information with regard to
the subject matter covered. It is sold with the understanding that the publisher is not engaged
in rendering legal, accounting, or other professional advice. If legal advice or other expert
assistance is required, the services of a competent professional person should be sought.
— From a *Declaration of Principles* jointly adopted by a Committee of the American Bar
Association and a Committee of Publishers and Associations

*This book is available at quantity discounts for bulk purchases.
For information, call 1-800-872-5627 (in Massachusetts, 617-767-8100).*

Visit our home page at http://www.adamsmedia.com

Contents

. . . .

Note: All pieces conducted by Geoffrey Giuliano are noted by the use of the author's first name in the interviews. The remainder of the content of this book consists of either press conferences, press releases, or other "fair use" and public domain materials.

Acknowledgments

The authors would like to thank the following for their kindness and selfless hard work in helping realize this book:

Editor: Laura Morin
Researcher: Brenda Giuliano
Associate researcher and editor:
   Steven Galbraith

Associate researcher: Julianna Jacoby
Photo researcher: Sesa Nichole
   Giuliano
Intern: Devin Giuliano

Jagannatha Dasa Adikari
Dr. Mirza Beg
Deborah Lynn Black
Stefano Castino
Clare
Vrndarani Devi Dasi
Robin Scott Giuliano
Sesa, Devin, Avalon and India
   Giuliano
His Divine Grace B. H. Mangalniloy
   Swami Maharaja
Jasper Humphries
ISKCON
Kashi Jones
Tyrone Jones
Myrna Juliana
Larry Khan
H.G. Sanjay Khemani

Dr. Michael Klapper
Donald Lehr
Julian Lennon
Andrew Lownie
Mark Studios, Clarence, New York
New Navadvipa Vaishnava
   Community
His Divine Grace A. C. Bhativedanta
   Swami Prabhupada
Scala Films
Self-Realization Institute of America
   (SRI)
Wendell and Joan Smith
Edward Veltman
Robert Wallace
Dr. Ronald Zucker

And, of course, John

Introduction
OF LOSS AND LENNON

John Lennon was just as lost, confused, and alone as any of us—perhaps even more so. But in his emptiness there were answers. Out of his pain and longing there was light. Fame, money, and even talent were ultimately only a diversion for the troubled musician. John was clearly a man in search of himself. That he gave in to the allurements of the world cannot now be held against him. The Beatles had virtually anything they wanted thrown at their feet by the time they were twenty-two. Who would not have become similarly entangled? Like Paul McCartney who lost his mother at fifteen, after Julia Lennon was killed in 1958 something inside of John was frozen. And however much he tried to trip, smoke, or copulate his way around it, the looming monolith of his mother's lost love was always before him. When Lennon cried out for love and peace it was because he needed it so desperately in his turbulent, emotionally empty life. The greater truth of John Lennon was ultimately about loss. The loss of his father and mother, of his youth, his innocence, his privacy, of the Beatles, of his freedom, of his masculinity and, most poignantly, of himself.

Why, then, does this talented, tragic hero so possess our thoughts even fifteen long years after his passing? It is because we are on the same journey of self-discovery. We too have experienced loss and longing, all themes clearly evident in John's soul-stirring music and challenging statements. For those who love John, the best way to express it now is to finish the great quest he started. Find yourself. Look inside. Let his powerful words and music guide you, but never lose sight of the final goal. The only certainty is our time together in life. Use it wisely. Give love. Live peace. Honor your highest self. Respect all life in every form. Transform yourself into a being of compassion and comfort for those in need. Do that, and you will not only pay tribute to the great, undying spirit of John Winston Lennon, but also to yourself. It's what John always wanted for himself and for us as well.

— GEOFFREY AND BRENDA GIULIANO
SEPTEMBER 11, 1996

I Read the News Today/ Newspaper Reportage 1962–1995

FINAL EXPERIMENTAL CONCERT HERE SET BY MISS YOKO ONO

Miss Yoko Ono, who will be returning shortly to the United States after a two-year stay in Japan, will give her final Japan concert on Tuesday, August 11, from 7 P.M. at the Sogetsu Kaikan, located near Aoyama 1-chome and the Canadian Embassy.

Miss Ono is well known in avant-garde circles in both Japan and the U.S. as a leading proponent of the post-John Cage school of creation in music and movement.

She will present her work, entitled "Strip-Tease Show," in three parts: Motional, Sprout, Whisper, assisted by Jeffrey Perkins and Tony Cox. Her work is quite experimental and, as such, controversial.

After graduating from Gakushuin Women's School and attending Sarah Lawrence College in New York, Miss Ono set out to establish a definitive style of her own. Her first concert in New York was marked by her appearance with Toshi Ichiyanagi and Toshiro Mayuzumi as one of a group of three contemporary Japanese composers at the Village Gate, produced by David Johnson in 1961. At her debut at Carnegie Hall she performed her own work, "Aos for David Tudor Opera" and "Strawberries."

During her stay in Japan, Miss Ono has performed at Ueno Bunka Kaikan, in Osaka, Sapporo and, most recently, in Kyoto.

The general public is invited to attend Miss Ono's farewell recital; admission is in return for a 100-yen donation. Miss Ono's recent 225-page book, *Grapefruit*, will also be on sale at the prepublication price of 1,000 yen.

1962

• • •

MOTHER FLIES HOME WITH SON'S BODY

An Aigburth mother returned home from Hamburg last Monday with the body of her son, who died suddenly. Mrs. Millie Sutcliffe, aged 54, of 37 Aigburth Drive, flew to Germany last Friday night after she received a telegram saying her 21-year-old son, Stuart, had died last Tuesday in the arms of his German fiancée while being sped in an ambulance to a Hamburg hospital.

Stuart's father, Mr. Charles Sutcliffe, was sailing from South America but cannot be told of the tragedy for at least another three weeks, as he has a bad heart and the news could prove fatal. The family has arranged for a padre to meet the ship in Buenos Aires and break the news to Mr. Sutcliffe.

Stuart, whose whole life was devoted to painting, went to Germany eighteen months ago with a city skiffle group, the Beatles. He intended staying in Germany for only three months, but while there he met 23-year-old Astrid Kirchner [sic], and he decided to stay on and enter Hamburg College of Art. They planned to marry when he had finished his course in June.

A former pupil of Prescot Grammar School and the Liverpool

College of Art, Stuart was described by a master as a brilliant student.

In a recent art exhibition in Liverpool, millionaire John Moores bought one of Stuart's paintings. Said his 20-year-old sister, Joyce, "Stuart lived for painting. His whole life was devoted to the subject, and his greatest wish was to have an exhibition of his own in Liverpool."

A few weeks ago he paid a surprise visit to his family, but his sister said he appeared very quiet and not at all his usual self.

Joyce added, "We had a letter last Monday saying Stuart had been taken ill and doctors could not diagnose the trouble."

A postmortem was made before Mrs. Sutcliffe flew home on Sunday with her son's body. A blood clot on the brain was given as the cause of his death.

APRIL 1962

• • •

HAIRCUTS DUE

Question: Are the Beatles men or girls? I heard they were girls dressed as men with wigs.

— *DARLENE PEFFER, NEW HOPE, PA*

Answer: The pride of the British Commonwealth are regular fellows. John Lennon, the eldest of the singing group, is married and a father. The boys' long, flowing locks are their own.

1964

• • •

BEATLES SEEK DIVERSION

"During filming," says Walter Shenson, "for *Help!* in which the boys run into a store. We decided to film it on location, using a good Bond St. store. We picked a Sunday and the boys did their scene.

"While the crew was changing camera locations to shoot the scene again, the boys stayed in the store. John took one look around, he is furnishing a new house, and said, 'I'll take that and that and that.'

"In the seven minutes it took for the new setup, John bought a desk, a grandmother's clock—he was very proud that it was a grandmother's and not a grandfather's clock—and leather-bound sets of George Bernard Shaw and A. A. Milne."

MAY 1965

• • •

BEATLE CRUSHED BY AWARD FUSS

LONDON—"It almost makes us wish we'd never got it," said Beatle John Lennon today of the fuss over Queen Elizabeth's award of royal citations to him and his three mop-top partners.

They were made members of the Order of the British Empire (MBE) last week. This entitles the Beatles to add an "esquire" to their names and wear a medal.

"I understand a few people saying they don't think much of it," Lennon said, "but for people actually to send back their MBEs to the queen, there must be something wrong with them."

Lennon's comment was the first from the Beatles since a howl of protest arose because the queen decorated the entertainers. British war heroes are returning their own royal awards in protest.

"I reckon we got it for exports, and the citation should have said that," Lennon said. The Beatles' personal appearances and record sales abroad have earned Britain several millions in various foreign currencies.

The award traditionally has been given for long and faithful service to Britain or for outstanding performance in the arts or professions. All such royal honors are made in the name of the monarch, but they are made on the recommendation of the prime minister.

JUNE 2, 1965

• • •

NINETEENTH CENTURY HAD "BEATLES"

CLYDE, N.Y.—Workmen who were tearing down a house here found a printed card announcing a dance at Perkins Hall, Tuesday evening, April 9, 1878.

The card also announced: "Music by the Beatles, full orchestra."

Nobody in this central New York village can recall the Beatles of '78 or Perkins Hall.

1965

• • •

JOHN PASSES L-TEST

Beatle John Lennon passed his driving test the first time at Weybridge, Surrey, today. He drove his white Austin Mini. "I left the Rolls at home," he said.

John had only seven hours' tuition before taking his test, taken by Weybridge's senior examiner, Mr. Scrine.

His instructor, Mr. Paul Wilson said: "He was one of the most apt pupils I have had to teach in my 30 years' experience of driving instruction. He has done very well in such a short time. He has been very quick."

Afterwards, John said: "I'm very pleased I passed."

John's wife, Cynthia, passed her test at the second attempt last October.

The Lennons live at St. George's Hill, Weybridge.

FEBRUARY 15, 1965

• • •

MISUNDERSTOOD, BEATLE ASSERTS

CHICAGO—"I'm sorry I said it, really. I never meant it as a lousy, anti-religious thing," apologized Beatle John Lennon.

He attempted to explain Thursday night his remarks about Christianity, which set off boycotts and bonfires in the United States.

The main thing, Lennon said, is that he was misunderstood.

"I wasn't saying whatever they're saying I was saying," he told a news conference. "I was sort of deploring the current attitude toward Christianity."

He added, "From what I've read or observed, it (Christianity) just seems to me to be shrinking, to be losing contact."

Paul McCartney added, "And we all deplore the fact."

Lennon said he was "worried to death" about the controversy aroused by his statements that the Beatles "are more popular than Jesus" and that "Christianity will go."

1966

• • •

LENNON'S STUDY—"BUT IT'S TRUE"

CHICAGO—John Lennon, of Britain's Beatles, said Thursday he was sorry he ever compared the popularity of the mop-topped quartet to Jesus Christ. But he insisted it was true, the Beatles *are* more popular.

Speaking before television cameras on the 27th floor of the plush Astor Hotel, Lennon said, "I suppose if I had said television was more popular than Jesus, I would have got away with it. I am sorry I opened my mouth."

Lennon went on to explain that in making the statement, he was "deploring" what seemed to be a decline of religious zeal.

"I'm not anti-God, anti-Christ or anti-religion. I was not knocking it (religion). I was not saying we are greater or better," Lennon said.

At this point another of the Beatles, George Harrison, said of Lennon: "I know him. He believes in Christianity. But I do agree with him that Christianity is on the wane."

The four Beatles agreed that public reaction, such as recent record burnings, worried them.

"I think it's a bit silly," Lennon said. "If they don't like us, why don't they just not buy the records."

In Indianapolis, meanwhile, about 1,000 teenagers threw Beatle records and souvenirs into a bonfire at a "Beatle burning" sponsored by the Catholic Youth Organization (CYO) of St. Catherine of Siena Church Tuesday night.

Police arrested two brothers, 14 and 15 years old, on charges of disorderly conduct and taunting an officer, after police tried to put out the bonfire with fire extinguishers.

AUGUST 12, 1966

• • •

JOHN BUYS A ROLLS

Beatle John Lennon took delivery of his rainbow-colored Rolls yesterday.

His £11,000 car has been painted mainly yellow, with bunches of flowers on the door panels. Blue, red, green and white have been used in the color scheme. The car also has the sign of the zodiac on the roof.

The work was done by a firm of coach builders and paint sprayers at Chertsey, Surrey.

Mr. John Fallon, aged 50, the firm's managing director, said: "It took about five weeks to do."

He refused to reveal the cost.

MAY 26, 1967

• • •

AT HOME WITH LENNON

The Lennon family home is in Weybridge, five miles outside of London. John paid a good deal of money for his magnificent old Tudor-type home, but he spent twice as much again making the interior the way he wanted it.

The grounds took a good bit of organizing too. Note the old caravan John had painted up for little Julian, and don't miss the large swimming pool. Now that we're here at the poolside, let's skip the formality of using John's front door. Just follow me through these sliding glass doors, and here we are in his living room.

What a fantastic collection of ornaments, posters and odd bits of furniture! Luckily the room is so vast, there's space for everything. Beneath it all there is this very fine, very deep carpet, luxurious suite and antique coffee table upon which John has left a game of chess half completed!

Cynthia Lennon looks after all her own cookery. Mind you, what woman wouldn't with such a marvelously furnished kitchen to work in!

1967

• • •

ONO SUFFERS MISCARRIAGE

Yoko Ono Cox, the Japanese artist and friend of John Lennon of the Beatles, has had a miscarriage in Queen Charlotte's Maternity Hospital W. Mr. Lennon has said he was the father.

NOVEMBER 22, 1968

• • •

DRUGS—LENNON FINED £150, BUT YOKO FOUND NOT GUILTY

Beatle John Lennon was fined £150 with £21 costs at Marylebone, London, today after admitting possessing the drug cannabis.

A charge against him of obstructing police in the execution of a search warrant, to which he pleaded not guilty, was dismissed after the prosecution offered no evidence on this.

His 34-years-old Japanese friend Mrs. Yoko Ono Cox, who was with him in the dock, was cleared of both charges against her, possessing cannabis and obstructing police, after the prosecution offered no evidence against her.

She had pleaded not guilty to both charges.

Lennon and Mrs. Cox stood side by side in the dock. He wore a black velvet jacket and black trousers, and she was in a white silk blouse with black trousers.

The clerk told them that they could be dealt with by the magistrate, Mr. John Phipps, or tried elsewhere. Lennon replied, "Here."

The charges were then read out to them, and they made their pleas.

Mr. Roger Frisby, prosecuting, said the pleas were acceptable to the prosecution. As far as the charge of possessing cannabis was concerned, they were found in a flat which was in their joint occupation.

"When the drugs were found, Lennon took full responsibility and by implication said Mrs. Cox had nothing to do with it. There is no evidence that she did, and in the circumstances

I think it right to accept the plea," commented the judge.

NOVEMBER 28, 1968

• • •

YOKO ONO SURGERY

LONDON—Artist Yoko Ono, wife of Beatle John Lennon, underwent a minor operation at a London clinic yesterday, a spokesman said. The spokesman said the surgery was for "a minor internal complication" following a miscarriage last October.

1969

• • •

BEATLES SEEN TRODDING SEPARATE PATHS

John Lennon has confided to associates he can imagine the day when he might not want his music on the same record with fellow Beatles Paul McCartney, his co-composer since the Beatles began, and George Harrison.

Even in his most "anti-establishment" moments, Lennon never has forecast that the album scheduled for release in January will be the last in which all four Beatles appear.

1969

• • •

GROUP "NO LONGER THOUGHT OF AS THE BEATLES"

Since the Beatles stopped making group recordings they had stopped thinking of themselves as Beatles, Mr. Paul McCartney stated in the High Court yesterday.

He was answering evidence filed by Mr. John Lennon, Mr. George Harrison and Mr. Ringo Starr, the other three Beatles, in opposition to his claim for the appointment of a receiver of the group's assets pending trial of his action to have the group legally broken up.

Mr. Lennon had stated in his evidence: "We always thought of ourselves as Beatles, whether we recorded on our own or in twos or threes." Mr. McCartney denied this.

He said: "One has only to look at recent recordings by John or George to see that neither thinks of himself as a Beatle." On his recent album John Lennon has listed things he did not believe in. One was, "I don't believe in the Beatles."

Mr. McCartney stated that when the four entered into their partnership agreement in 1967 they did not consider the exact wording or give any thought to the agreement's legal implications. They had thought that if one of them had wanted to leave the group he would only have to say so. On the way in which the four had sorted out their differences in the past, he denied that it had been on a three-to-one basis. If one disagreed, they had discussed the problem until they reached agreement or let the matter drop. "I know of no decision taken on a three-to-one basis," he added.

Mr. McCartney denied that he and the Eastmans, the father of Mr. McCartney's wife and her brother, obstructed Mr. Allen Klein in the preparation of accounts. Nor, he said, had the Eastmans been contenders for the job of manager of the group. He said he wanted them as managers, but when the rest of the group disagreed he had not pressed the matter.

Mr. Lennon challenged his statement that Mr. Klein had sowed discord within the group. Mr. McCartney recalled a telephone conversation in which he said Mr. Klein had told him: "You know why John is angry with you? It is because you came off better than he did in *Let It Be*.

He added that Mr. Klein also said to him: "The real trouble is Yoko. She is the one with ambition." Mr. McCartney added: "I often wonder what John would have said if he had heard the remark."

When the four had talked about breaking up the group, Mr. McCartney said Mr. Harrison had said: "If I could have my bit in an envelope, I'd love it."

Mr. McCartney also recalled the negotiations to acquire one of the NEMS companies for Apple. Mr. Klein, he said, had told the Beatles at the outset: "I'll get it for nothing."

That, Mr. McCartney went on, was a typical example of the exaggerated way Mr. Klein expressed himself to them. He added: "I became more and more determined that Klein was not the right man to be appointed manager."

Mr. McCartney ended his evidence by stating that none of the other three Beatles seemed to understand why he had acted in the way he had.

The short answer was that the group had broken up, each now had his own musical career, there were still no audited accounts and they still did not know what their tax positions were. None of these points, he added, had been denied by the other Beatles.

The hearing was adjourned until Monday, when counsel will make their final submissions.

1969

• • •

LENNON'S HUR COAT

John Lennon has taken to wearing hair on his back. His latest favorite garment is a "hur" coat, a shaggy black coat made from long human hair, thirty Asian girls' worth. Clothesmaker Fran Cooney, who made the coat, is planning to make blonde "hur" coats for chicks. They'll be backed with suede and sell for $700. Lennon's "hur" is backed by thin knit wool, since he refused to wear animal skins.

1969

• • •

LENNON SAYS YOKO PREGNANT, URGES PEACE

LONDON—John Lennon told thousands of rock concert fans yesterday that his wife, Yoko Ono, may be pregnant and cited that as one more reason for world peace.

Speaking over a telephone hookup from his home, Lennon told 12,000 persons gathered in London's Bethnal Green for a rock concert that: "I think she is pregnant."

1969

• • •

Yoko Named in Divorce Bid

Beatle John Lennon is being sued for divorce.

His wife, 27-years-old Cynthia Lennon, has filed a petition in which she alleges her husband has committed adultery.

The woman named in the petition is 34-year-old Japanese actress Yoko Ono.

Solicitors acting for both 27-year-old John and Yoko have entered an appearance denying Mrs. Lennon's allegations.

John and Cynthia were married in 1962 and have a five-year-old son.

Their home at St. George's Hill, Weybridge, Surrey is up for sale at £40,000.

Yoko is married to American film producer, Anthony Cox.

The hearing of the petition is expected to be before the end of the year. Meanwhile solicitors for John and Cynthia are negotiating financial settlements.

August 22, 1968

• • •

No Ticket to Ride for Lennon

SAN FRANCISCO—Beatle John Lennon, whose hit songs include "Ticket to Ride," was definitely without one Friday.

The management of an airport limousine service said Lennon was permanently banned from their vehicles following Thursday's ride from the airport to the Hilton Hotel.

Bob Higi, assistant manager of Carey Limousine service, said

Lennon left a woman employee in tears after swearing at her and swore at a driver who recognized him.

1969

• • •

Lennon Has a Brand New Bag

John Lennon and Yoko Ono have formed their own record, film and book publishing organization under the title of Bag Productions. The new venture will work within the framework of Apple but will, it is said, "funnel their creative energy into the world markets." The Beatles lost their bid to win control of Northern Songs, the company which controls the copyright of almost all of their hits to date. Plans for John Lennon to sail to America at the weekend to launch Bag Productions fell through because the U.S. Embassy has not granted him a visa. The Beatles' first *Please Please Me* LP is to be re-released on a cut-price label.

The first project from Bag will be two books, one by Yoko Ono and one by Lennon, which will be published in America shortly. British publication will follow.

The Beatles' battle for Northern Songs was lost on Monday due to a teaming-up by their biggest opponent, ATV, with a consortium of brokers representing other shareholders.

The successful shareholding groups now plan that six new members will join the board of Northern Songs, four representing ATV, one the brokers, and one the Beatles themselves.

"It's nice of them to give us one," John Lennon said this week.

1969

• • •

LENNON HELPS GYPSIES

Beatle John Lennon and his wife, Yoko Ono, are to buy a caravan school for gypsy children.

The £1,000 caravan will be installed on an unofficial gypsy camp site and manned by volunteer teachers.

John and Yoko offered to pay for it after an approach from an official of the Gypsy Council, Mr. George Marriott.

Mr. Marriott explained yesterday: "I wrote to the Beatles' firm, Apple, to tell them of our plan to put a caravan school on every gypsy site in Britain. Back came a telegram from John and Yoko, saying: "We are behind your project. Will send money immediately."

The caravan, complete with a plaque reading "From John and Yoko with Love," will go to a site at Caddington, near Luton, Bedfordshire.

1969

• • •

LENNON AND YOKO TURNED BACK AT PORT

Beatle John Lennon and his girlfriend, Yoko Ono, were turned away from a cross-Channel ferry last night.

They arrived at the Thoresen company's foot-passenger terminal in Southampton just before the ferry Dragon was about to sail to France.

But after they had bought their tickets, they were turned away by immigration authorities over passport irregularities.

Behind them in the queue was Mr. John Hooper, of Portsmouth, who said: "There was some kind of argument over their passports. Just as the ship was leaving, the couple, together with another man who seemed to be carrying a guitar, left and got into a taxi."

A police spokesman at Southampton dock confirmed that they had been turned away. "But I don't know why," he said.

1969

• • •

JOHN "JETS" YOKO TO £8,000 QUIET WEDDING

John Lennon and Yoko yesterday proved that a Beatle can get married quietly. But it cost £8,000 to do it!

They did not want a repeat of Paul McCartney's wedding last week. So they slid away to Gibraltar on a private jet from Paris, where they had been since Monday.

Only two other people were there—Beatles personal assistant Peter Brown and photographer David Nutter.

Immediately afterwards John, aged 28, and Yoko, 34, flew 3,000 miles back to Paris to their honeymoon suite in the Paris Athea Hotel.

John's first wife, Cynthia, divorced him last year.

Yoko's divorce from American film director Tony Cox was granted in the Virgin Islands.

The couple arrived on the Rock at 8:30 A.M. They collected their two witnesses and arrived at the registrar's office just after 9 A.M. to meet the registrar, Sir Cecil J. Wheeles. The ceremony took three minutes.

They both wore white. Yoko was in a mini dress, a high-crowned hat with wide brim and wooly knee-length socks.

John had on a white suit. Both wore white tennis shoes.

MARCH 20, 1969

• • •

TULIP POWER HITS JOHN AND YOKO

Teenagers stormed the Lennon Rolls-Royce when Beatle John and his wife of one week, Yoko Ono, arrived in Amsterdam from Paris.

As the couple walked from the car to their hotel, teenagers pelted them with tulips.

1969

• • •

VICE SQUAD WARNED OF LENNON LOVE-IN

AMSTERDAM—Vice squad police here began taking a close interest today in the honeymoon "love-in" announced by Beatle John Lennon and his bride Yoko Ono.

But as police warned that they may be forced to step in, the Amsterdam Hilton Hotel was keeping diplomatically mum about the "way-out happening" the couple have promised will be staged there.

Friends of Lennon and Yoko—married six days ago in Gibraltar—are being invited to witness the couple's love for each other in their Hilton haven.

No Information

The vice squad boss here, Chief Inspector Perrels, started delving into the intended "love-in" today. If people are invited to such a "happening," the police "would certainly act," he said.

Lennon and Yoko, both dressed in white, arrived last night in a white Rolls-Royce and took over the Hilton's best rooms, the presidential suite.

Lennon said: "We came here to seek some peace and rest. We want to stay in bed for seven days if we can."

In London today, a spokesman for the Beatles' organization, Apple, said: "We are not giving any information to the press. The love-in will be continuing through the week—why not go take a look?"

MARCH 1969

• • •

COME IN, WE'RE JUST MAKING LOVE
The Lennons Begin Their Bed-in as Protest Against Violence
"Couple of Freaks? We're Happy"

Beatle John Lennon and Yoko Ono, his bride of five days, took to their bed yesterday for the "special happening" which they promised would surprise the world.

And that really was that, for the only surprise was that they did practically nothing at all except clutch a tulip each.

They plan to stay that way for seven days, just sitting around in bed as a protest against war and violence in the world.

Many of the reporters and photographers who breezed through their £20-a-day suite at the Hilton Hotel in Amsterdam were puzzled at first by the lack of action.

Winked

John—reading their thoughts, perhaps—winked and said: "I hope it's not a letdown. We wouldn't make love in public—that's an emotionally personal thing."

In his white pajamas the 28-year-old Beatle said: "This is our protest against the suffering and violence in the world." Yoko, 34, in a white, high-necked, old-fashioned nightie, said: "We want to tell the youth of the world that we are with them."

She added: "We will be in bed for seven days, and we hope to conceive a baby."

John said: "We're happy to be called a couple of freaks."

MARCH 25, 1969

● ● ●

MRS. LENNON'S SURPRISING GIFT

Beatle bride Yoko Ono is wearing a new wedding ring today—drawn on her finger in ink by loving husband John Lennon.

Yoko's real ring—valued at £3 10s—is too large for her and has been sent to an Amsterdam jeweller.

John used a ball-point pen to draw a substitute ring on Yoko as they lay in their Hilton Hotel love nest.

He explained: "It is unlucky not to wear a ring, but it wasn't because of superstition that I drew it.

"It was just a romantic thing to do. We are two love-birds."

Beatle John and his bride told me the story of the ring when they invited me into their room this morning, where they are spending seven days in bed in protest against violence.

And with no other journalists present (for once), John also explained the reason he decided to marry again: "We have been living together for a year, but to get married was important.

"I used to say, 'Ha ha, marriage,' but the marriage ceremony was beautiful. It gave our relationship something."

John and Yoko are easily installed in the £25-a-day presidential suite of the Amsterdam Hilton. On the walls are messages proclaiming "Bed Peace," "Hair Peace," and "Grow Your Hair."

The couple have not been entirely idle during the lie-in. They have put the finishing touches to a new LP. It features words from newspaper cuttings set to music. Yoko sings on the record.

The record contains a recording of a baby's heartbeat. "And there is a minute's silence, which I have copyrighted for the baby, and for all violence and death," Lennon told me.

MARCH 1969

● ● ●

BEATLE SENDS ACORN TO KING

AMMAN, Jordan—A handful of "acorns for peace" sent to King Hussein of Jordan by Beatle John Lennon and his wife Yoko Ono have been planted at the king's orders in the grounds of the Royal Villa.

Palace sources said Lennon and Yoko sent the acorns to Hussein several months ago as part of a "world peace campaign" and asked the Jordanian monarch to have them planted as a gesture against war.

The sources said that, like many gifts and mementoes, the acorns were put aside, and Hussein did not know they had been sent until a secretary working at the palace came across them.

1969

• • •

YOKO AND JOHN PUT SACHER'S IN SUCH A TIZZY

Sacher's, one-time home from home of the Hapsburgs, still regarded as one of the world's most exclusive hotels, is in a rare state of panic.

Management and staff are in close consultation to decide whether to roll out the red carpet or pull up the drawbridge.

They have only just realized that the reservation for a double apartment on the first floor, which was made by the Austrian television service, is for the two great lovers John and Yoko Lennon.

The couple, who are due to arrive from Amsterdam any minute, have called a press conference at the hotel for the evening.

They are here to watch the world premiere of their television shocker, *Rape*, which is intended to show the effects on a girl of the kind of news

television treatment the Beatles have been receiving in the past few years.

It shows the girl pursued by reporters, pleased with the attention she is receiving on the first day, but as the days go by, breaking down—a result of the constant pursuit.

The highlight of the film is a 20-minute scene in which the girl is struggling violently and attacking the TV camera.

Whatever the effects of the play, it can be nothing compared to the atmosphere prevailing in this sedate, elegant hotel.

Although, once upon a time, the private dining room here served a young Austrian prince and kings as a rendezvous with the ballet girls from the opera across the road, the very idea of a love-in by the long-haired couple horrifies the management.

They are worried, lest by tonight the sedate scene will be transformed into a turmoil which threatens to make the old Emperor turn in his grave, just around the corner.

1969

• • •

BEATLE NAME CHANGE

Beatle John Winston Lennon today changed his name to John Ono Lennon at a brief ceremony on the roof of the Beatles' Apple Company Headquarters, at 3 Savile Row, London W1. The change of name was effected by Señor Bueno de Mesquita, Commissioner for Oaths.

YOKO ONO LENNON
JOHN ONO LENNON

John says: "Yoko changed hers for me. I've changed mine for her. One for both, both for each other. She has a ring. I have a ring. It gives us nine 'O's between us, which is good luck. Ten would not be good luck. Three names is enough for anyone. Four would be greedy."

APRIL 22, 1969

• • •

STAY AWAY FROM POT

Beatle John Lennon warned teenagers to stay away from drugs in a television interview in Toronto yesterday.

Lennon said his time on drugs was when he had no hope, and when a person was on drugs it was harder to find hope.

The Beatle and his Japanese-born wife, Yoko Ono, appeared on the Canadian Broadcasting Corporation program "Weekend" as part of the couple's campaign for peace.

They are arranging for a "pop peace festival" at the Mosport auto race track, near Toronto, next July.

Lennon described Canada as the first country to help with his peace movement. He was astonished when Canadian reporters treated him and his wife like human beings.

JANUARY 17, 1970

• • •

BEATLE LENNON, WIFE YOKO GET HAIRCUTS

VUST, Denmark—A female barber cut off Beatle John Lennon's long locks yesterday and cropped his hair to crew length.

The Danish hairdresser, 27-year-old Aase Hankrogh, said she also clipped the heads of Lennon's wife, Yoko Ono, and her five-year-old daughter, Kyoko. She did not say how short their locks were clipped.

"He was gentle and full of good humor," Miss Hankrogh said. "He said he wanted the haircuts so he could mingle with people without being easily recognized."

JANUARY 1970

• • •

LENNONS FAST FOR FIFTH DAY

FJERRITSLVE, Denmark—Beatle John Lennon and his wife, Yoko Ono, yesterday were too absorbed in fasting and meditation to care much about the big fuss over the new Lennon haircuts, Danish associates reported.

On the first day of what could prove twenty days of fasting, the couple were said to have taken no other nourishment than water and fruit juice at their North Jutland rural retreat.

Friends of the couple said the Lennons were "pretty tired from the self-imposed discipline of fasting and thinking and took little interest in the fact that official photographs unveiling the new closely cut Lennon hairstyles had been distributed worldwide.

The photographs were taken by American movie producer Anthony Cox, Yoko Ono's former husband, who is now host to the Lennons in a remote Jutland farmhouse. Also at the farmhouse are Cox's wife, Belinda, and his five-year-old daughter by Yoko Ono.

Aage Rosendahl Nielsen, head of the so-called "World University," an unorthodox college assisting the Lennon meditations, said the Beatle and his wife were continuing their fast.

"They may go on with the fast and the meditation until February 7th, but also they could cut it short," Nielsen told a newsman. Associates of Lennon said Thursday he would remain in retreat until February 7th.

JANUARY 1970

• • •

JOHN, YOKO TAKE A TRIMMING, BEATLEMANIACS MOURN

AALBORG, Denmark, Jan. 21—Very short, yeah, yeah, yeah. That was the verdict today on Beatle John Lennon's new close-cropped hairstyle.

The once shaggy Beatle and his wife, Yoko, both were shorn of their locks in a North Jutland barn Tuesday.

But mourning Beatlemaniacs need not despair. The hair is being kept in plastic bags, although for what purpose was not known.

Aaga Rosendahl Nielsen, head of the new experimental college Mr. Lennon has joined, said Mr. Lennon told him he sent for a hairdresser "because I just felt like shedding all that hair and because a new haircut might enable me to move about anonymously."

Looking at the crowd of newsmen and photographers, Mr. Rosendahl Nielsen added:

"Of course, there is something symbolic in the haircut, but anyone is free to guess what the symbolism may be. Personally, I like him better with the new haircut. It makes his personality come out much more strongly."

Mr. Lennon and Yoko came to Aalborg at Christmas to see her daughter, Kyoko, who has been living at the experimental college with her father, American movie producer Anthony Cox.

The last time Mr. Lennon had his hair cut short was in 1967, for a role in Richard Lester's antiwar movie, *How I Won the War*.

JANUARY 1970

• • •

JOHN LENNON GOT CHEESED OFF

LONDON—With only slightly less tumult than usually attends a royal birth, John and Yoko Lennon gave their newly shorn hair to a worthy cause.

The celebrated hair was presented to Black House, an interracial community center in North London, to be auctioned off to raise funds for the center's work.

Appropriately dressed all in black, with the beginnings of a new beard, John obligingly brandished the two hanks of hair overhead like an Indian for the photographers. Then he and Michael Malik, the light-brown leader of Black House, who styles himself Michael X, both held up the hair and a large pair of blood-spotted white boxing trunks supposed to have belonged to Muhammad Ali.

Yoko, also clad all in black, stood in the middle and looked boyish in an unruly crew cut brushed forward to a point.

Sounding a little choked up, Michael X said he'd like to "keep and cherish" the Lennons' hair but reckoned it would be auctioned off along with the boxing trunks. John referred to Ali's trunks as "the undies."

Michael X said the center needs £120,000 ($288,000). John joked the sale of the hair ought to bring in about £119,000. "Maybe some American will buy it," he said.

At a press conference, John said he cut his hair because "I got cheesed off at it."

1970

• • •

LENNON AND PICASSO WORKS COMPARED

A Picasso lithograph and a catalogue of Picasso drawings were produced at Marlborough Street Magistrates' Court yesterday for comparison with a series of prints by John Lennon, seized by the police from an art gallery. The Picasso exhibits were shown by Mr. David Napley, defending Mr. Eugene Schuster and London Arts, Incorporated, of which Mr. Schuster is a director.

They pleaded Not Guilty on a summons alleging that between January 15 and 16 at the London Arts Gallery, New Bond Street, W1, they exhibited to public view eight indecent prints "to the annoyance of passengers" contrary to Section 54(12) of the Metropolitan Police Act, 1839, and the third schedule to the Criminal Justice Act, 1967.

Mr. Kenneth Horne, for the prosecution, said that on January 15 the gallery opened, free to the public, with an exhibition of prints by John Lennon. The fourteen prints were for sale at £40 each, or £550 for the complete set.

As soon as the public were admitted, complaints were received by Scotland Yard. Detective-inspector Patrick Luff, of the Central Office, New Scotland Yard, said that when he went to the gallery on January 15, about forty people were viewing the prints.

Inspector Luff said: "I saw no display of annoyance from the younger age group, but one gentleman was clearly annoyed."

Mr. St. John Harmsworth, the magistrate, asked: "Did he stamp his foot?" Inspector Luff replied: "Anger was registered on his face."

Inspector Luff said that when he returned the next day with a warrant, about twenty people were in the gallery. "I decided to take action when we went in," he said. They took possession of eight lithographs and told Mr. Schuster that the facts would be reported to the Director of Public Prosecutions.

Mr. Napley, handing over a set of the lithographs to the court, commented: "I hope the officer will not mark them, because no doubt by the end of this case they will be worth more than £550."

1970

• • •

LENNON "BEATLES FED UP"

John Lennon, in an interview in the pop music journal *Rolling Stone*, says that Mr. McCartney's attempts to dominate the group led to its breakup.

Mr. Lennon said all the Beatles got "fed up being sidemen for Paul."

Mr. Lennon listed his experiences with drugs and said he stopped using LSD because he just could not stand the bad trips. He started taking it in 1964 and made about 1,000 trips. He was on pills when he made his first film, *A Hard Day's Night*, and had turned to marijuana when he made the second film, *Help!*

He said: "*A Hard Day's Night* I was on pills—that's drugs, that's bigger drugs than pot. I started on pills when I was fifteen, no, since I was seventeen, since I became a musician. The only way to survive in Hamburg, to play eight hours a night, was to take pills. I've always needed a drug to survive."

DECEMBER 31, 1970

• • •

JOHN BLAMES PAUL FOR THE BUST-UP

Beatle John Lennon, in a frank interview in the U.S. pop music journal *Rolling Stone*, blames Paul McCartney's attempts to dominate the group for leading to its breakup

and claims the other Beatles insulted his Japanese-born wife, Yoko Ono.

Lennon also had some outspoken things to say about the solo albums recently issued by his former colleagues. Ringo: "Good, but I wouldn't buy any of it." McCartney: "Rubbish." George Harrison: "Personally, at home, I wouldn't play that kind of music."

Lennon, who has just issued his own solo album, said: "I prefer myself. I have to be honest, you know."

"Ringo was all right, so was Maureen (Ringo's wife), but the other two really gave it to us. I'll never forgive them."

Lennon said all the Beatles got "fed up of being sidemen for Paul."

Lennon listed his experiences with drugs and said he stopped LSD because he just could not stand the bad trips.

He said he started taking LSD in 1964 and made about a thousand trips.

Lennon said he started on pills at 17 and was on pills when he made his first film, *A Hard Day's Night*, and had turned to marijuana when he made the second film, *Help*.

Paul McCartney yesterday started High Court proceedings to end the Beatles partnership.

In a writ issued in the Chancery Division yesterday, he claimed a declaration that the partnership "The Beatles and Co," formed in April 1967, "ought to be dissolved and accordingly is dissolved."

JANUARY 1971

• • •

BEATLE LENNON AND YOKO NOW VISITING LOS ANGELES

WASHINGTON—Beatle John Lennon and his wife, Yoko, have received U.S. visas and are now in Los Angeles "for business discussions," State Department officials said yesterday.

The Lennons will be in New York between May 7–16 "for further business discussions," the officials said.

1970

• • •

BEATLE WINS STAY

WASHINGTON—Watergate tactics had been used against John Lennon, one of the four musical Beatles, to oust him from the United States.

Our revelations, combined with the superb legal work of attorney Leon Wildes, have persuaded the Government to consider letting Lennon stay here indefinitely.

The attempt to deport him was based upon a minor drug charge brought against him in England. The former Beatle pleaded guilty in 1968 to the unwitting possession of a tiny amount of hashish.

Wildes came up with proof, however, that the United States harbors hundreds of ex-felons, many with far more serious drug records, under the "non-priority" status that permits them to stay in the country. For that matter, murderers, rapists, robbers and even one bigamist are allowed to remain for "humanitarian" reasons.

Impressed by this evidence and stung by our Watergate charges, Federal prosecutor Paul Curran has written to the judge handling the case that the Immigration Service will "undertake a review of the question of possible non-priority status" for the singing star.

Curran made plain that none of the immigration officials who participated in the Watergate tactics would be permitted to work on the review. What all this means is that Lennon now has a better-than-even chance to stay in the United States as long as he wishes.

Meanwhile, we have obtained startling additional documentary proof of our charges that Lennon was singled out for special Watergate treatment.

The deportation attempt, as we previously reported, came out of the Senate Internal Security Sub-committee, which still continues to stir up the old witches' brew of the McCarthy era in a dark corner of the Senate basement.

The staff prepared a smear sheet against Lennon, falsely linking him with militants who were supposed to be plotting at the time to disrupt the 1972 Republican convention.

The false memo was slipped to stern old Strom Thurmond, R.-S.C., who forwarded it in a "Personal and Confidential" letter to Atty. Gen. John Mitchell on Feb. 4, 1972.

Addressing Mitchell as "Dear John," Thurmond urged: "This appears to me to be an important matter, and I think it would be well for it to be considered at the highest level . . . Many headaches might be avoided if appropriate action be taken in time."

At the bottom of the letter, in Thurmond's military scrawl, is his signature, "Strom," and his comment that "I also sent Bill Timmons (a White House aide) a copy of the memorandum."

1976

• • •

LENNON: WHY BEATLES GOT INTO SHOWBIZ

The only reason the Beatles and most other rock musicians go into show business is to meet girls, former Beatle John Lennon admitted in a New York interview this week.

"That's why most musicians are onstage," Lennon said. "It's the quickest way to meet girls, and that's an incentive for any performer.

"The Beatles always had girls. They were always hanging around.

"As kids, we used to go to the Elvis Presley movies in Liverpool and noticed all the girls going to the shows, screaming whenever he came onstage.

"We thought, 'Hey, that's pretty good. That's for us.'"

Actually, according to Lennon the people who work for the artists meet even more girls than do the performers.

"They screen the girls and tell them, 'If you want to see Elvis—or whoever—you have to see me first.'"

Boredom

Lennon said it wasn't jealousy but boredom that finally broke up the Beatles.

"We'd been together a lot longer than the public realizes. Actually from the time we were kids. We became stale in a musical sense.

"Paul McCartney was always the most popular of the Beatles, but none of us were jealous about that.

"When we broke up, most of us were worried about Ringo. He isn't dumb, like a lot of rumors say he is, but he doesn't have much writing ability, and we were worried how he'd make out on his own.

"Now he's actually doing better than I am," he grinned.

Millionaires

In addition to the girls, there were other hangers-on, said Lennon. People waiting to get some of the big money the group attracted.

"We saved what we could get our hands on, but we made a lot of millionaires around the world," he said bitterly.

NOVEMBER 1970

• • •

UN MAKES APPEAL
Beatles May Stage Boat People Benefit

UNITED NATIONS—The United Nations is urging the Beatles to get together again for a concert to benefit Vietnamese "boat people" and other refugees, a UN spokesman said today.

The Washington Post, in today's editions, quoted a UN official as saying George Harrison, Paul McCartney and Ringo Starr have agreed to play the concert, probably in New York, and that the fourth Beatle, John Lennon, was considering the proposal. The *New York Post* said Lennon had agreed only to working on the same bill as his three former partners and not to performing with them.

SEPTEMBER 2, 1979

• • •

WIFE WAS PLANNING TO DIVORCE JOHN LENNON WHEN HE WAS SHOT

The bullets that cut down John Lennon also cut short a surprising plan by his wife, Yoko Ono. She was intending to divorce him.

And despite Yoko's long-running show of grief since the tragic assassination, another man moved into the Lennons' apartment with her just months after John's death!

Those are the shocking disclosures of sources close to the 49-year-old widow.

"She brought up her divorce plans repeatedly," says Yoko's former hairdresser and makeup man, Luciano Sparacino.

"I spent a lot of time with her during the five months John was in the Bahamas writing his part of the music for their last album, *Double Fantasy*, and she was home writing hers.

"She told me, 'I'm bored with John, and I'm tired of the Lennon name and living in his shadow.

"'As soon as this album is off the ground, the marriage is over. I'm planning to leave him.'"

Another source who knows Yoko confirmed, "She made no bones about it. She was going to leave John. I heard her say, 'I'm bored with John.'"

Sparacino, 31, who quit working for Yoko several months after her ex-Beatles husband was gunned down in cold blood in December 1980, explained:

"After all the years she and John had been together, the spark had gone out. There was nothing left.

"She also was fed up with John just lying back and not wanting to work.

"He didn't even want to do *Double Fantasy*, which won a Grammy Award for them, but she pressed him into it."

Yoko began saying even back in 1979, a year before Lennon's brutal murder, that she wanted out of the marriage, another insider revealed.

"She said she was bored with everything, with John, with her life, with being known as Mrs. Lennon instead of as a person on her own. She said she wanted a new life," the insider confided.

And when Lennon was murdered, Yoko got that new life she'd wanted.

Revealed one New York insider, "It's well known that it was only six months or so after Lennon's death that interior decorator Sam Habitoy, who'd been decorating her apartment, moved in with Yoko.

"But that's the last thing she wanted her fans to know. She and

Sam made every effort to avoid being photographed together."

Added Sparacino, "Habitoy has moved in lock, stock and barrel. He's doing nothing but living at the Dakota and escorting Yoko around."

1980

• • •

THREE BEATLES RECORD

LONDON—Beatles George Harrison, Ringo Starr, and Paul McCartney have cut a new record, friends said yesterday.

The record, "All Those Years Ago," is Harrison's new single, recorded on his own Dark Horse label. It will be released May 15, the friends said. The single is part of Harrison's new album, *Somewhere In England*, which is to be released in June.

Harrison sings the vocal and plays lead guitar. Ringo plays the drums, and McCartney and his wife, Linda, provide background vocals.

Friends said this was a one-time affair and does not mean the group was back together again. What it means, they said, is that they are still good friends and will always try to help each other's recordings when they can.

Former Beatle John Lennon was murdered outside his New York apartment in December.

1980

• • •

THE REAL LENNON

NEW YORK—Slain Beatle John Lennon was a compulsively jealous husband with a "huge inferiority complex," his widow, Yoko Ono, revealed.

Says Ono, "After we were together, he made me write out a list of all the men I'd slept with before we met. I started to do it quite casually, then I realized how serious it was to John."

Ono also said that after they began living together, Lennon's jealousy was so great he once insisted she accompany him to the men's room in a recording studio because there were other men in the studio.

"He didn't even like me knowing the Japanese language, because that was a part of me that didn't belong to him. After a while, I couldn't even read any papers or magazines in Japanese."

Despite Lennon's musical talent, Ono said, "he had this huge inferiority complex. He was brilliant as an artist, but he didn't think he was capable of it.

"John used to say he'd had two great partnerships. One was with Paul McCartney, the other Yoko Ono. 'And I discovered both of them,' he used to say. 'Not bad going, is it?'"

1980

• • •

Psychic reveals . . .

I TALK TO JOHN LENNON

A Psychic has tape recordings of what he says are his conversations with the murdered Beatle John Lennon, and a skeptical reporter who heard the tapes has been converted into a steadfast believer!

The psychic, Bob Stayton, of San Diego, claims he has made contact with Lennon and recorded some of their paranormal talks.

The voice purporting to be John Lennon said that in heaven he had met Brian Epstein (the Beatles' manager who committed suicide) as well as his own mother, Clark Gable, John Wayne, Harry Truman, and Golda Meir.

He had tried to contact his wife, Yoko Ono, said the voice, but in vain.

Composing

He went on to say he was starting to compose again, although there were no musical instruments in heaven, and music had to be communicated spiritually.

And he hoped to get a peace message to the world somehow, perhaps by appearing on TV if he could find a way to do it.

Heavenly sex

Asked how people socialize in heaven, Lennon replied: "The word gets around, 'Let's have a party.' Carole Lombard was at one party, and I took to her. I really took to her."

Asked about sex in heaven, Lennon replied: "We do the same thing here but without the body. We love sex as much as anybody who's got a body.

"The sensations are a bit different, with an interplay of energies. We don't concern ourselves with planned parenthood, since spirits can't propagate a baby spirit."

Lennon described his death as devastating. "It took me off guard. I had a flash in the skin and then I was out. It's not so bad, once you let go. The idea is to accept that you're really and irreversibly dead."

Yoko

Lennon went on to say that he had met a group called the Guides, who had helped him to adjust to the idea of being dead.

He said: "I've tried to make contact with Yoko. I think she sensed my presence but has difficulty understanding what I'm trying to say."

In planning for a TV appearance to promote peace, Lennon revealed that he might attempt to materialize during a prime time TV show, adding, "That would draw attention to me. I may try to do it this year."

Meantime, Lennon says he is writing a book called *Little Pearls from John Lennon.*

1981

• • •

YOKO SAYS SHE WILL WED NEW LOVE—WHEN JOHN LENNON'S SPIRIT SAYS "OK"

Yoko Ono, the widow of murdered Beatle John Lennon, is telling pals that she will marry interior designer Sam Habitoy as soon as Lennon's spirit gives her the OK.

"I never thought I would fall in love again after John, but now Sam has made me come alive again," Yoko told a close friend.

"I'll never stop loving John, but I've discovered I can love Sam and go on with the rest of my life until I meet John again in the spiritual world."

A confidante of Yoko said, "Yoko loves Sam very much. She's told me many times she wants to marry him.

"But Yoko is very spiritual. She's remained in touch with John. She told me that John approves of her romance with Sam so far.

"She just wants to make sure it's all right with Lennon, then she will marry.

"Yoko's just waiting for John to give his okay."

A close pal of the tall, handsome Habitoy said, "Sam would marry Yoko tomorrow. He's madly in love with her."

The couple first met when Lennon was still alive. He hired Habitoy to do interior design work for him and Yoko in their New York apartment and at their Palm Beach, Florida, estate.

But after Lennon was murdered by a madman in December 1980, Habitoy lent Yoko his shoulder to lean on, said a source close to her. "The love grew slowly between them, because Yoko was totally dedicated to John and his memory."

Said an insider, "Yoko believes that she communicates with John's spirit and that he is still with her. But now she loves Sam dearly."

At first, Yoko and Habitoy would walk together in New York's Central Park so apart that observers thought he was her bodyguard. But now Yoko is beginning to show her affection, they say.

"Now they hold hands or have their arms around each other," said a source. "When they think nobody is looking, they hug and trade warm kisses and embraces."

And another observer revealed, "The last time I saw them, it was like a total change had taken place. They were very playful and full of fun. Yoko was hugging him, fixing his collar, touching his hair."

Yoko has been spotted all over New York with Habitoy in the past few months. They attend Broadway plays and share intimate dinners in posh New York restaurants. And they've been traveling together.

"I love Sam. I really love him," Yoko told the close source. "If he can just bear with me a little longer, we'll get married."

Added the source, "The only thing stopping them is Yoko's lingering feelings toward John. This is complicated by the fact that she still feels emotionally and spiritually bonded to John. She still feels his presence around her. She wants John to give her his personal okay before she marries Sam."

1981

• • •

JOHN LENNON'S SEARCH FOR HIS LOST SISTER

If one were to believe his closest family members, John Lennon went to his grave never knowing the existence of his illegitimate half sister, Victoria. The secret, unveiled in 1985, five years following his death, sent shock waves not only through the tight-knit Lennon clan but the rock legend's many devoted followers as well.

Unearthed from thousands of entries in London's Central Births Register was found a birth certificate that dramatically documented the existence of a third, previously unknown sister. A baby girl named Victoria Elizabeth, born to John's mother, Julia, in 1945, was apparently the product of an illicit wartime romance. The infant was quickly and discreetly put up for adoption and for the next forty years remained a skeleton securely locked away in the Lennon family closet. Sadly, this was the sister John would never know.

In March of 1964, following the Beatles' first whirlwind assault on America, Lennon returned to Liverpool. Paying a visit to his aunt, Harriet Birch, John began reminiscing about his lighthearted and carefree mum, Julia. The anguished Beatle confessed he wished she'd have lived to see his phenomenal fortune and success. "You know, Harrie," he ventured, "there was also a very grey side to Mummy. I remember often going into her bedroom and seeing her crying. She seemed very sad at times."

Mrs. Birch then made a bold decision. "John," she said, "you're a man now, and it's time you knew the truth. Your mother had an affair during the war while your father was away at sea. She became pregnant and gave birth to a little girl when you were just four years old."

"It completely blew him away," a Lennon family insider, who was told the story by Clive Epstein, brother of the Beatles' manager, Brian, reveals.

According to Epstein, as time wore on, Lennon became increasingly obsessed with his long-lost sister. Brian observed John's self-occupied, depressed state and finally confronted the obviously troubled Beatle. Lennon then confided his discovery with the declaration, "Look, Brian, I want to try and find her. I'd like to do something for her if I can. Perhaps set up a trust fund and maybe eventually get to know her."

The Beatles' manager immediately hired private detectives working in both London and Norway, paying for the investigation out of his own pocket. "He wanted to keep his boys happy," explains Beatles expert Geoffrey Giuliano. [He] "issued a memo to his staff directing that the matter be handled under the strictest confidentiality. To this day, none of the many Beatle insiders have ever said a word."

It was eventually uncovered that Julia Stanley Lennon had a six-month affair with a Welsh army gunner named Taffy Williams while her husband, Freddie, a ship's steward, was away at sea. When Williams discovered Julia's pregnancy, he urged her to make a life with him. However, he refused to take along four-year-old John in the package. "To her credit," says Giuliano, "Julia would not abandon her son, and she and Taffy soon parted company." Freddie, however, eventually turned up and learned the unhappy truth. The canny Julia then devised a story that she was raped by the Welsh soldier. Later that evening, Freddie and his younger brother,

Charlie, confronted Williams, who vehemently denied the accusation. Forcibly hauling him across Liverpool to Julia's, Charlie Lennon recalls the hysterical woman laughing in poor Williams' face, crying, "Get out, you bloody fool!"

Julia's unbridled conduct in those days was viewed as a disgrace the ultraconventional Stanley family tried desperately to conceal. As Charlie tells it, "Fred had an evening pass to come up and sort things out with Julia. He got as far as her door, and Judy told him to beat it. So John's dad said to me, 'I'm sure there's something going on in that house, but I can't put my finger on it.'

"Back on ship Freddie made several calls to Julia's sister, Mimi. The story he got from her was, 'Oh, take no notice, there's nothing wrong.' Now, she must have known there was something going on. People coming in and out all the time, men, soldiers, civilians, which was certainly happening."

Julia Lennon, liberated, lusty woman though she was, could not easily escape the iron fist of her straitlaced father, George "Pop" Stanley. John's sister, Julia Baird, explains, "Pop had all the hallmarks of the classic Victorian father, for that's how he had been brought up. Deeply concerned about the effect an unexpected pregnancy might have on both John's and my mother's welfare, Pop took charge of the situation and said it would be best for everyone if the baby was adopted as soon as possible. From what I gather between my grandfather and Mimi, the pressure

was on to have the baby adopted. Initially, it was suggested that perhaps one of Mummy's sisters might take the child, but after due consideration, the only real option seemed adoption.

"She didn't go into Sefton General to have Victoria, where John, Jacqui, and I were born. Arrangements were made with the Salvation Army for the confinement to take place in Elmwood, their hostel in North Mossley Hill Road."

The child was born June 19, 1945, and within a month, a home was found for the lively little girl. "Oddly enough," states Giuliano, "it was Bobby Dykins (later to become Julia's common-law spouse) who located the adoptive parents. Bobby worked at the Adelphi Hotel in Liverpool, where one evening he met up with an old mate, a wealthy Norwegian sea captain. Ironically, the captain and his wife were desperately seeking to have a child. The arrangements being agreeable to all parties, Victoria was soon whisked away to Scandinavia to begin her new life."

Years later, Epstein's detectives were able to track the girl, now nineteen, to Oslo, where she was believed to have entered nursing school, apparently with the intention of one day becoming a doctor. But the trail grew cold when it was discovered the adoptive parents had changed Victoria's Christian name, thereby making the task of checking the records of various schools all but impossible. After six months, the search was reluctantly called off. "By then," says Giuliano, "John became drawn into other emotional traumas in his life, and the matter was subsequently dropped."

Lennon's Liverpool family were astounded upon learning the facts of this extraordinary story. "I found out not in a very nice way," admits Julia, "via a journalist who happened to mention it to me, then stopped short in his tracks when he looked at my face and realized I didn't know. I was quite upset about it. I brought it up to Nanny (one of the five Stanley sisters) and she told me only what she thought I needed to know.

"Basically, none of us children ever had any idea of what really went on in our family, including John. It wouldn't surprise me at all if John had never been told. He might have been a Beatle, he might have been a multimillionaire, but he was still one of the children; and as such, he wouldn't have been told. As Nanny told me, 'Look dear, that was your mother's life, and it's none of your business.'"

Looking back on her youth, Julia recalls her mother's "puzzling" episodes of deep melancholy. "She used to pick me up in the mirror and put her face next to mine and cry. Obviously what was going through her mind was that she had another daughter somewhere, another little girl. I'm not saying she didn't love me; I got it *doubly*, excessively, lots of hugging and loving. I honestly think I got the love of two children.

Dr. Leila Harvey, John's cousin, points out that Julia's four sisters, headed by the eldest, prim and proper Mimi, had considerable clout over the decision to give up the child. "We were a very conservative family, and Julia was undoubtedly pressured by them, because at that time it would have been quite a scandal."

Baird agrees. "I think my mother must have suffered enormously because of the social pressures. It's not regarded the same way now as it was then. It affected her whole life. It wouldn't happen that way today."

John's sister insists it wasn't really in their mother's nature to give up the infant, pointing to Julia's exceptionally compassionate and loving spirit. "Her husband disappeared into the mists of America, she was alone with John and living at her father's," notes Julia. "She already had John, didn't she? There was no money coming from his father, and Pop was already helping to keep them. Maybe this is why my mother had so many part-time jobs. Mummy already had one child, and here she was having another. Who was going to keep this one? What was going to happen to this child?"

Little did the often whimsical Mrs. Lennon know how dearly she would pay for her imprudent behavior. Shortly after Victoria's birth, while still legally married to Freddie Lennon, Julia settled in with John Dykins in a tiny flat in the Liverpool suburb of Gatachre. Once Mimi got wind of their so-called love nest, though, she demanded John immediately be surrendered into her care.

"Mimi was upset," relates Julia. "She cited Mum's 'indiscretion' with

Victoria and charged her with being an unfit mother. My mother, of course, wanted him desperately. As far as I know, Mimi came to get him but had to go away the first time."

More determined than ever, the eldest Stanley sister returned, this time with a social worker in tow. Once the official discovered that John was sleeping in the same bed with his mother and Dykins, young Lennon was quickly handed over to Mimi.

Adds Leila, "Julia did not go and dump John, saying, 'Mimi, you take John.' Mimi wanted him. John was a very sweet little boy, very cute. She didn't have children, and she wanted him. I was in the room when Mimi said to her (and she won't deny it), 'You are not fit to have this child!'"

Wrenched away from his mother at the age of five, and then again at sixteen to lose her in a tragic accident, created a lifelong torment for Lennon. "The profound attachment to his mother heightened the sense of loss John felt for his sister," says Giuliano. "The notion of her being out there somewhere gnawed at John. The only place he could reconcile his trauma was through his music. Just as he had penned the poignant "Julia" (off the Beatles' *White Album*) as a tribute to his mother, the touching ballad "You've Got to Hide Your Love Away" likewise expressed his feelings of unrequited love for Victoria."

Julia Baird recalls a "freaky" experience in 1974, when a man in his early twenties came to her door. "This might come as a bit of a shock to you,

but I'm your brother," declared the stranger, who identified himself only as "Tony."

"No, I actually have a brother and it sure ain't you," Julia replied impatiently.

The man persisted in his disturbing allegations. "Have you never heard that your mother had another child? Your mother was Julia, wasn't she? Your mother had another baby. Your mother had four children."

"Look, I have a sister, Jacqui, three years younger, and there's nobody other than that."

He insisted, "Oh yes there was. Yes there was."

Haunted by those words, Julia confided the incident to John by phone during their first contact in four years. "I told him that I had somebody here who thought he was our brother. John replied, 'What a load of rubbish. You don't know how many brothers and sisters I've got!'"

Though John laughed off the incident, looking back on the conversation, Julia now wonders if there had maybe been a hint about Victoria dropped in the cryptic line?

These days Julia can't help but speculate—if Victoria is indeed still alive, does she have any idea of her unique family heritage? Does she realize her elder brother John was one of this century's most celebrated artists? Or that she still has two younger sisters living on Merseyside?

Curious as she is, Julia admits she won't be following up where John's search left off. "Too many years have flown and too many loved ones have come and gone to ever seriously con-sider looking so far back over my shoulder. My priority now has to be with my own children. Though I cer-tainly feel a lot of love for my anony-mous big sister, I have learned the hard way how to say goodbye."

Were Victoria to come forward, however, Giuliano suggests there may be more waiting for the now forty-five-year-old woman than a loving family reunion. Would the tightly closed will of John Lennon have somehow provided for his illegitimate sibling? Could she possibly stake a claim to a portion of the multimillion-dollar estate of rock's most famous legend? Perhaps one day Victoria Elizabeth will step out of her shroud of mystery, and the world will at last meet the sister John Lennon never knew but never forgot.

In a strange footnote to the story, Giuliano received a mysterious phone call in 1988. The party identi-fied himself as the natural son of Victoria's adopted parents—her younger brother. "He had heard me on the American radio show," says Giuliano. "I appeared with Julia Baird to promote our book, *John Lennon: My Brother*. He told me he was a stu-dent at New York University and that following Victoria's adoption, his par-ents discovered they were able to have children after all."

According him, his sister eventu-ally became a pediatrician in Oslo and never married, giving herself instead to her work with the home-less and helpless children of Norway's capital city. "Her big brother, one imagines, would have been extremely proud."

1995

Square Circle/
Lennon on the Beatles

Even if I'm friends with Paul again, I'd never write with him. There's no point. I was living with Paul then, so I wrote with him. It's whoever you're living with. He writes with Linda, he's living with her, you know. So it's just natural.

• • •

It's very important to me for people to know that I actually had a mother. She just happened to have a husband who ran away to sea when the war was on, and so she had it very rough for a while. I wasn't an orphan by any means, though. My mum was very much alive and well and living only a fifteen-minute walk from my aunties. I always saw her off and on. I just didn't live with her full time, that's all.

• • •

You can't tell George anything. He's very trendy and has the right clothes and all that. But he's very narrow-minded and doesn't really have a broad view. One time I said something to George and he said, "I'm as intelligent as you, you know."

• • •

I have a great fear of this so-called "normal" thing. You know, the ones that passed their exams, the ones who went to their jobs, the ones that didn't become rock and rollers, the ones that settled for it, settled for "the deal." That's what I'm trying to

avoid. But I'm sick of avoiding it through my own destruction.

I've decided now that I want to live. I'd actually decided it long before, but I didn't really know what it meant until now. It's taken me many years to get this far, and I'm not about to give it up. I want to have a real go at it this time.

• • •

I've never claimed divinity. I've never claimed purity of soul. I've never claimed to have the answer to life. I only put out songs and answered questions as honestly as I can, no more, no less. I cannot live up to other people's expectations of me, because they're illusionary. And the people who want more than I am, or than Bob Dylan is, or Mick Jagger is . . . Whatever wind was blowing at the time [the sixties] moved the Beatles too. I'm not saying we weren't flags on the top of a ship, but the whole boat was moving. Maybe the Beatles were in the crow's nest, shouting "Land ho!" or something like that, but we were all in the same damn boat.

• • •

I've withdrawn many times. Part of me is a monk and part a performing flea! The fear in the music business is that you don't exist if you're not at Xenon with Andy Warhol. As I found out, life doesn't end when you stop subscribing to *Billboard*.

• • •

Whatever made the Beatles "the Beatles" also made the sixties. And anybody who thinks, "If John and Paul got together with George and Ringo, 'the Beatles' would exist" is out of their skulls.

• • •

Talking is the slowest form of communicating anyway. Music is much better. We're communicating to the outside world through our music. The office in America says the folks there listen to *Sgt. Pepper* over and over, so they know what we're thinking in London.

• • •

I was getting into that established, fat, professional-pop-star-can-do-no-wrong, worker genius, a record every few months, and that's all right. A few Hare Krishnas here and there and I've done my social bit.

• • •

Some people discovered a new reality and really do feel confident about the future. Everybody's talking about the way it's going with all the decadence and the rest of it, but nobody's really noting all the good that came out of the last few years. Look at the vast gathering of people

at Woodstock. It was the biggest mass of people ever gathered for anything other than war! Nobody ever had that big an army without killing somebody. Even Beatles concerts were more violent than that, and they were only fifty thousand.

• • •

I'm not afraid of dying. I'm prepared for death, because I don't believe in it. I think it's just getting out of one car and getting into another.

• • •

Touring's like the army, whatever the army's like. One big sameness which you have to go through. One big mess. I can't remember any tours. We've had enough of performing, forever. I can't imagine any reason which would make us do any sort of tour again.

• • •

We would rather be rich than famous. That is, more rich and slightly less famous.

• • •

We were a band who made it very big, that's all. Our best work was never recorded.

Watching Rainbows/ Lennon on the Music

This was one of the first songs I ever finished. I was only about eighteen, and we gave it to the Fourmost. I think it was the first song of my own I ever attempted with the group.

"HELLO LITTLE GIRL"

●　●　●

That's me again, with the first backwards tape on any record anywhere. Before Hendrix, before the Who, before *any* fucker. Maybe there was that record about "They're coming to take me away, haha"—maybe *that* came out before "Rain," but it's not the same thing.

"RAIN"

●　●　●

That's me, because of the *Yellow Submarine* people, who were gross animals apart from the guy who drew the paintings for the movie. They lifted all the ideas for the movie out of our heads and didn't give us any credit. We had nothing to do with that movie, and we sort of resented them. It was the third movie that we owed United Artists. Brian set it up, and we had nothing to do with it. But I liked the movie, the artwork. They wanted another song, so I knocked off "Hey Bulldog." It's a good-sounding record that means nothing.

"HEY BULLDOG"

●　●　●

That was written about a guy in Maharishi's meditation camp who took a short break to go shoot a few poor tigers and then came back to commune with God. There used to be a character called Jungle Jim, and I combined him with Buffalo Bill. It's a sort of teenage social-comment song and a bit of a joke. Yoko's on that one, I believe, singing along.

"THE CONTINUING STORY OF BUNGALOW BILL"

●　●　●

I was trying to write about an affair without letting my wife know I was writing about an affair, so it was very gobbledegook. I was sort of composing from my experiences, girls' flats, things like that.

I wrote it at Kenwood.* George had just got the sitar, and I said, "Could you play this piece?" We went through many different versions of the song, but it was never right, and I was getting very angry about it—it wasn't coming out like I wanted. Finally I said, "Well, I just want to do it like this." So they let me go, and I played the guitar very loudly into the mike and sang it at the same time. Then George had the sitar, and I asked if he could play the piece I'd written, but he wasn't sure, because he hadn't done much on the sitar but was willing to have a go. I think we did it in sections.

"NORWEGIAN WOOD"

●　●　●

---

* John's home at the time, on Sunningdale Road, St. George's Hill, Weybridge, in Surrey.

That was a piece of unfinished music that I turned into a comedy record with Paul. I was waiting for him in his house, and I saw the phone book was on the piano, with the words "You know the name, look up the number." That was like a logo, and I just changed it. It was going to be a Four Tops kind of song—the chord changes are like that—but it never developed, and we made a joke of it. Brian Jones is playing saxophone on it.

"You Know My Name (Look Up My Number)"

• • •

I often sit at the piano, working at songs, with the telly on low in the background. If I'm a bit down and not getting much done, then the words on the telly come through. That's when I heard, "Good morning, good morning"—it was a corn flakes advertisement.

"Good Morning, Good Morning"

• • •

"Cold Turkey" is self-explanatory. It was banned again all over the American radio, so it never got off the ground. They were thinking I was promoting heroin. They're so *stupid* about drugs! They're always arresting smugglers or kids with a few joints in their pocket. They never face the reality. They're not looking at the *cause* of the drug problem. Why is everybody taking drugs? To escape from *what*? Is life so terrible? Do we live in such a terrible situation that we can't do anything about it without reinforcement from alcohol or tobacco or sleeping pills? A drug is a drug, you know. Why we take them is important, not who's selling it to whom on the corner.

"Cold Turkey"

• • •

This was about my dream girl. When Paul and I wrote lyrics in the old days, we used to laugh about it, like the Tin Pan Alley people would. And it was only later on we tried to match the lyrics to the tune. I especially like this one. It was one of my best.

"Girl"

• • •

Often the backing I think of early on never quite comes off. With "Tomorrow Never Knows," I'd imagined in my head that in the background you would hear thousands of monks chanting. That was impractical, of course, so we did something different. I should have tried to get nearer to my original idea: the monks singing. I realize now that was what it wanted.

"Tomorrow Never Knows"

• • •

It just came to me. Everybody was going on about karma, especially in the sixties. But it occurred to me that karma is instant as well, as it influences your past life or your future life. There really is a reaction to what you do now. That's what people ought to be concerned about.

Also, I'm fascinated by commercials and promotion as an art form. I enjoy them. So the idea of instant karma was like the idea of instant coffee: presenting something in a new form. I just liked it.

"INSTANT KARMA"

• • •

I was having a laugh because there'd been so much gobbledegook about "Pepper"—play it backwards while standing on your head and all that. Even now, I saw Mel Torme on TV the other day saying that "Lucy" was written to promote drugs and so was "A Little Help from My Friends," and none of them were at all. "A Little Help from My Friends" only says "get high" in it. It's really about a little help from my friends, it's a sincere message. Paul had the line about "little help from my friends." I'm not

sure, but I think he had some kind of structure for it. We wrote it pretty well fifty-fifty, but it was certainly based on his original idea.

"GLASS ONION"

• • •

This was one of my favorite songs, but it's been issued in so many forms that it missed it as a record. I first gave it to the World Wildlife Fund, but they didn't do much with it, and then later we put it on the *Let It Be* album.

"ACROSS THE UNIVERSE"

• • •

That's about the Maharishi, yes. I copped out and I wouldn't write, "Maharishi what have you done, you made a fool of everyone," but now it can be told, Fab listeners.

"SEXY SADIE"

Life with the Lions/
The Interviews

Part One

Big John Beatle

PRESS CONFERENCE

North America, 1964

QUESTION: Do you fight amongst yourselves?

JOHN LENNON: Only in the mornings.

QUESTION: What do you miss most now that your fame prohibits your freedom?

JOHN: School, because you don't have much to do there.

QUESTION: What impresses you most about America?

JOHN: Bread.

John Lennon
Press Conference
· · · · · · · · · · · · · · · · · · ·
London, 1966

QUESTION: How do you write your books?*

JOHN LENNON: I put things down on sheets of paper and stuff them in me pockets. When I have enough, I have a book.

QUESTION: Why do you kill people off in your books?

JOHN: That's a good way to end them. I suppose they were manifestations of hidden cruelties. They were very *Alice In Wonderland* and *Winnie-the-Pooh*. I was very hung up then. I got rid of a lot of that. It was my version of what was happening then. It was just the usual criticisms, as some critic put it.

QUESTION: What were you really trying to say in your book? Why don't people understand it?

JOHN: *I* understand it. If I wrote it in normal spelling there would be no point. I'm not saying anything. There is no message.

---

* *In His Own Write*, published on April 27, 1964, and *A Spaniard in the Works*, published July 1, 1965.

John Lennon

BED-IN PHOTO-OP CHAT

•••••••••••••••••••••

Amsterdam, 1969

JOHN LENNON: Here come the photographers. Good afternoon, I hope you're not disappointed.

PHOTOGRAPHER: We're not.

JOHN: Because I heard some rumors going around.

PHOTOGRAPHER: Do you mind if I get close?

JOHN: No, as long as you don't climb in bed with us.

PHOTOGRAPHER: (*Singing*) We've come all the way from London.

JOHN: (*Singing back in the same melody*) Oh, you're expecting something else—we've heard all about you! You've got a bad image, you know, the press. So I'm looking after you.

REPORTER: Thank you very much, John.

JOHN: Hey, for old times' sake, sing "Remember When We Were in Bed Together in Amsterdam!"

REPORTER: Do you remember when we were in bed together?

JOHN: That's it, lads.

REPORTER: Thank you.

John Lennon and Yoko Ono
BED-IN PRESS CONFERENCE #1
Amsterdam, 1969

John Lennon: We'd had the idea to do this event before we even got married. We'd stay in bed for seven days and grow our hair or go to the Albert Hall and just grow our hair live onstage. We had four days in Paris before anybody knew we were there. We were walking around the streets. We got married in Gibraltar and came back to Paris.* So we didn't announce it or see anybody.

Question: Has your recent relationship with the Beatles changed?

John: I mean, that's said of any pop star that's gotten married. I can't build my life around what other people's reactions are going to be. I must lead my life as well as I can, and whatever the reactions are, I'll make the best of it. I can't be aware of every twelve-year-old and what they're going to say about what I do. It's always been someone else's job, even Beatlemania. Even if the audience changes, there will always be people who know what we are doing.

Question: What do you mean by "event"?

Yoko Ono: Everything we do is a happening. All of our events are directly connected with society. Even if you cough, that will affect the whole world. With anything we do, we're responsible to society too. We would like to communicate with the world. They're the people who share the same feelings about peace. This event is called "Bed Peace," and it's not p-i-e-c-e, it's p-e-a-c-e. Let's just stay in bed and grow hair instead of being violent.

Question: How about that story in the British papers that indicated you are going to make love in public?

John: That's *your* idea. I think it's a possibility for someone else. We'd produce that show rather than be in it! We're a bit reserved. Derek† might have hacked it up a bit. I wouldn't put it past him, but I don't really think he would.

Question: Then you deny it?

---

* The Lennons spent their honeymoon in the City of Light for seven days, from March 25–31, 1969.

† Derek Taylor, the Beatles' longtime press representative and close friend who works for Apple to this day. Over the years, Lennon carried out a long and semi-regular correspondence with the former Liverpool newspaperman.

JOHN: I do deny it. I doubt it very much. I haven't communicated with him much, because he's having a baby and I don't know what he's doing. I doubt very much he'd say that. He probably said, "You never know."

YOKO: But then conceptually we are making love. You talk about making love in just one way. Conceptually we are all making love, and it should be like that, instead of making babies.

QUESTION: I noticed your wife is wearing a wedding ring and you are not.

JOHN: Well, in England it isn't so often the man wears a ring, but occasionally they do. I found it irritating, but I'll do it if Yoko wishes me to. We just never thought of it. I know on the Continent they both wear a ring, but it's not a thing here . . . Back me up, back me up! Do they both wear rings in Wiggam?

QUESTION: I've not seen any man in Wiggam wearing a ring.

JOHN: I think it's a self-conscious English thing. It may be good to change it.

YOKO: It's an old ritual. It's symbolic, saying, "You belong to me now."

JOHN: Yeah, but I should wear one as well.

QUESTION: Why was it important for you to get married?

YOKO: It's the best happening yet if you are really in love.

JOHN: When we got divorced, we weren't aware of how great it was to have a piece of paper saying, "You're free." We felt free anyway and didn't consider the paper or not. It would just be nice to have a legal divorce.

QUESTION: If you're marriage should fail, would it change your ideas on marriage?

JOHN: That's like saying, "If there is an earthquake"—that's what that question means to me. I can't speculate if this marriage is going to work, or if you're going to die.

QUESTION: Do you want a baby?

JOHN: Yeah, if we have babies, we have them. We're not trying not to, though. We think it might be nice to conceive in Amsterdam. It's a beautiful place, with the youth doing all their things. It's a beautiful city to look at—if you live here, you know it. We all went round a bit in the early morning, and you can smell it. Even in this room you can smell it.

QUESTION: You have no plans to go out and see the city this time?

JOHN: Well, the whole event is for us to stay in bed, and we know it's quite hard to stay in bed. I did it in India. It's very hard to stay in one room.

QUESTION: You learned it in India?

JOHN: I did it because I wanted to. We consider the small sacrifice of staying in a room worth it because of the effect we think it will have.

QUESTION: You have a certain image, and you've changed your image.

JOHN: *You* change it, I don't. I am just myself, and the image I project, like how much hair I've got, or whether I wear blue or green glasses, or whether I paint my nails, is a matter of choice. I know we had a Beatle image, and we had a pre-Beatle image and after-Beatle image. I had a Lennon image and a John image, two separate things. And there was a Paul image and a George image. We can't be conscious of these things. The more time you spend wondering about these things, you can't do the work.

YOKO: We're just being—especially John, who is always very honest and one of the greatest men I know. He's just being himself.

QUESTION: Can we talk a second about Apple? Do you have any plans to open another boutique here in Amsterdam?

JOHN: No. We've no boutiques in London either. Apple is going to be a production company.

QUESTION: Is it true Apple is doing badly financially?

JOHN: I made that statement, but since then we brought in a man called Allen Klein, who's sewing it all together. He's the only man who has the ability to replace Brian. He also handles the Rolling Stones. He's the only man we've met out of all the people over the last two years, as we've been floundering about trying to do it ourselves, that could possibly replace Brian on a personal and business basis.

QUESTION: How much have you lost at Apple?

JOHN: I haven't a clue. I just knew it was slipping away. We wasted it—it could have been used better. We were trying to do something and couldn't do it. We have to have businessmen to do it. We're not businessmen.

QUESTION: But when you mention Apple, it's the whole of Apple, not Apple Records, which is apparently going really well.

JOHN: Yeah, Apple Records is doing fine, with the hits and all that, but as a company, we were spending too much money to produce the things. We could have done it much cheaper and more effectively, but we've learned.

QUESTION: You've kept the name?

JOHN: Sure! The concept of Apple is what we created. Apple is beautiful—we wanted to do something nice with it. Only the function of it, doing it, didn't turn out too well. It wasn't disastrous, but the statement I made was, "If we went on for another six months it would be near the line and we'd have to do some spectacular work to pull it out."

YOKO: John was being too honest by saying that in six months Apple might go broke, and the press reported, "Apple is broke," which wasn't true.

JOHN: There's no point having a business that keeps telling you how great it is and then goes broke. It looks even more foolish, I think. We could have kept up an image of it going fine and gotten away with it. But I figure, be straight with it. If it's not going well, say in the adverts for Apple that "the company's losing this month, so please buy." It's like that rental car agency saying, "We're second best." It's that kind of honesty.

QUESTION: How long would you say, in seven days, your hair will grow?

JOHN: I don't know. We might have to get the scientists in for that one.

QUESTION: Will you keep protesting your whole life?

JOHN: Sure, in our own way, until it changes.

QUESTION: Are there any protest songs on your record?

JOHN: All of our albums have protest songs on them, even the early ones.

QUESTION: But not all of the Beatles have the same idea of protesting as you do.

JOHN: No, we are all individuals, but we are all aware that the Beatles as a whole have some effect on people, and we'd prefer it to be a happy effect, not a bad one. There's enough between us to sustain them.

QUESTION: Is this your last marriage?

JOHN: I hope so. I believe it is.

YOKO: I hope so too. It's just the greatest happening. Everything you do in life is an event.

QUESTION: Are you eating normally while you're here?

JOHN: No, we don't eat meat or fish.

QUESTION: But will you do it *normally* during this event?

JOHN: They're getting food for us while we're here. All we need is brown rice and vegetables, that's enough. Seeing how we're to stay seven days, it would be better if we had a stricter diet because it makes you higher, and then we can face the seven days better. It's a permanent trip eating brown rice.

QUESTION: You once said you were more popular than Jesus. Any comment?

JOHN: I'll leave that for you to judge.

QUESTION: Is God part of your marriage?

JOHN: Sure. *God is everything.*

QUESTION: How's Apple at the moment?

JOHN: Fine, thank you.

QUESTION: The Beatles are staying together?

JOHN: Sure, the Beatles are a good vibration. That's one reason to stay together—to produce the effect Beatles has.

QUESTION: Do you get along well together?

JOHN: Sure we do, and we fight like anybody else, and we get along well. But as everything is, the fights are exaggerated. George has an argument with Paul and it's in the papers that George and I have a fistfight. We're human, we'll stay together. We're not going to kick a gift horse in the mouth.

QUESTION: Do you see a development towards a more Oriental sound in your music?

JOHN: I don't perceive where I'm going and what the next sounds are going to be. They're the people who come and go every week, because they're thinking, "What's going to happen next? I must get in on this craze," and the craze is gone by the time they've realized it. Crazes aren't created by sitting down and thinking about them. They happen, and the people who make them are the people who invented them, even if they consciously don't try. The people who sit behind desks and try and invent images and pop figures don't last long, usually. Before the next war they should let all the soldiers take their pants off and fight and see how funny that is. It'd be great.

John Lennon and Yoko Ono
BED-IN PRESS CONFERENCE #2
Amsterdam, 1969

JOHN LENNON: We're promoting peace for the whole world, but mainly aiming towards the youth. We are appealing mainly to people with violent inclinations for change. We believe violent change doesn't really accomplish anything in the long term, because in the over two-thousand-plus years we've been going, all the violent revolutions have come to an end, even if they've lasted fifty or one hundred years. The few people who have tried to do it our way, unfortunately, have been killed, i.e., Jesus, Gandhi, Kennedy, and Martin Luther King. The way we might escape being killed is that we have a sense of humor and that the worst, or the least, we can do make people laugh.

QUESTION: Can you give some examples of things you dislike?

JOHN: We're mainly antiviolence in all forms, and antisuppression.

QUESTION: Not war and those big problems, but . . .

JOHN: The big problems are the only ones to handle! It's no good changing the local post office when the government is the thing responsible for it. We're all responsible for what happens and to change people's altitudes to what's going on, first, and then they'll see that society's aims are wrong. We don't have to live with ten cars. There is no object having all the things we're programmed to want by the government and big business. We don't need those things, and it's no good writing to me and saying, "Well, you've got then!" Until I, or people like me, change society, I'll work within the framework and try and change it or *build around it* rather than smash it.

QUESTION: Is there a specific message for those who come home after work, watch television, and live strictly within the realm of society?

YOKO ONO: That's another thing. You don't think we have to work, but we're always working. We only took a two-week vacation.

JOHN: Any working-class people could do what we're doing.

YOKO: Working people in this age have at least two weeks' holiday, even office girls. Students who are marching in the street can stay in bed. Even if they have community bed-ins, something the establishment won't react violently to. It will have more effect, because if they provoke violence in any form, they will engender more violence. It's just a fact, action and reaction. If you do certain things, the reaction will be violent.

YOKO: We don't believe in revolution, we believe in evolution. It will change. And many young people are impatient. "We can't wait for evolution, we have to have revolution." They're very impatient about it. Ten years now was like a hundred years in the nineteenth century—it goes very fast. So, for instance, it's now possible in this age for a young, unknown girl like Mary Hopkin to make it overnight all over the world.

JOHN: We've had lots of telegrams from people of all ages, you know. Priests, hotel owners, all sorts of people. Even if they're not going to do it themselves, they're wishing us luck. I believe the vibration they're sending us is effective. I believe there are a certain amount of people who are protecting us through their minds. I believe in those kind of vibrations too, and because we've set ourselves up on the ninth floor of the world, a lot of people in different countries are saying, "Oh, yes, that's what I think." Even if they just say, "Yes, I believe," that is effective. You know, as Yoko said the other day, "When you cough, it affects the room, affects the world." If you speak, what you say doesn't end here. I believe scientists could prove that vibrations go on and on infinitely, and therefore every action goes on and on infinitely and has its effect. If you carefully think out the effect you're going to create, there's more chance for all of us. It's hard to think of your every move. But your attitudes to life will have an effect on everyone—and, thereby, the universe.

YOKO: There were many pacifists before us—Gandhi, and so forth, and gurus who meditate high in the mountains. I think those vibrations are very important, too. Or Martin Luther King, who preached, and John Kennedy, who did it with politics, those vibrations are all very important too. But the difference between those people and us is the fact that we're funny. We're not just meditating on a stone, we're in bed, which is the most human thing you can think of. We are sending a conceptual lovemaking vibration all over the world! So it's not like meditating with just water and air in the mountains. There's a big difference—this is very human and today. For the young people to change the world, they shouldn't try to change it by preaching, politicking, or even being a guru. *Everybody's a guru.* You can meditate right in your bed. Our religion is based on the basic principles of Christianity, Hinduism, Buddhism, Communism, any "ism" that's been invented. Most of them are in vented by a man with good intentions—it's the distortion of the facts we're against. So we are Christians, Buddhists, and Communists. We believe the message was the same throughout the world.

QUESTION: But before you thought this you were Catholic?

John: I was brought up Church of England, which means you lived in England and went to the local church.

Yoko: I went through all sorts of phases, and I'm sure John has too. This is typical of this age, because everybody goes through *Das Kapital*, Zen Buddhism, and everything. This is the age where everybody gets acquainted with all sorts of wisdom.

Question: You don't use the word "religion"?

John: We don't want to be in a bag or an "ism." All "isms" we accept on their basic principles. They're all the same, they all say the same thing.

Yoko: In other words, coexistence. Once you make a statement, you immediately become dangerous. A statement is dangerous, because that immediately kills other statements.

Question: Like what John said about Jesus. Did this paint you in a corner?

John: Yes.

Yoko: If you believe in Jesus so much, you're immediately put in a position to kill Buddhism, or whatever, and that's dangerous. Why not let all the "isms" coexist and build a future around them? We're just saying, "Hello, we're with you." Maybe we can call it "Bed-ism" or "Hairism" if you'd like, "Nowism," if people insist on a tag for it.

Question: What did you learn from your Eastern adventures?

John: I learned a bit about Hinduism and Zen. I asked Maharishi many questions because he was a good teacher and knew a lot about philosophy, which I didn't. My education wasn't so hot—it ended at sixteen, really. So I learned a lot about the "isms," and I've noticed the similarity between Christianism, which I was brought up with, and Communism, which I've read about, etc. So I learned a lot there. I learned meditation, which was the main thing. I needed to be told to meditate and relax myself.

Question: So why did you quit?

John: I quit the "ism," but meditation I still do. I still believe in the principle of Maharishism, but I don't want to belong to the group.

Question: It seems funny you can be so antiestablishment when, on the other hand, you stick with them by marrying. It would be of more consequence if you had said, "We are in love, that's all, and there's no reason for marriage."

John: We wanted to marry, that's the difference. People should be allowed to marry or not if they want. I don't think people should be ostracized for being illegitimate. But we can't do this in Parliament with a law that says homosexuals may get married, or you. So you must do it by law and change people's minds. If you could change their minds, I think it would be better. Then the law wouldn't have to exist. Then we should be allowed to get married or not. If we want to be married in a church, or by you, maybe that would be functional. If there had been some way we could have said, "John Lennon and Yoko Ono hereby announce they're married—we possess each other." That would be enough for me if the state was not going to take her from me and send her back to Japan, or not allow her certain rights as my wife.

QUESTION: But you both know what marriage means—you were married before.

JOHN: Yes, but I wasn't in love like this. I got married for many reasons before, but I've never been in love like this. I always used to think, "I'll never get married again. If I get out of this, I'm going to be the biggest bachelor in the world." Of course, when the opportunity to become a bachelor came, I didn't want it. I'd found somebody, and I wanted to live with her and have the ring.

QUESTION: What are your feelings on sex?

JOHN: As long as it doesn't' interfere with people's coexistence. I think homosexuals should be free. They're more free in Amsterdam than anywhere else, it seems. Sadism and masochism is okay as well, as long as it doesn't interfere.

QUESTION: Fascism?

JOHN: I don't know much about fascism except the result, so I can't really comment. As long as it doesn't interfere with other people. I'm not saying there should be sadism in the streets, unless everybody said, "Okay, lets have sadism in the streets." I think it should be a community allowance. People should be allowed to do whatever they like.

QUESTION: But your opinion about sex is different, because issues you talk about, like communal sex . . .

JOHN: I think communal sex should be allowed if people want it.

QUESTION: For you especially?

JOHN: For me, I don't want it. I don't mind if there was communal sex going on over there. We'd watch it.

QUESTION: You'd watch it?

JOHN: Yeah, sure. But being in love is different. We're very possessive about each other's bodies. Conceptual sex we'll share with the world, but how do you approach it individually? I think you should be allowed to have communal sex if you want it, if it doesn't interfere with other people. If it interferes with a neighborhood—where people are having communal sex in the fields next to somebody's house that doesn't want it—it shouldn't be allowed for that person's sake. If they can have a children's playground, then they can have adult sex grounds.

QUESTION: There were years when money was very important in your lives, especially when you didn't have it.

JOHN: It was only important to have enough to last the week, but even when I earned ten pounds, I spent it. I let it go. I didn't save it or plant it, so I was always loose and easygoing with money.

QUESTION: Do you feel a lot of people are hooked by money in a way?

JOHN: Lots of people are addicted to money. People used to ask us this when we were the Beatles. We're not saying we never wanted to earn money, but the object was to be the best rock 'n' roll band, or be like Elvis, and the money was secondary. When we got it, it was just like what we'd read from other rich people, saying, "Money isn't everything." They were right. It didn't do a bloody thing for you except get you on a plane instead of a boat. How many suits can you wear, or how much food can you eat? But when I was sixteen and some rich guy said, "It's nowhere being rich, it's no good," I'd say, "Oh yeah? Well, give me the money and let me find out!" I don't preach to people "Don't try to find money," because I remember having no money and thinking, "Give it to me it you don't want it." Which is no good, to be handed to you on a plate, because you're the son of a rich man. That's a hard life to lead, being born with money, which Yoko was. I think it's just as hard as being born without it.

YOKO: There's always a catch to it. I personally didn't have money. My mother had some, but that's a terrible situation because she would try to control me in many ways. The fact that your surroundings are rich doesn't mean anything because you lose freedom. The terrible thing about this society is that money buys certain freedoms for you—that's why people want money. Money is a concept of freedom. You get your freedom ticket.

John Lennon and Yoko Ono

BED-IN PRESS CONFERENCE #3

Amsterdam, 1969

QUESTION: The things people have said about you haven't been very kind lately. Does this bother you?

JOHN LENNON: It's so much, it's past depressing. It's a bit depressing, however, the way they keep picking on Yoko.

QUESTION: What about the Beatles? You've gone through many phases, from four clean-cut young men to long-haired and strange.

JOHN: Well, prior to Brian, we were young, long-haired, and scruffy, and I used to go onstage in my underpants in Hamburg with toilet rolls around my neck. Then Brain cleaned us up to sell us to the public, and once we were sold, we relaxed and became ourselves.

QUESTION: So what phase are you entering now?

JOHN: I've no idea. Perhaps I should ask you.

QUESTION: Do you remember anything from Amsterdam when you were here in 1963?

JOHN: Yes, I remember being held up in a hotel.

QUESTION: What are your plans for the future?

JOHN: Well, we have a few films we're going to make. This looks like the start of one. We have an LP coming out and new things we're thinking up all the time.

QUESTION: Nice room.

JOHN: Yeah, we were thinking about conceiving a child here and calling it Hilton Lennon or Peace Lennon. It would be great to call it Peace Lennon.

QUESTION: You say everybody is equal, but some people are more equal than others.

JOHN: But they are all infinite. They all have infinite possibilities, my friend.

QUESTION: You would subscribe to that philosophy? Personally, I am not much of a philosopher.

JOHN: No, me neither.

QUESTION: Just a plain reporter.

JOHN: Just a plain singer.

QUESTION: I get the impression you're very sensible.

JOHN: Well, I'm pretty old and she's pretty old, but we still have a sense of humor.

John Lennon and Yoko Ono
BED-IN PRESS CONFERENCE #4
Amsterdam, 1969

QUESTION: Will you see Holland at all?

JOHN LENNON: We're giving Holland a chance to see us.

QUESTION: Have you heard these reports from London in the *News of the World*?

JOHN: I don't know any more about it than you do. Somebody phoned me in the middle of the night to ask if I'd had an offer to play Christ, and I said, "No, I haven't got an offer."

QUESTION: Would you consider it if you did?

JOHN: Sure, I'm just the right age. As the *Daily Express* put it Sunday, I look "forty and worried."

YOKO ONO: I think that because we are part of the world, anything we do is part of the world. We'd like to create a vibration and communicate with the world about peace.

QUESTION: Do you think that the Hilton Hotel is a very good place for a vibration?

JOHN: Sure, sure. If the Hilton has a bad vibration, then it's our job to come and give it a good one.

YOKO: The Hilton is very functional for us. If we had to stay in a small house, then we couldn't go out and we wouldn't eat.

JOHN: We wouldn't have people to control people if we lived in a house. It's very functional for us to live here. It's comfy, and we can afford it. We might as well use our money for the things we believe in.

QUESTION: Is there a new Beatle record coming out soon?

JOHN: Yes, we've done about twelve tracks, and Paul's in New York still, so we're all meeting up in seven days. I'll use the Beatle-free seven days to do this event and our honeymoon to speak to you.

QUESTION: When does it go on sale?

JOHN: Well, we've got to go back, remix the eight tracks and record the other four. So it should be around the summer, I suppose.

John Lennon and Yoko Ono
BED-IN PRESS CONFERENCE #5
Amsterdam, 1969

QUESTION: What is a Beatle?

JOHN LENNON: I don't know, I haven't a clue. I suppose it's something four guys turn into when they get together and project "Beatle."

YOKO ONO: The Beatle image is something other people created.

JOHN: I think of the Beatles as a separate entity—we all do. I often say to Anthony* or Neil,† "See what the Beatles think."

QUESTION: When did you get to that point?

JOHN: It's always been like that. We say it to each other: "What do the Beatles think?"

QUESTION: There's John and Yoko, the private people; there's you, John Beatle; and there's the Beatles as four boys together.

JOHN: It's always been the same—it just depends what I'm doing. I'm always John and Yoko. That never stops. We're a twenty-four-hour couple. So whenever I'm doing something with the Beatles, Yoko's sitting on my shoulder like a parrot. There are no four guys together like there used to be, you know.

QUESTION: Why are you willing to take it all for us?

JOHN: I'm doing my own thing, and it just happens that way. Maybe we're masochists or something. You probably go through exactly the same torture I do, but it's not publicized. Everything I do and Yoko does is publicized, so we only *seem* to go through it for other people. All we are doing is sharing our sorrow and joy with the rest of the world. It helps us get through whatever we have to, to know other people understand, because lots of people certainly do. People write to us and say now they feel together because they're in love, or they want peace or they like my music. So we're not alone in the world. We're going through it for them as much as film stars on celluloid. People relive the experiences of other people onscreen, and they tend to do that with us. But they also have to

---

* Anthony Fawcett, John and Yoko's then personal assistant, who later went on to write an excellent book on his illustrious employer, entitled *One Day at a Time*.

† Neil Aspinall, the Beatles' lifelong personal assistant and road manager, who these days is managing director of Apple.

do their own thing. But if they associate with us it's all right, because we associate with them.

QUESTION: But every time *I* do something, you get punished for it.

JOHN: I don't know about that, mate.

YOKO: Nobody's really alone. We all influence each other. Everything you do affects us, of course, but everything we do affects you as well. The world is one big entity, actually.

QUESTION: Are you then simply showing us who we are?

JOHN: We're not trying to show anything. We're just living, just sort of vegetating. It's a vague, vague existence. Anything you get from us is only a reflection of yourselves. We're not trying to project any kind of definite image. You're getting something out of us that probably is already in you. It's enough responsibility living up to your own image of yourself. Like George is always quoting Gandhi: "Make and preserve the image of your choice." We can see these images being made. Like we made a peace image and a Plastic Ono image and, to an extent, we've got to live up to them. It's like action and reaction [karma]. But we're not sitting back thinking it out, we're just drifting along with it.

QUESTION: You told me once in Amsterdam that you're using the media. How are you doing so, and for what ends?

JOHN: By exposing ourselves. I'm not having a press conference that lasted two hours, where the mighty Beatle spoke, but to let the press in Amsterdam and Montreal ask and ask and ask. They had no time limit.

YOKO: No matter how we try to expose ourselves, there's still many layers left. But an attempt to expose ourselves is an attempt to not avoid things, to face up to it.

QUESTION: Did you actually make that decision as a thing to do?

JOHN: The idea happened over years of maturing. It's about suddenly realizing there is a responsibility we all share for the entire world.

QUESTION: But why play the clown role?

JOHN: I've always been like that. I was the class clown. That was my way of getting love or attention. Whatever I do, I have to be myself to a degree. So now, because of Yoko's encouragement to be myself completely, I'm more like I was when I was eighteen when I went through the Beatles thing. We were all wrapped up in show business.

QUESTION: You "*went* through the Beatles thing," past tense?

JOHN: Yes. The Beatles was sort of a cocoon for growing up, and now here I am being me, and the next objective is karma, and I take it like dice-throwing. I mean, people keep coming up with an idea for the Biafra thing for us to do. There's no avoiding it, it's just in our heads.

QUESTION: Does being funny save you from taking yourself too seriously?

YOKO: What we're doing is natural—this isn't acting. We're not calculating whether it will be good or bad. We're doing our best.

QUESTION: The thing with the Beatles has always been, "It will be all right, as long as we act naturally." I don't see how it's possible to act naturally without becoming an actor.

JOHN: It's a danger. With the Beatles, it was natural. We were the four lads from next door, but it was an *unnatural* naturalness we got into. The next *unnatural* natural act we could get into was the intellectual art bag. But Yoko has been through that, and I definitely have such a working-class chip on my shoulder, so I won't allow it. I hope we'll save ourselves from that, even though we've been going to all the artsy films.

QUESTION: Are you balancing each other the same way the four Beatles used to balance each other, the sharing of egos?

JOHN: Yeah.

YOKO: The thing is, they came from the same district [Liverpool], and we come from opposite ends of the world. Also, if you think because we declared our love we must always be lovers, it's quite the opposite. We just forget the fact we are in front of people and sort of say things to each other, instead of being very cynical or something.

QUESTION: Do you want to be leaders?

JOHN: No. "I am he and you are he and you are me and we are all together." We are all one, but I can't keep saying it in each song.

QUESTION: Donovan tried to explain the same thing to me the other day.

JOHN: George came up to me after I'd written the lyrics for our latest song, "The Ballad of John and Yoko," and said, "You should have made it easier on yourself by changing them to 'crucify *us.*'" But because the lyrics happened so naturally, while I was half asleep, I woke up, wrote them down, and that was it. So I thought, "Sod it, it came out naturally." We have said it a lot of times, "I believe we're all one or interconnected." Paul and I just knocked it off in one night without the other Beatles, and it had to get out quick because it was like news, a ballad of today. Usually I play around with them and push a little word in here and there. But this was like news, like there would be spelling mistakes in the paper the next day, or five hundred dead when there was only four hundred and sixty. I didn't have time to work out other people's reaction to things. I just had to get it out.

QUESTION: But people go around in soft voices saying, "He's looking more like Christ every day."

JOHN: Well, that's a joke. There's many of them that look like Christ. But I do think Christ was a groove.

QUESTION: Well, there's got to be another Christ, doesn't there? And these days he must come from the media. It's the only place to look.

JOHN: Well, if there was one around I'm sure we'd know about it. I went through acid trips where I thought, "Oh, I must be Christ," but it was just discovering my responsibility of being in the world.

YOKO: We have come to the conclusion we really don't have to know. All we have to be is ourselves and somebody will decide later, or maybe never decide.

JOHN: Christ never said, "I'm anything"—just the son of God or the son of man, *and we're all that.* So it was all the others that laid the Beatle image on him, wasn't it?

QUESTION: If someone gave you power instead of influence, what would you do? The power to command people instead of merely suggesting.

JOHN: I don't think it would work. Like being prime minister, I guess. If being prime minister gave you the power, which I don't think it does, I'm not sure where that power lies. I'd just say, "Stop that war" and "Stop selling arms" and all that.

QUESTION: He has the power to command armies by force?

JOHN: Well, I wouldn't have armies. The first thing I'd say is, "Get rid of your arms and get some forks and shovels and start digging the land. Use them as an army to go and dig up the desert or something, and help other countries."

YOKO: It's not just John. Anybody who's written a bestselling book would have more influence than any prime minister. I believe that is a mental power which he has already. John already has much more power than any prime minister. Artists have more power, I'm sure, than any politician.

QUESTION: When Hunter Davies* left you, you were apparently egoless and leaning on the rest of the group and in a rather unhappy state. When I see you today though, you seem fine. What were the changes?

---

* Hunter Davies was the author of *The Beatles' Authorized Biography*, published worldwide in 1967. Thus he has been the only author given exclusive, intimate access to the group.

JOHN: Yoko. That was the change. When we first did the acid bit, the religion, and all of that, it was our ego that was interfering with our relationship together as Beatles. We suddenly saw each other back to when we were fifteen. We saw each other at that age, what we were back then, and what we've developed into. And then it was all reading the different books, the Leary handouts talking about ego, and we all got into the bit where we thought ego was bad. I had a tremendous ego that got me where I was, but I spent two years killing it stone-dead. And it took me two years to get it back again.

QUESTION: How was it without one?

JOHN: It was terrifying, because I'm a naturally nervous and paranoid person, and without an ego, I was nothing. It was terrifying. I just leaned on Paul or one of the other Beatles who hadn't destroyed themselves as much as me.

QUESTION: What's your star sign, John?

JOHN: Libra, so it's pretty difficult weighing me up anyway. I just thought, "Get rid of the ego and I'll just be the B-side of the record and I'll let Paul run the other out. I won't be that guy back in school who was pushing and started the group. I'll be someone else." I was just coming out of it before I met Yoko. India helped a lot, three months out there, and then the breakup.

QUESTION: The actual meditation?

JOHN: The meditation was fantastic. The meditation was as big as acid trips and changing me whole thing. Suddenly I was tapping this source of power inside myself and vast vistas of creativity, if I could just hold it and get back. If I hadn't come back and met Yoko, I would have been swamped by this whole scene. I tend to lose it all again and think I can't do anything. But then she came along, and I thought, "Oh, great, I like your drawings, I like everything." So she built me up again.

QUESTION: Did you realize what you did for him, Yoko?

YOKO: I don't know. I was unconscious of it. That's what I think was really great about us, because I'm an egotist, too. I'm a big ego!

JOHN: I had to get an ego to counteract hers, or it would have been impossible. It's all right leaning on a group of guys, because they play it very subtle, but she had to have a sparring partner.

YOKO: I was just coming to the point where I was doing everything I wanted, and it was very lonely. Then I met John, and if I usually meet a man my ego would always stand in between, and I could never get over that. I was really taken by him. It's a really corny expression, but "Love did it." Without love, the ego could never disappear. I thought, "I'm not going to fall in love or anything, because that's disastrous, that's death for me," so I was trying to escape it. So I didn't know what I was doing for him at all, really. I thought I was destroying myself, and it was a great thing for both of us.

QUESTION: What in God's name is it like to be a Beatle?

JOHN: I don't know.

QUESTION: How do you possibly live with it and make it bearable?

JOHN: It's so long since I've not been one. I was trying to re-create the feeling of buying Elvis's records in the old days. I was trying to not be me. It's just impossible. It's like being permanently in a white bag, and people are looking, but they don't ever see. So I'm on like a permanent trip, with everyone's voices slightly in the distance. I'm in a permanent high state. If people worship something, it rubs off on them. So with what I've done and what people have done to me, they've cocooned me, my life and my wife, in this sort of bag. So I'm immune to a lot of things and very un-immune—it's a bit of both. Like when you're in a white bag, there's a risk you'll get kicked when you're sitting on the floor, because people are so interested. But there is also the womb thing. I'm in this sort of polyethylene womb, and every now and then something gets through and I actually get touched. And I say, "What are you doing in my kitchen, or demanding my arm?" And then I have to think about that, but mostly it's just a kind of high or a low. If it's a low, I never go anywhere without being attacked. And then I think, "If you really wanted to, you could shave your hair bald, shave off your mustache, and go to Egypt or India, so who are you kidding?" But I want to live in England. I was born here, and I wouldn't be myself.

YOKO: But that's like losing your identity, so that works out two ways.

QUESTION: But you have more freedom now, in that respect. You're still John Lennon, and there is still a crowd of people out here.

JOHN: Of course, there's less because there isn't Beatlemania going on, and I'm acting more naturally. I don't have to keep up any image. I'm an artist now, an individual. I'm not responsible for a Beatles image or anybody else's, and I don't have to sign an autograph unless I feel like it. They're beginning to accept that, though one or two people still get uptight. I had to stop it, because as a Beatle I had to sign everything and be everything they wanted and always smile and react to "Hi" and all of that. Or we went the other way, which is hiding, and wouldn't see anyone, wouldn't see the press, kept the gates locked. But now I do it on whim, just let it roll.

QUESTION: Is everybody a stranger or a hanger-on? Your friends are still the old ones?

John: The only friends I've got are the Beatles and Derek [Taylor], Neil [Aspinall] and Peter Brown, who have been with us over the years, and a few more people we picked up here and there. People can be hangers-on as well as friends. I've had hangers-on that have been friends that have dropped off because we didn't have enough to give each other. I must have something from a friendship. We picked up a few more from Yoko's life, who are so determined not to be hangers-on, which is a relief. They pretend the Beatles don't exist.

Question: How would you describe your relationship with the people at Apple?

John: Well, Derek sort of put it in a nutshell the other day. He's a good, intelligent friend, whether he worked for us or not. I mean, there are certain things I'd ask his advice on or discuss with him or be pleased to see him about. When you're younger, you just need somebody to go to the pictures with or get pissed with, but when you're older, the relationship has to sustain a few years. I could go away for four years and come back and relate the story to Derek, and there wouldn't be a big gap between us. Hangers-on would stay at the level they were when we last had them hanging on—the glory rubs off on them, and they turn into something and go off into swinging London. But I'm a sucker for people. I go by people's faces, and if they look straight, I believe in them. I've had a lot of bad experiences like that. It hasn't hurt me much—just sort of, "Oh really, that's what they wanted." So between us, we try to watch for it. We discuss everything in minute detail about everyone we meet—"Are they conning us?"—because I've been conned all my life since I was a Beatle.

Question: Did I ask you when you stopped that?

John: Stopped being conned?

Question: No, stopped being a Beatle.

John: I haven't really stopped.

Yoko: Everything has a natural course, and when it's necessary they exist, and when it's not, it passes. So the fact that it's going on means there's still the necessity.

John: The Beatles are always discussing, "Should we go on or shouldn't we? What are we together for now?" And when it gets down to it, I like playing rock 'n' roll. I like making rock records. I've played with other musicians very rarely, but I've occasionally played with them, and it needs work to get anything good going. I don't like session men, so I try not to use them. I don't like violinists or anything these days. I try not to use anybody but the Beatles. If I wanted to make a record, I'd choose the Beatles. I can say to Ringo, "Give me 'Bee-Bop-A-Loo-La.'" Even from a commercial point, what's the biggest-selling name? The

Beatles, or John Lennon and the Fabs, or George Harrison and the Fabs? Our biggest market is obviously the Beatles. Who are our closest friends? Beatles! Who do we have the most arguments with? Beatles! So Beatles is it, until it becomes too much.

QUESTION: What has happened with Apple since its inception?

JOHN: It's done everything under the sun. Everything you can imagine has happened to it. I can't describe it, I'm too involved to describe it. Maybe in two years I can answer that. I don't know what it is, what it's for, or what the hell it's going to do or what it's about or anything.

QUESTION: And Brian, is he still missed?

JOHN: I don't think of him very often. I mean, he's certainly missed when we realize we have to solve all the business things. I'm one of those "out of sight, out of mind" people, really. I've a real resistance to sorrow. I forget about things the next day, which is very lucky. I remember odd things, but really I've got a good buffer, a protective thing in my mind.

QUESTION: So you'll stay where you are in the foreseeable future?

JOHN: Yeah, until we get into the next bag. I hopped into this bag with Yoko, and it's always changing. We keep changing our bags. If the bag gets bigger, then that's the bit. I've got out of one bag, a Beatle pop bag, and she got out of her avant-garde bag, and we got into a bigger bag, so there's more room to breathe. So the game is to keep expanding the consciousness of the bag.

John Lennon and Yoko Ono

ROOM CHAT

• • • • • • • • • • •

London, 1969

AIDE: So what this bloke is apparently saying, John, is that the Immigration Department is inviting you, and they're offering to charter a plane to take other people over, for this massive concert. They want to do a peace thing, and they're offering to put you up in a castle this weekend.

YOKO ONO: When is this?

JOHN LENNON: In a castle?

AIDE: Why it's suddenly all happening I don't know, but I've asked the Immigration Department to ring us within the next half hour from Canada.

JOHN: Sounds great. If only we could get Eric and George and a few people. It sounds very good, this Canadian thing.

YOKO: Yes, it does.

AIDE: I've got Ritchie Yorke* from Canada outside.

JOHN: Who's Ritchie Yorke?

AIDE: The *Rolling Stone* reporter with the ginger walrus mustache.

JOHN: Oh, we saw him out there.

AIDE: He wants to pay his respects because he's interviewing George on Monday.

JOHN: Maybe he knows a bit about Canada.

(*Yorke enters the room.*)

JOHN: Hi, how are you? Maybe you could help us here. We just *seem* to be getting lies from Canadian Immigration saying they'll give us a chartered plane to go play a rock concert this weekend.

RITCHIE: Oh, tomorrow, yeah.

YOKO: And put us up in a castle or something. What is this?

---

* Ritchie Yorke is the noted rock journalist and author who went on to work as a personal assistant and peace envoy to John and Yoko in 1969. After returning home to his native Australia in the late eighties, Yorke once again resumed a successful career as a broadcast/print journalist.

Ritchie: There's a "Toronto Rock 'n' Roll Revival" on tomorrow which has Jerry Lee Lewis, Gene Vincent, and Little Richard. They got them all together, and Kim Fahey and the Doors. A nice little scene. I know the two guys who are running it, but I didn't know . . .

Yoko: Is it people who's running it, or the State Department?

Ritchie: One of the Eatons is involved, I know. They probably have pretty good legal connections through their fathers.

John: Well, we seem to be getting invites from the Immigration Department, but I'm not sure about it.

Yoko: Do you want to find out? I mean, do you think you can find out for us? It would be very nice of you.

Ritchie: Yeah, sure, I can call them up.

Question: What's his name?

Ritchie: John Brower.*

Aide: He's the one who was on the phone just now. He was just talking to Bill upstairs.

Ritchie: Good God.

Question: Well, we can give him a ring back. Do you know his number?

John: Find out how much, too!

Aide: (*Speaking via an interoffice intercom*) Hello? Bill, was that John Brower that just phoned? It was? Ritchie, have you got his number?

Ritchie: Here we are.

John: It won't turn into a rocker's festival, will it?

Ritchie: Oh, no, it's not that sort of thing.

John: It would be nice if we could get a group together to take over. I wonder if George would do it? No, I doubt if he'd come all the way to Canada. I don't really need Ringo, I need a group, you know.

Aide: Would Paul go?

---

* Of Brower and Walker, a successful Toronto-based group of rock promoters in the late sixties. Also planned by the firm was a "Peace Festival" with John and Yoko, which eventually came to nothing.

JOHN: No, no. George is the only hope. He was going to do the Hyde Park thing with me.*

YOKO: George and Eric might go.

JOHN: Eric might come. Could you ring George and ask if he can get me a group together for tomorrow night in Canada?

---

* This refers to a heretofore unknown, though obviously planned, free concert in London's Hyde Park by John and Yoko. Earlier shows had featured the Rolling Stones and Blind Faith.

John Lennon and Yoko Ono
BED-IN PRESS CONFERENCE
Montreal, 1969

QUESTION: Mr. Lennon, in 1941 and Hitler was in power, the Americans came to the aid of the British nation. Would you have preached your philosophy to the American people then?

JOHN LENNON: I would have preached it to Hitler.

QUESTION: Would you have succeeded?

JOHN: I can't speculate.

YOKO ONO: If I were Hitler's girlfriend, things would have had many changes. The reason why there is war or a dictatorship is that people don't communicate enough and people don't give love enough. If everybody loved Hitler, "love" meaning really communicating and opening his mind and turning him on, then he wouldn't have been there. He was there because he had a typical condition for a dictatorship, which is isolation. It's everybody's responsibility.

QUESTION: They say Hitler loved children. He was very fond of his nieces and nephews.

JOHN: Those were the remnants of the Christ within him.

QUESTION: Was there a need for the Americans to help Britain after Hitler came to power? Was there a need for that war?

JOHN: I think what happened then was right for that moment. If you believe violence can solve the problem, that's up to you. I don't. You might have a few instances, but no one ever tried the peace thing. Just tell me any sustained peace propaganda or nonviolent movements that ever lasted.

QUESTION: The civil rights movement in America.

JOHN: It started off nonviolent, and look what happened—every time they marched it was chaos. I think marching is old hat. I think it's time they put their heads together and tried something new. They've been marching since the thirties, or maybe before, and it's okay for the workers to be marching, it was where their heads were at, but it's a new age. It's gimmicks and salesmanship, and if that's what it takes to put it across, then that's the way to do it. Whether you're protesting the conditions you live in, the conditions you work in, or the conditions of the whole world, I think there are better methods to be used. I'm not saying, "Everybody lie in bed." I mean, it would be a nice idea if they all did, but it's suitable for us. We hope it gives some suggestions to people to do something else. We're selling it like soap. You've got to sell, sell, sell, until the housewife thinks, "Oh, there's peace or war, that's the two products."

Yoko: The thing is, you are criticizing the establishment. It's dirty and filthy, but the point is, they are people, too. One way or another, we are stuck with them. We are living in a small ghetto. The whole world is like a ghetto, and we have to live with it. We have to face them, we can't ignore them. The only way to change the world is to change their minds. If the makers of Coca-Cola can condition everybody in the world to drink Coca-Cola, why can't we do the same? The establishment is like a retarded child—you're stuck with the retarded child. You go to the retarded child, and instead of killing the child, you start to open up the retarded child's mind. You're the one that has to extend your hand. If you don't extend your hand to the establishment, how do you expect the establishment to extend its hand to you?

Question: You have made a compromise taking the Queen Elizabeth Hotel.

John: What's the compromise there?

Question: You'd have to know what it's like to come up here and see you.

John: Do you have a suggestion where else we could hold this event? Tell us! Tell us a better place we can do this.

Question: I accept it for what it is. All I'm saying is, do *you* accept it as a compromise?

John: No, we don't. I want you to explain to me why it's a compromise to be in the Queen Elizabeth Hotel.

Question: Because of the procedures involved in being here, because of the procedures involved in getting to meet here.

John: So what do you see as a compromise?

Question: Establishment procedures.

Question: Do you condemn civil rights marching?

John: No, I'm not condemning them, I'm with them. I'm just saying, isn't it about time they thought of something else? They've been marching for sixty years. I think it's ineffective. The CNB people came to us in England and said, "We agree with you, it's ineffective, what do you suggest?" I said, "You've got women, don't you? Use sex!" Every day in the popular papers they have bikini-clad girls. Get the CNB girls in there. Use sex for peace.

QUESTION: Do you include campus violence and building takeovers? Do you condemn them as well?

JOHN: A sit-in is okay. I don't see why they have to destroy a building to take it over. Either sit in it and take it over or leave it, take no notice of it. You don't need the building.

QUESTION: Are you condemning the methods used at Harvard, Berkeley, and City College?

JOHN: We're not condemning anything. We're just saying, how about thinking of something else? If you're successful, we congratulate you, and if you've missed, think of something else.

QUESTION: If they are successful by using violent means . . .

JOHN: No, I can't agree with you, because violence begets violence.

John Lennon and Yoko Ono

TELEPHONE CONVERSATION WITH RIOTERS

Berkeley, CA, 1969

JOHN LENNON: Listen, there's no cause worth losing your life, brother. I don't believe there is any cause worth getting shot for! You can do better by moving on to another city or moving to Canada. Go anywhere—then they've got nothing to attack and nobody to point their finger at. Sing "Hare Krishna" or something, but don't move about if it aggravates the pigs. Don't get hassled by the cops, and don't play their games. I know it's hard. "Christ, you know it ain't easy, you know how hard it can be, man!" It is hard. So what? Everything's hard. It's going to be hard tomorrow, and it's going to be hard the next day. So what? It's better to have it hard than to not have it at all. If those squares can sell one kind of soap to the housewives, so can you!

YOKO ONO: The only way you can get them to understand you is to extend your hand and really try to open their minds and give your love. That's the only way they will come around.

JOHN: Entice them, entice them, and con them. You've got the brains, you can do it. You can make it, man, we can make it, together. We can get it together! We can get it together, now that's all!

John Lennon
BED-IN PRESS CONFERENCE
Montreal, 1969

QUESTION: How's Yoko?

JOHN LENNON: She's beautiful.

QUESTION: That's wonderful. Do you plan to come back to the United States soon?

JOHN: Well, I applied for a visa yesterday at the Montreal U.S. Embassy, and I'm hoping, you know, just hoping.

QUESTION: How long will you be in Montreal doing your number there?

JOHN: We plan on doing the Bed-in for seven days, and I think this is the fourth day. I'm not sure—there's so much going on in this bedroom. We snuck out yesterday morning to the American Embassy to apply for a visa, but it was a great secret.

QUESTION: What are the chances of it coming through?

JOHN: Well, I really don't know. It's in the air. I just hope for the best.

QUESTION: What if the visa does come through and you are granted permission to come into the U.S.? Where will you go?

JOHN: I originally planned to go to New York, but it all depends. We've thought about Washington, Berkeley, and San Francisco. It's really just us making a decision.

QUESTION: I think you've had a lot to do with the peace movement in Berkeley going on today.

JOHN: We've been screaming like madmen for them not to kill themselves. No bit of grass is worth that, no park is worth dying for.

QUESTION: Are the Beatles connected with the English publication *The Beatles Monthly Book?*

JOHN: They're vaguely connected to it, yeah. I mean, we don't own the rights to it or anything, but it's our magazine.

QUESTION: What is "Hey Jude" all about?

JOHN: Anything you like.

QUESTION: What about the future of the Beatles with Northern Songs Publishing now that ATV controls it?

JOHN: We never had control. All we ever did was try and prevent someone else from taking control. We never had a controlling interest in Northern Songs, ever. When someone new came in, we just tried to stop them, and did stop them, from getting complete control. They only have three-quarters.

QUESTION: What city would you like to live in—Berkeley, San Francisco, or Los Angeles?

JOHN: I've spent time in L.A., so maybe I'd go for 'Frisco.

QUESTION: On "Get Back," you credited Billy Preston. Why did you bring in an outside person on a Beatles song?

JOHN: We've often used other musicians on millions of records. I can't understand it. We just named Preston because Billy was playing a pretty funky piano solo, that's all. He used to play in the Ray Charles Band, and he came over and signed up with Apple, and George is doing an LP with him. He's a groovy cat. He just comes in and sits in on a session and lays it on you. Anyway, it says, "with Billy Preston," not "Billy Preston *instead* of the Beatles."

QUESTION: You cut this record, "The Ballad of John and Yoko." What message are you trying to portray in this song?

JOHN: I'm telling a story, like a newspaper. I'm just portraying a song about John and Yoko, and therefore everyone, because we are all one: "I am he as you are he and you are me and we are all together."

QUESTION: What about the flip side, "Old Brown Shoe"?

JOHN: Well, that's George's song, and I just did the sound. I haven't really got into the lyrics. "I'm getting out of this old brown shoe, baby I'm in love with you"—that's good enough for me.

QUESTION: Are you and Yoko doing a film together?

JOHN: We've made about seven films so far, and we've got them in a brown paper bag at the moment. We're trying to get distribution.

QUESTION: Anything in the near future about a film?

JOHN: Yoko and I are filming all the time. We're making a film of this event, and it will be an amazing film when you see the goings-on in the bed.

QUESTION: Really!

JOHN: (*Laughing*) Not that kind of thing, now! Lay off that. We've got radio stations in here, we've got people chanting "Hare Krishna," we've got people coming one after the other in strange outfits. It's really fantastic.

QUESTION: Will this show in the U.S.?

JOHN: Well, we just got to get distribution.

QUESTION: With the Beatles, you shouldn't have any trouble getting distribution.

JOHN: Are you kidding? I couldn't even get *Two Virgins* out on Apple.

QUESTION: Well, maybe things are changing for the better.

JOHN: I believe it. "They're getting better all the time!"

QUESTION: In the past it was difficult to get in touch with you, and now you've made yourself readily available. Is there any reason for this change of heart?

JOHN: Peace! Okay? That's the reason. I'm selling a product, so I'm back again.

QUESTION: What are your plans? Are you going to go out on tour? Are you going to perform? When can we see you? Where can we see you?

JOHN: I don't know. You get me into the States and I'll let you know. The Beatles are four middle-aged teenagers who have to make a democratic decision on whether they'll go on tour, and we're not agreed on it, so I don't know when. But John and Yoko will definitely perform.

QUESTION: What are the other guys doing now?

JOHN: Paul was driving through Europe, last time I'd heard; Ringo is in the Bahamas, half filming and half on holiday; and I don't know what George is doing—probably working.

QUESTION: I understand the group recently purchased a Moog synthesizer, right?

JOHN: Yeah. Actually, George has it in his house right now. The thing is like Hal out of *2001*.

QUESTION: Are you going to use it on any upcoming sessions?

JOHN: He's made an LP with it.* We've got this new output on Apple, called "Zapple." John and Yoko have just made a new album on it which will come out in a few weeks, and George's electronic album comes out at the same time. We'll also have poets on it. It's called "Zapple," so you know you'll get a surprise when you buy it!

QUESTION: What about a new Beatles LP? What's in the works now?

JOHN: Well, we finished it, and the most finished number on it was "Get Back." It was just a rehearsal for a show we never finished, so we just put it out. It's

---

* *Electric Sound* was issued on Zapple Records in 1968.

sounds okay—it's got chatting and messing about on it. Then we got halfway through another album. We stopped that—we got tired and took a break.

QUESTION: Will the new LP be a double album, like the last one?

JOHN: It will be a single one, but this one comes with a book about making the LP. We also made a film of it at the same time, so we've got to get that together.*

QUESTION: Tell me about the film.

JOHN: Well, we've got sixty-eight hours of film, so we've got a lot of work to do. It shows all the trauma and paranoia. All the things that happen to you when you're trying to make a record.

QUESTION: Is there great hopes about this maybe being a movie production, or will it end up like *Mystery Tour*?

JOHN: It may end up like *The Magical Mystery Tour*, but this time it will be on the air!

QUESTION: What about the future?

JOHN: I just plan to turn the people on to peace.

QUESTION: How?

JOHN: Through music, painting, books, and dancing.

QUESTION: Have you devoted any time to writing songs?

JOHN: Yeah, I've got a couple coming out. I've also written a couple since I've been on the road with Yoko. One of them is called "Give Peace a Chance," which I'm going to record as soon as I can.

QUESTION: Why suddenly go on this kick?

JOHN: It just was a gradual development over the years. I mean last year was "all you need is love." This year, it's "all you need is love and peace, baby." Give peace a chance, and remember love. The only hope for us is peace. Violence begets violence. You can have peace as soon as you like if we all pull together. You're all geniuses, and you're all beautiful. You don't need anyone to tell you who you are. You are what you are. Get out there and get peace, think peace, and live peace and breathe peace, and you'll get it as soon as you like.

---

* *Let It Be*, originally titled *Get Back*.

John Lennon and Yoko Ono
LIVE PEACE IN TORONTO PRESS CONFERENCE

London, 1969

QUESTION: How did your appearance at the Toronto Rock 'n' Roll Revival happen?

JOHN LENNON: We were sitting in our office at Apple, and a call came through from Canada saying, "There's a 'Rock 'n' Roll Revival' over here, would you care to come?" Before they were finished talking, I was already saying, "Get me Eric Clapton, get me George, and get me a band together." Then the guy said, "We would like you to preside over it." We're saying, "What! We're not going to preside over it, we're not that old. We're just playing." That was Friday night, and we flew over Saturday morning. There was a bit of a hang-up trying to find Eric, because he was living in the trees. We got him at nine o'clock in the morning. He said, "Okay," and we went. We tried to rehearse on the plane, which was stupid, because with electric guitars you can't hear anything. I didn't know any of the words to anything. Luckily it was a rock 'n' roll revival, because I don't know the words to any songs except ones from when I was a kid. Then we tried to rehearse backstage. We ran through it twice and went onstage. It was a great session because there were good musicians, and they really got into it, as you can hear.

QUESTION: That was the first time you'd played live with a group for quite some time, wasn't it?

JOHN: Four years. No, actually Yoko and I performed together at Cambridge. That was different though—it was only us two.* And the Stones' *Rock 'n' Roll Circus*, which never came out.† I think it was me and Yoko, Keith Richard, and somebody and somebody,‡ I can't remember.

QUESTION: I know there are a lot of contractual hang-ups with people in the Plastic Ono Band. Are they likely to appear with you permanently as a group?

JOHN: I wouldn't have another permanent group. The scene isn't going that way. Musicians are freeing themselves and playing with anybody, now we're going out

---

* "Cambridge 1969" was a live performance of avant-garde "unfinished music" by John and Yoko. The soundtrack was eventually released on their second album together, *Unfinished Music Number 2/Life with the Lions*.

† An unreleased film by the Rolling Stones that also featured the Who, Jethro Tull, and Taj Mahal.

‡ Hendrix drummer Mitch Mitchell and Eric Clapton.

in the open. Instead of calling Eric Clapton "Tommy Flenge," or whatever, like they used to. We know people have got to have contracts, but there must be some kind of a contract with a certain amount of leeway. That's what musicians want, and nothing's going to stop them. I like to have fresh people around all the time. I like jamming instead of finished music.

QUESTION: What kind of possibilities are there of the Beatles doing a concert again?

JOHN: You'd have to ask us all one by one. The last time I heard, we weren't. I go off and on it, personally, anyway. But for the Beatles to perform, it's like four Bob Dylans coming on or expecting Buddha to play. With us, they expect Buddha *and* Jesus to perform. There would be so much expectation no matter what we did, it would be a letdown unless we burnt ourselves or something. So it's a bit nerve-racking to perform with the Beatles, but to perform just as John and Yoko is easy. They don't expect anything from me, whereas with the Beatles, they do.

QUESTION: To the LP itself: the first side is certainly a purely rock 'n' roll affair. Throughout your career, it's been said you are really a rock 'n' roller at heart.

JOHN: That's the age I come from. There was a jazz age, and I'm from the rock age, so it's instilled in me. But I think records like "Come Together" or "Cold Turkey" are the rock of today.

QUESTION: The first track on the album is an old standard, "Blue Suede Shoes." You did this quite often in the early years, right?

JOHN: Yeah, I'd been singing it for three or four years. I'd given it to George before the Beatles got big. So it was George's song, but it was originally mine. I like Carl Perkins and Elvis. I've sung it many times, but I've only just remembered the words.

QUESTION: It sounds like there was quite a large audience over there in Toronto.

JOHN: I haven't a clue. It was two hundred thousand something, but it was very peaceful. During the intro they said something like, "Here comes the Plastic Onos, light up your matches," and as we came on people lit up matches, which was fantastic, because it was so dark onstage.

QUESTION: The next track, "Money," was always a Beatle favorite.

JOHN: It's simply a matter of what songs I knew and which would be easier for a band who'd never played together before. So we pretty much stuck to twelve bars, which most musicians can gig along with, and that's why I vaguely knew "Money." I knew a couple of verses, and I had Yoko holding the words for me. I didn't use them. If I didn't know the words, I just made them up. Obviously, it's a matter of necessity for four people who have never played together to pick songs that are pretty easy to play.

QUESTION: Yoko, how involved did you become when the rock 'n' roll side of the concert was on?

YOKO ONO: I grooved on it. It was a fantastic vibration. It was very nice.

QUESTION: "Dizzy Miss Lizzy" is also one of the big rock 'n' roll songs the Beatles did. I guess the same thing applies—it was another song you knew.

JOHN: Yeah, I know this one because the Beatles did it on every tour, for the same reason. We all knew it was a cinch, especially if you were nervous, because the backing was so solid. I always enjoyed singing it, though, because it just grooved along. You can hear I'm more relaxed on that track than the others.

QUESTION: Did you perform any songs aside from the ones on the LP?

JOHN: No, everything thing we did is exactly how it happened onstage, including all the bits and pieces in between.

QUESTION: There was also a film made of this. Are we likely to see it here in Britain?

JOHN: Yes, as soon as we can get it together. Some guy was filming it, and we somehow managed to get the rights. I think they'll make a film with all the other people in it, like Richard and Berry and the others. I don't really know what we're going to do with our piece of film, but we'll obviously show it.*

QUESTION: I think a lot of people have been waiting for an LP, certainly following the success of both singles! The new single has been taken off the market. Can you tell us about this?

JOHN: Well, that was an old Beatles track we did in 1967, which is a bit camp. It's something we'd do in between takes. It's a song for which I had only two lines: "You know my name, look up the number." We played in all sorts of rhythms and gagged about on top of it. A few months back I remembered it, and Paul and I sang the lyrics and put a few gags over it. Originally we did a gag backing, but nobody wanted to do it, so we just forgot about it. I thought this would make a good Christmas record, because it's a real laugh, or you hate it. I thought the Beatles wouldn't want it, because they don't want another record out at the moment, so I'll have it, but of course they did. I just wanted it out—I don't care what they call it, the Beatles or Tom and Jerry, just get the bloody music out! It will probably come out in January with a track from *Get Back*. Something like "Let It Be" backed by "You Know My Name."

---

* The film was not officially released until several years after Lennon's death.

QUESTION: Do you find any conflict now that you are virtually part of two groups and doing things with Yoko as well?

JOHN: Not really. No more than when I did *How I Won the War** or I wrote my two books. I have an individual life, as does each of us, but now it's more public. Like me with Plastic Ono and the events, the peace thing, Ringo with his films, Paul with his artists, and George with his.

QUESTION: We now move on to the first of your own compositions, which is from your double album† called *Yer Blues.*

JOHN: We sang this because I'd done it on the Rolling Stones' *Rock 'n' Roll Circus*, and therefore I had an idea of how to do it live. Also, Eric had also done that one, and the other people in the group almost knew it, as you can hear.

QUESTION: All this talk about not knowing songs and learning them leads me to wonder, does most of your songwriting happen in the studio?

JOHN: Yeah. Usually I learn them for the occasion, or I know them before I come to the studio. But when you're on the road, you only learn numbers to play on the road. You don't have time to learn new ones. In the old days, when we used to play four or five hours a night, you'd have to know a lot of songs, and these hung around in my head almost complete. I had a vast repertoire in the old days, and it's practically vanished. The Beatles only ever did twenty minutes onstage. So you had less need of learning new songs, except for recording purposes.

QUESTION: This particular track, "Yer Blues," has a classic blues formation. It's rather unusual to hear on your LPs, because it's more a heavy rock sound than previously.

JOHN: It really goes more with the "Money/Dizzy" tradition.

QUESTION: Moving through the Toronto LP, we get to the sound that was the single. This, in fact, was the first performance of "Cold Turkey," wasn't it?

JOHN: Yes. In fact, I hadn't decided on an arrangement or anything. I just sang it to the group, and because it was basically a three-chord song, they picked it up quite well. It was just verse-chorus, verse-chorus. Here, too, Yoko was holding the words, but just out of sight. So I had to dodge off the mike to try and get one of the verses. It's entirely different than the single, but you can see where the single came from. A more professional version of this would be more commercial, but that's how I wanted the song to go.

---

* Richard Lester's disappointing antiwar film, in which Lennon appeared as the character Musketeer Gripweed.
† The Beatles' four-sided LP popularly known as the *White Album*, released on November 22, 1968.

QUESTION: There has been some comment about the lyrical content, the antidrug references, and the screaming at the end. Enlighten us.

JOHN: The screaming effect is only a progression from the end of "Strawberry Fields" or the end of "Walrus" or "A Day in the Life." The expression "cold turkey" isn't only known around drug addicts, but "cold turkey" is also known to ordinary people, and not just the meat. It's not only exclusive to drug addiction. I like words or expressions, and "cold turkey" just happens to be one of them. I wrote the song "I'm a Loser" after I'd picked up the expression. "Kick out the jams" is a nice expression—I'd write that if there already weren't so many of them. "Day Tripper" I made up out of hearing about trips before I had anything to do with tripping. Cold turkey means suffering—it can mean a three-day flu or dying in Biafra. It means many things that have nothing at all to do with drugs.

QUESTION: Speaking about Biafra, the next song is "Give Peace a Chance," which gives us an opportunity to talk about you returning your MBE.

JOHN: Well, for the last year or two I've been seriously considering returning it, privately. People say I should have done it that way, but what they don't understand is that there is no real way to return an MBE privately. Therefore, rather than wait for the story to break, I made use of the stories that were going to be in the paper anyway. Look, if I have an accident and I have to go to hospital, it's going to be in the press. So on the way to the hospital, if I can change it into a peace event, I will. I'm getting press anyway, whether I like it or not. I found that out a long time ago, so I might as well get used to it.

QUESTION: Some people felt your reference to "Cold Turkey" as one of the reasons for returning it took a little edge off the peaceful reasons you did it for. Was this a cynical shot at everybody?

JOHN: It was a gag. I'm not too serious a person. People get bored with seriousness. Had I just done it like some silly old colonel, it would have had that effect.

John Lennon and Yoko Ono
WAR IS OVER POSTER PRESS CONFERENCE
London, 1969

QUESTION: Could you please explain your "War Is Over" poster campaign?

JOHN LENNON: It's part of our advertising campaign for peace.

QUESTION: Do you really believe such actions will contribute to world peace?

JOHN: It's like asking Mr. Coca-Cola, "Do you really believe your advertisements are contributing to selling Coca-Cola?" It certainly does contribute. We believe in advertising. On a David Frost program the other night, we saw this firm making adverts against racialism. The adverts weren't too good, but the idea was. We thought we'd invented the idea, of course, but somebody had thought of it. It's a very good idea to advertise for peace and against racialism. You must advertise them. That's what everybody else does.

QUESTION: I see the posters in Spanish and French and German. In which places are you campaigning now?

JOHN: Of course in Amsterdam, but we haven't got a copy of that one. Tokyo, New York, L.A., Montreal, Toronto, Berlin, Rome, Paris, Amsterdam, Athens, London. I think that's it. Eleven places altogether.

QUESTION: Why not Cairo, Tel Aviv, Saigon, or Hanoi?

JOHN: We had enough trouble getting them about in London!

QUESTION: What is the cost of such a campaign?

JOHN: I don't want to think about the cost of such a campaign, but I'll have to write a song or two to earn me money back.

John Lennon and Yoko Ono

Toronto Peace Conference

* *

December, 1969

QUESTION: There are a lot of experts around the world trying to promote world peace. Why do you feel that you can succeed where they have failed?

JOHN LENNON: It's like saying, "Why bother keeping on with Christianity because Jesus got killed?" We don't think people have tried advertising before. We can start there. If anybody brings out a new product—say, pretend peace is new 'cause we've never had it—they start advertising it to sell. Whatever gimmickry and irrelevancies that are going on during the advert, it's the drink or the car they buy at the end of it, whether there's chicks in it, white horses, or snow. The product sells, and we believe in selling, you know.

QUESTION: If the whole idea *is* to advertise, why are you almost a semi-recluse when you're here in Canada.

JOHN: When? Well, I've been here one day . . . I wouldn't call that "semi-reclusive." We got up this morning, and here we are.

QUESTION: What do you intend to do for the rest of the week?

JOHN: We'll probably see press, you know.

QUESTION: A few months ago, you had a campaign going to have a peace ship in the Mediterranean.

JOHN: Well, this is somebody else's gig, and we're helping him out with it. He's in New York now, trying to raise money for the ship. We did what we could out of America—we couldn't do much. We could only say, "We're with you, and you can put our name on the ad and try to use us as best you can." His plan is, he has this ship, he's got a lot of kids to paint it, he's in New York, and he needs some kind of transmitter, which costs a lot. I'm not like *that* with him, because I met him for five minutes. I liked him, I believed in him, I believed in his campaign, and we've done what we can for him. He's still in New York, and that's still on.

QUESTION: Last time you were here, in Montreal, you mentioned you had the acorns . . .

JOHN: King Hussein planted his, he's the only one!

QUESTION: Is this still a part of your campaign?

John: Yes, we'll keep sending them until everybody's planted one. We've sent them to all the world leaders' addresses we could get together. We've had about twenty replies from here and there. I don't know who, so it's no good asking me, because I can't remember. But we've had replies saying, "Yes, thank you," and some just saying, "Yes, we got it." So the ones that said "Thank you" we guess are sort of the peaceniks.

Question: Do you intend to go anywhere else in Canada besides Toronto?

John: We'll go down to Montreal to dedicate these radio stations to peace in a few days, probably, yes.

Question: What about Ottawa?

John: That's not on the schedule at the moment.

Question: We're trying to arrange a meeting with the prime minister, as we did last time. If we could arrange it, would you be interested in going to Ottawa?

John: Yes, of course we would, but we don't want to hassle him and press him into things, because obviously, if our lives are anything to go by, his is a lot more delicate and pressurized. And I don't want to do all this "They're gonna give him acorns, and they're gonna do this," because that spoils it. I'd rather not talk about it. If it's possible, of course, we'd enjoy it.

Yoko Ono: But you'll hear about it in a week or so.

Question: You say "we." You mean your husband and yourself?

Yoko: Yes, and also anyone in the world.

Question: It's a public event?

Yoko: Yes, it is.

Question: What about the lithographs? Can you confirm that you'll personally be signing? From what I've heard, if they're that erotic, they may have some trouble passing through Customs.

John: I have no idea, that's the publisher's problem. He asked me to do some lithographs, I did them, and they can handle it themselves.

Question: You're personally going to sign them?

John: Yeah, with lithographs you've got to sign them.

Question: Get back to Biafra for a minute. Is it true that you were planning on going there a few months ago?

John: Yeah. At the time Yoko was pregnant and we decided not to go, and she had a miscarriage then. And we thought and thought about it. We're scared of going to somewhere where it's happening, because we don't want to be dead saints. I'm scared of going to Vietnam and Biafra, and until I'm convinced that I'd do better there than I can do outside of it, I'll stay out. Like I'd go to Russia, but I'd think twice about China, because I don't want to be a martyr. I'd like to play it safe and be around.

Yoko: And he did a lot of good, I think, as far as Biafra's concerned, with returning the MBE.

John: Another thing we're doing with this Peace Festival is to try and set up a "peace vote" for all the youth in the world, which would be like a petition, but it'd be a vote. You just vote for peace or war, and we'll set up a thing where all the youth votes, or anybody votes.

Question: About your vote for "peace or war." How do you answer accusations that that kind of thing is bordering on naiveté?

John: If anybody thinks our campaign is naive, that's their opinion, and that's okay. Let them do something else, and if we like the idea, we'll join in with them. We're artists, and we do it in the way that suits us best, and this is the way we work. Publicity and things like that is our game, because the Beatles' thing was that, and that's the trade I've learned. And I'm using it to the best of my ability.

Question: What is the point of having this "peace/war" vote?

John: Why do people have those Gallup polls? Every politician in England is saying, "84 percent want hanging," and Nixon said, "We claim the silent majority." Well, by the way, *we* claim it. *We're* claiming the silent majority. (*Delayed laughter*) Why do they have polls? If we get a vote from around the world of millions and millions of kids who want peace, that's a nice gallup poll—we can wave *those* figures around. It's a positive movement—all we want is a "Yes."

Question: Have you given any thought to the possibility of using the Peace Festival in the way they are using festivals in the States now, especially the Earth People's Park, using the proceeds from the festival to buy a piece of land, a thousand acres or something?

John: Any ideas like that, please bring them to us, all suggestions like that. The thing is only in the baby stage now. We've come here to think about it and to say that we're setting it up, we've got a place to do it, we hope it'll be well. The stage is gonna be a bed, and where the proceeds go and how we'll work that out will be worked out with the help we can get from Rabbi [Feinberg] and anybody else who's got more of an organized brain than we have. We're not organizers—that's the kind of help we need. Any ideas like that we're open to. What to do with money if we get any money, and how to use it, we'd have to decide then. But *all* ideas are welcome, so please approach us through John and Ritchie.

QUESTION: Do you think something like *Hair* is a source of entertainment that sells peace effectively?

JOHN: The *Hair* thing probably did some good. I don't really know. I think it's all right, it was nice reflection. Everything positive is nice. I like it. Just the effect it had on people was good, I think.

QUESTION: Do you ever try to pitch your colleagues in the Beatles into doing tours that are strictly peace-oriented?

JOHN: Well, no, because this is the first time there's been an actual peace-oriented idea, a festival for peace. I'll try and hustle them out, and maybe I'll get one or two. I got George on the other night for UNICEF, and a lot of other people. I can't speak for the Beatles, 'cause I'm only me, but if I can get them, if I can get Elvis, I'll try. I'll try and get 'em all.

QUESTION: Does that mean Apple isn't involved in your peace work either?

JOHN: Well, I'll probably get all the Apple artists, I'll tell you that.

YOKO: Same thing.

JOHN: I'll try and make Apple pay for a few things, you know.

QUESTION: Did you see the press for the one in California a few weeks ago, where four people . . .

JOHN: The Stones one? Well, that was bad, and I've heard a lot of things about that concert, and I think it was just a bad scene. Ours won't be like that, God willing.

YOKO: But we must be very careful, you know.

JOHN: Well, I don't know. I believe in the way a thing is set up. I think they created that, whether subconsciously or whatever, and that it was the result of the image and the mood they create. And I think if you create a peaceful mood, you stand a better chance. But we have six months to prevent that.

QUESTION: How's Paul these days?

JOHN: I haven't seen him for months, he's been on holiday. He's in the Bahamas, actually.

QUESTION: What about people helping, say, in this area, just people in Toronto?

JOHN: Any help that you have or want to give, you contact John Brower or Ritchie Yorke here, or Rabbi Feinberg, and channel it through them. They're John and Yoko in Canada, and they're in constant touch with us.

QUESTION: Have you got anything to say about music? Anything coming up?

JOHN: Well, we have an album out today, folks. It should've been out two weeks ago, but they hustled it out today.

QUESTION: How about the next Beatles album?

JOHN: The next Beatles album is out in January, one after that in March or something. Plenty of product, you know. Ask EMI.

QUESTION: I remember you saying sometime you thought we'd have peace by the year 2000. Do you still think that?

JOHN: I'd sooner say by 1970. I believe in that positive thinking bit, so I try to knock all the negative thought out. Let's say 1970, and then when it's '70, we say, "Oh, we're wrong, it's 1971." I think we get it as soon as people realize that *they* have the power, and the power doesn't belong to Mr. Trudeau, Mr. Wilson, or Mr. Nixon. The people are the power, and as soon as people are aware they have the power, they can have what they want. If it's a case of they don't know or they don't know what to do, let's advertise to them to tell them that they have an option.

QUESTION: What can they do?

JOHN: They've got the vote, haven't they? I mean, you'll *have* the vote, you *will* be the Establishment. There's no good attacking it and breaking it down, because you'll have to build it up again, that's all we're saying.

QUESTION: Were you serious when you said yesterday that you'd send the bill to President Nixon?

JOHN: I was coming out of London airport, and they said "How much did it cost?" and I said, "Anyway, I'll send the bill to Nixon." It was a joke, you know. It's an idea, but it's a joke.

QUESTION: Back to Biafra for a minute—you said you had planned on going until Yoko was pregnant. What had you planned on doing in Biafra if you had gone?

JOHN: We had an invitation from somebody connected with Biafra, and they wanted us to just go there and film. Publicity is what they want, for their side of the story, and for it to come from somebody that isn't particularly politically one side or the other—somebody independent who can go there, see it, and come out again. That was the idea behind it.

QUESTION: Can I ask you a question about the Beatles? Do you ever expect to perform again? I know you had a bit of a hang-up not wanting to.

JOHN: It's like, a few months ago, George didn't. Now he's just been on tour with Bonnie and Delaney and Eric Clapton. And I go off it and on it. And so there's four of us, you know, and I don't know how Ringo feels about it now, but I'm gonna try and sew him up for July, you know.

QUESTION: What about the future of the Beatles—do you expect to remain a foursome?

JOHN: I've no idea. If we are comfortable and enjoy being the Beatles, we'll do it—and when we don't, we won't. That's always been the case. The last four years, every time we've made a record, it's been a decision of whether to carry it on from there. The point is, in the old days, Paul and I would knock off an LP and write most of the songs and do it. Nowadays, there's three of us writing equally good songs, wanting that much space. The problem now is, do you make a double album every time, which takes six months of your life, or do you make one album? We spend three or four months making one album, maybe get two or three tracks each, that's the problem. You know, it's just a physical problem, and whether we do it or not I've no idea.

QUESTION: Do you ever fear that your name coupled with the word "peace" could be used for other means?

JOHN: There is always a danger of that, but if anybody tries to use us, we have you people there, and if we find out, we'll say, "That man used us." Our only protection against being used is to tell you.

QUESTION: Are there any circumstances in which you personally could support a war?

JOHN: No.

QUESTION: I'm wondering what your attitude would've been. For example, you're younger than I am. . . .

JOHN: Yeah, in 1939. I can only say, "Don't talk to me about '39, talk to me about 1930."

QUESTION: But the death of six million Jews in itself is not . . .

YOKO: But it was the responsibility of everybody.

JOHN: It was all our responsibility, it wasn't just the Germans. The Germans say, "Oh, it was Hitler," and the world says, "Oh, it was the Germans," etc., etc. It was *all* our responsibility then. I know for people that were there then and all that—I was only a child being bombed, and it is different. But I just don't believe it. I believe it was all our responsibility before it happened, you know. That's all I can say about it. I don't believe in killing.

QUESTION: How seriously do you consider the possibility that in your pursuit of peace that your manner of clothing and hair would alienate more people than it would ever convince to come over to your side?

JOHN: Yes, I understand that. Many people say, "Why don't you get a butch hair-cut and a suit." (*Laughter*) And the thing is, that's what politicians do. I try and be as natural as I can under the circumstances. We do. Now how many members of the public are gullible to politicians with the nice picture of the family, the dog, and a whore on the side, church on Sunday. Now, I could do that. I don't think people would believe it. That is the politicians' way—youth certainly doesn't believe it anymore. We have an intuition about "leaving one gate open." There's an old Chinese saying that "The castle falls from within." Say like America, no Communists are going to overrun them—the place'll collapse from inside. Always to leave one door open. If you have every door shut in the castle, the enemy will attack from every side, and you stand a chance of losing. If you leave one door open, they'll concentrate there. Our door is hair, or mentioning "Cold Turkey" on the MBE letter to the queen, some kind of irrelevancy to distract, so the attack doesn't hit us. And we try and be natural, you know. If I feel like cutting it, I'll cut it.

QUESTION: We've heard a great deal about hidden significance in some of your records—you know, this thing where if you play a certain record backwards it says, "Turn me on, dead man." Is there anything to this?

JOHN: No, all those things are beyond me. I believe that anything—like with this cigarette packet, you can read something into it if you want, and nobody sees the same picture, and all lyrics mean everything people want. There was never any specific "Turn me on, dead man," or the other famous one I won't repeat, where you played it backward and got a secret message.* If it's imagery, it's imagery. If it's straight lyrics, it's straight lyrics. But of course, you can read anything into anything—that's why there's so many versions of the Bible.

QUESTION: How did the death rumor about Paul get started?

JOHN: I have no idea. I'm now being credited as the creator of a great publicity campaign for the Beatles. Now, if I'd thought of that idea, I don't know how I would've put it into action, and whether I would've done it or not, I don't know. I don't know how it started. It started, seems to me, the same way as the guy that resurrected my comment about Jesus and got publicity for himself and his

---

* Here Lennon is referring to the song, which, if played backwards, allegedly said, "I'll fuck you like Superman." Most likely, this is a load of old cobbers.

station, and it just got out of his hands. I think it's the same kind of thing. I don't know, I can't understand it myself.

QUESTION: Do you think you will have more power reaching the new generation through a peace movement than trying to change the grown-up people's minds?

JOHN: Yes, we're aiming at youth. Our hope is with youth, because they will be the Establishment.

YOKO: The old people will come around too, if all the young are watching. Say if there's a Hitler in this world, somewhere in this world, we're hoping this time we can stop him from doing something, because all the youth is watching, and it's very difficult for Hitler to operate.

RABBI FEINBERG:* John, you are now endowed with more influence over young people in the world than all the bishops and rabbis and priests put together. That is true. Do you ever feel any sense of fright at the power that you have?

JOHN: It's an abstract power. If we have something specific we'd like to use the power for—say we wanted to plug a certain product that wasn't peace, and I contact any press I know and try to get it over—there's a good chance it won't work. So I haven't got a power that I can really get hold of and do something with.

RABBI FEINBERG: But you're using it now for peace, and I think the whole world should be very grateful to you and Yoko for doing it.

JOHN: Well, thank you for that, you know.

QUESTION: At the same time, do you not feel obligated to carry this message to Russia and China?

JOHN: Sure, sure, but we must believe you start with two people, like in your own village, and our village happens to be the West, really. Of course we want to go to Russia and Czechoslovakia. We have to decide how we go and what we go as. They don't really know much about us there. Do we just get on a train and arrive in Moscow as tourists, or do we try and take this Peace Festival? I think that might be a good way. But the world is quite large still, and we've got to get a good team going here first, and then when we're a bit more organized maybe we can go over there. I'd like to go somewhere over there, so as to stop that question from arising again, before the end of '70. I think there's a chance we might go to Czechoslovakia, and there's a good chance we can take this Peace Festival to Russia, I think. I believe they might allow pop stars to sing and play now. And I've heard it's easier to get in there than the States!

---

* Rabbi Feinberg briefly held court with John and Yoko during various visits to Canada in 1969.

QUESTION: Have you ever considered making a financial request to the Establishment? For example, a man like Henry Ford II?

JOHN: Sure, sure. When we get a bit more organized. See, what we didn't want to do was become leaders. I believe in Wilhelm Reich, who says, "Don't be a leader." We don't want to be the people saying, "It was your fault we didn't get peace," or "It was your fault this happened." We want to be part of it. Like people said, "The Beatles *weren't* the movement, the Beatles were only ever *part* of a movement." We were influenced as much as we influenced, and John and Yoko refuse to be the leaders of the youth movement for peace.

YOKO: That's dictatorship.

JOHN: That's dictatorship. We want everybody to help us. We're just saying, "Listen, this is our flag, it's a white flag, anybody else in the game?" And then we can get something together. It takes time for this sort of news to get through to, say, Henry Ford or Onassis or somebody like that, because they'll be reading last year's papers or whatever, or the financial page. They probably still think I'm on tour with Paul or something like that. When we get something functional and organized, and a few people that aren't just John and Yoko, like Rabbi here and a few others . . . if you don't mind me calling you "straights," we can approach from that angle and say, "Listen, man, we've got so much money, will you double it?" because we know they all do charity things.

QUESTION: The point is, you won't call them this trip over?

JOHN: Not this trip over, but of course I think of that—there's a lot of money around.

QUESTION: Do you believe in God?

JOHN: Yes. I believe God is like a powerhouse, like where you keep electricity, a power station, and that He's a supreme power. But He's neither good nor bad, nor left, right, or black or white. He just is, and that we tap that source of power and make of it what we will. Like electricity—you can kill people in a chair or you can light the room with it. I think God *is*.

YOKO: Also, we talk about having a belief in youth, but youth includes everybody that is youthful, naturally. Then this voice said, "Well, what can we do?" and this question was always coming up, even when we had the Bed-in in Montreal and all that. But just imagine what's happening now. For instance, maybe it was twisted around a little by reporters, but the Woodstock Festival or the Isle of Wight Festival, those were festivals with thousands and thousands of people, and there wasn't any violence. Maybe there were some mishaps, but no real violence, and that's fantastic. It's very historical, because before that, when that number of people gathered, it was only for war or something violent. If it were for war even, the reasons why people were quiet was because maybe the colonel or major or something were telling them to be quiet! We were at the Isle of Wight and it was beautiful! That's starting to happen now, and all we can do is gather and show that we're very quiet, and show the noisy people, the violent people, to just make them ashamed to be violent.

JOHN: Right.

QUESTION: It's been said Jesus Christ made the mistake of trying to save the whole world as one man. Do you think this, and is this why you don't believe in leadership?

JOHN: I don't know about that. I just believe that leaders and father figures are the mistakes of all the generations before us, and we can't rely on Nixon or on Jesus or whoever we tend to rely on. It's just a lack of responsibility that you expect somebody else to do it. It's, "Oh, he must help me, and if he doesn't help me, we kill him, or we vote him out." I think that's the mistake, just having father figures. As long as we keep moving about, we will never be leaders.

YOKO: And *you're* the leader—everybody in this room has to lead the next world.

JOHN: It's just that, you know. The Beatles were never leaders, but people imagined they were, and now they're finding out. And I *won't* be a leader, and leaders are just, "Okay, I will be then, " and they have the badge on. Well, I'm not doing that.

QUESTION: Could you give us your personal definition of peace?

JOHN: Peace? Just no violence, and everybody grooving, if you don't mind me using the word. Just no violence. Of course we all have violence in us, but we must channel it.

QUESTION: Do you remember the Cavern?

JOHN: Yes.

QUESTION: Do you think the kids are really as interested in peace as they were in the olden days?

JOHN: Well, I don't know what they were interested in at the Cavern.

YOKO: I think they're getting to be very interested.

JOHN: We consider this like we're in the Cavern now—we're in that stage. We haven't got out of Liverpool yet with this campaign, and we've got to break London and then America. I feel exactly the same as I did then about the Beatles as I do about peace and what we're doing now. I don't care how long it takes and what obstacles there are, we won't stop, you know.

QUESTION: Is there any one incident that got you started on this peace campaign?

JOHN: It built up over a number of years, but the thing that struck it off was, we got a letter from a guy called Peter Watkins who made a film called *The War Game*. It was a long letter stating what's happening: how the media is controlled, how it's all run, everything that everybody knows, that bit. But he said it in black and white, for hours and hours on pages, and it ended up, "What are you going to do about it?"

YOKO: "What are *you* doing?"

JOHN: He said, "People in your position and *our* position"—'cause he's a filmmaker—"have a responsibility especially to use the media for world peace." We sat on the letter for three weeks, thinking, "Well, we're doing our best"—you know, "All you need is love," man, and all that. Finally we came up with the Bed Event after that, and that's what sort of sparked it off. It was like getting your call-up papers for peace. We got it, and we sat on it for three weeks while we worked out what to do, and then we did the Bed Event.

QUESTION: Is there any significance to these black clothes you're wearing?

JOHN: We just like them. We like black and white, and they're warm.

QUESTION: What about Biafra?

JOHN: Well, you know what we think about Biafra. We want to try to make Britain aware of its responsibility in Biafra, and that's what we're about.

QUESTION: Mrs. Lennon, one reads in the newspapers that your own home country of Japan is building up a certain industrial military capacity. Is this so, and what do you think about it?

YOKO: Well, we're doing something in Japan, too, and it's a surprise. I'm sure that you'll hear it maybe in a week or so.

QUESTION: You and your husband will do doing something?

YOKO: We're doing something now at this moment.

JOHN: By remote control.

John Lennon and Yoko Ono
MOON LANDING PRESS CONFERENCE

London, 1969

YOKO LENNON: I hope the Americans don't start getting aggressive and feel imperialistic about this event and try and colonize the moon, which they usually do. They make a colony of anything they get their hands on. Maybe something interesting might happen. The greatest fear I have is, "Are they going to start colonizing and become aggressive again?" The other thought was, "Are the States together enough for that?" America doesn't have much of a reputation for being together.

QUESTION: Why do you think we went out there? Do you think it's human nature?

JOHN LENNON: It's done them good politically, because of the fear the Americans have that the Russians would take it and bomb them and vice versa. I was hoping they would have both landed there at the same time. They've been planning this ever since they got rockets from the Germans.

QUESTION: Do you think it was as calculated as that? "We can shoot the Russians better from there?" ·

YOKO: We all have dreams about going to the stars and the moons. Nothing is going to be done unless some scheme is pushed, especially in America. I'm sure there is a big government push behind it.

JOHN: It wasn't as verified. The Kennedys or the Johnsons said, "Let's really push it," and they really pushed it. They had to come up with the goods within so many months, and they did. So it was just a matter of them all deciding, "Let's do it," and they did. People thought of it from reading all the science fiction books.

YOKO: All children dream about it. It's the children who thought of it before the government.

John Lennon and Yoko Ono

PRE-BAHAMAS BED-IN PRESS CONFERENCE

London, 1969

JOHN LENNON: We've been trying to get into the States to do a peace mission and get visas. It doesn't look like we're getting them so far. So we're going to the Bahamas to sort of blast off from there and to do a Cuba. For instance, we've written Bertrand Russell to try to get him to help us. The behind-the-scenes concerning the visas we'll let you know in the Bahamas.

We want to go and do a peace mission. We want to give acorns to Nixon, and that's all we want to do, but someone doesn't want us to. So the Bahamas are the best deal we could think of. We'll probably do a Bed-in down there like we did in Amsterdam, which is stay in bed for a week. We call it a Bed-in and our second honeymoon, which we're having rather quickly after our first one. We'll be doing that from the Bahamas, in bed for a week, then we'll be out and about a bit, waiting to hear about the States. I'm trying to get friends inside to help us. I think they think I'm going to go there and run around the streets naked.

QUESTION: That's not your plan?

JOHN: No, that's not our plan. Our plan is simply to promote peace in a nonviolent fashion, and the States need it. It's the right time for two nonviolent people to go and promote nonviolence. The situation is serious enough for them to be with people who are going to say to the kids, "Don't break it." Which is a bit explicit in that letter. The kids are shouting, "Kill the pigs." We're saying get off that and get back to "Make Love Not War"—it's the only way out. And that's it really, in a nutshell.

YOKO ONO: We're not trying anything special, you know. It's just something to remind them, "Remember love and peace."

JOHN: And give peace a chance. That's really something to be frightened of!

QUESTION: Did you actually board the QE2 last week?*

JOHN: No, we never got on.

QUESTION: Did you think you could go over to the States?

---

* Lennon is referring to a proposed cruise to the United States aboard the QE2 he and Yoko were supposed to take. In the end they were turned away at the dock due to a fairly recent drug bust, and Derek Taylor sailed instead.

JOHN: Well, I was given to understand that within a reasonable space of time there's a good chance of me getting a visa. The circumstance that kept me out was the British drug charges, but the judge accepted the mitigating circumstances. I can't see why the States can't.

QUESTION: America is under the impression it's the British that won't let you out.

JOHN: And the British are under the impression it's the Americans that won't let me in. It's just a game that's going on, and it's called "delaying tactics." So we waited a week. We almost wasted ten days trying to go out there, so now we're going to get as near as we can.

QUESTION: So you have no trouble going to the Bahamas?

JOHN: No, it's British.

QUESTION: If and when you get into the States, what do you plan?

JOHN: Well, we hope to have an audience with Nixon and give him some acorns to plant as a symbol of peace. We think of it as a positive move towards peace. We hope to go around the world doing that. We thought we'd start with America, as it was an English-speaking nation and because of the violence going on there. If we have any influence over the kids and youth, which we do, I am there. They think we're going to enflame the youth, but we're not. We want to pacify everyone as much as we can.

QUESTION: I don't think I understand exactly what you're going to do in the Bahamas.

JOHN: We'll do seven days in bed, in which we'll hold a press conference for anyone who is interested at the radio stations, TV, press, school magazines, and we'd like the press from the North America as well as the South.

QUESTION: What, if anything, do you think was accomplished in Amsterdam by your Bed-in?

YOKO: Peace and happy vibrations. Mainly communicating with the youth. We've got letters from people that actually had Bed-ins.

JOHN: We've got thousands of letters from people who have been influenced by it, and that's apart from the good stuff in the press, like cartoons, etc. We appreciate the cartoons, whether they're for us or against us—it gives people a laugh. A laugh is a release of tension, so we don't mind being Abbott and Costello for the world—we'll do that if it relaxes people. Anything we can do, we'll do it. And so, cartoons and everything are worthwhile. Any kind of picture of us, whether it's us getting off a plane or sitting in the office, whatever, because we're talking about the essentials of life, and most newspaper headlines are not that essential.

So we think our propaganda is as important as the next man's, because we're talking just about peace and not about what size table.*

QUESTION: How do you feel about the criticism that says that you should perhaps take more positive measures?

JOHN: This is the most positive thing that our two minds, which are pretty well ticking, could think of. Whether we appear as freaks or clowns, the effect here was that everybody of that period was talking about peace, and since then we threw a stone in the water, and the ripples are still going around. We've had various approaches from various peace movements asking, "What can we do?" Looks like the marches are going nowhere, which is what we're saying—all you get is front-page headlines of violence after the march. We'll think of a few gimmicks for them, too. What we did was say, "John and Yoko are available for peace functions," so that's what we did. It doesn't matter if they think we're freaks—we are freaks, in their eyes. But who's to judge what a freak is?

YOKO: It gives a great uplifting beat to the whole world, and the world is so tense, and you just kind of smile again.

JOHN: It started out, if the world was a party and if it was a bit miserable or a bit intellectual and everyone got onto one subject, and someone comes in a bit pissed or happy, it can change the whole atmosphere, even if it's for five minutes. And that's all we're doing: take the world as one big party. Everybody's talking about what to do and not doing anything. We say we are doing something. We're the guy that comes in the room and cheers everybody up, at least. Even our friends the British press, they're always knocking us, and they're friendly faces. I know them—they've been seeing me coming for years. And I know them as people, and what they write is vaguely what they think. It's not the same, we know what the game is. In "The Ballad of John and Yoko," it's the Beatles' new song, and I say the press said, "It's good to have the both of you back"—they actually said that.

QUESTION: What could be the most constructive or the best outcome of your mission in the U.S.?

JOHN: Inspire the kids into protesting in a nonviolent way. We think violence begets violence, and the establishment knows how to fight violence, but they don't know how to fight candy. We just want to tell them here's an instance of how to protest by staying in bed. Everyone says, "Well, that's all right for you, staying in bed," but what we did the first time was give up our honeymoon—anybody could do that. If some old woman up in Lancashire did it and

---

* An allusion to the peace talks held between the United States and Vietnam in which extensive arguments took place over what shape the negotiating table should be.

announced it to the local press before we'd done it, all the local press would say, "What the hell," and go down to see what this freaky old woman is doing, and that's the argument against people saying, "It's all right for you two." It is the best way for us two, but if some old woman wants to do something, she could do something else. We're giving people incentive to do something for peace.

QUESTION: It's not a lost cause—there is more peace than war.

JOHN: Yeah, more disgrace, more noise. But I don't think the situation is going to get like the First World War, where everyone is happy to go to war. Like the whole of Britain was coming into the first war thinking they couldn't wait to get out there for the three-day fight and come home with the spoils, a bit of rape and it's all over. So what we're doing is reminding people of that: don't be conned by fighting the good fight.

QUESTION: Are you particularly protesting the Vietnam war?

JOHN: Not particularly at all—all violence. Whether it's local violence in the back alley, or student violence, or any violence. Vietnam is really a manifestation of the world's violence, like the First World War was, or like Hitler was, and we're antiviolence, full stop.

QUESTION: I understand you're keeping banker's hours these days.

JOHN: Yeah, I've always kept twenty-four-hours-a-day hours. It just so happens I find it convenient to keep them here, because it's a twenty-four-hour job. The Beatles and the peacenik freaks, John and Yoko, it's the same gig, it's our business as well, so we do both—the Beatles, Apple, and this.

QUESTION: Will this jaunt to Bermuda interfere with your Apple business?

JOHN: No, no. Apple business is doing okay now that we have Klein and good people to look after it—David Plathes. And the Beatles have taken a break at this point in time. I should have been in America at this time, because George and Paul are on holiday, and I think Ringo is in the Bahamas too, so I might spoil his holiday for him.

QUESTION: George and Paul are in New York?

JOHN: No. George has been banned from the States as well.

QUESTION: Paul is in the States?

JOHN: No, he's been and gone. So, I'm taking a few weeks' holiday time, and we'll come back to do Beatle business.

QUESTION: You've just finished an album?

JOHN: Yeah, the Beatles album is finished now, and we're half through with the next one, so we feel we can take a break, and we'll use it for one of our ends. We want to . . . I'm using it for peace. And we'll be back to finish the Beatles film, which is half through—the Beatles TV film, which is the title of the album.

QUESTION: Do you miss the touring days?

JOHN: I'm on tour now, aren't I? I'm on tour now.

QUESTION: What next, other than your film and album?

JOHN: That's all for the Beatles now, the film and the album. And for us, we hope to go around to the major areas of the world and promote peace.

QUESTION: How long do you expect this tour to go on?

JOHN: It could be over a whole year. We'll do it whenever we get the chance or whenever we get invited somewhere. We're choosing which exact place to go in the Bahamas.

QUESTION: I didn't quite get your comment about Cuba.

JOHN: Cuba is a little guy waving a flag, and we're going to do a little Cuba in the Bahamas.

QUESTION: Do you honestly feel that you could get an audience with the president?

JOHN: Sure. I mean, if Duke Ellington can, why can't we? And the pope—anyone, all of them.

QUESTION: Do you want to summarize?

JOHN: We're not allowed to get into the States, and the reasons we're given are various. We're going to the Bahamas to promote peace. We're trying to get into the States to promote peace with only nonviolent protest. The States are afraid we're going to go over and rouse the kids up, which we don't intend to do at all. We intend to calm it down, you know. I think the States need us, and we can help. I don't see what reasons—okay, there's the offense, but they allowed Donovan in, and it's the same bit.* There were mitigating circumstances allowed by the judge here—why can't they accept that? Anything more about the visa, I could let your people know in the Bahamas, but there is still a chance today of getting it. I'm going to keep trying a bit nearer this time, a bit more publicly. There might be a bit more on the visa, which I'll tell you about in the Bahamas, backstage details.

QUESTION: What are you going to be doing in the Bahamas?

---

* He is referring to sixties' singer Donovan Leitch who, like John, was slapped with a minor drug charge.

JOHN: We're going to do seven days lying [in bed] again and talk to the press and all the people that are interested in the communication world—radio, TV, newspapers, anything—and tell them a few stories about peace.

QUESTION: You definitely think you achieved something by doing this in Amsterdam?

JOHN: Sure we did, we achieved a lot. We relieved some tension in the world by giving a laugh. We got many, many, letters from all walks of life backing us. Today we've been approached by many of the major peace movements to see if we can inject any life into them as they go around in circles. And that's just the start. We threw a stone in the water and the ripples are still rippling. And now we're going to throw another stone in, the same message tied to the stone, and see what happens, and we don't intend to stop until peace is declared. And the main complaint about the bed event is that, "Oh, yeah, it's okay for them two to stay in bed, they can afford it," but anybody can afford to stay in bed, especially on their honeymoon or on holiday. If some old woman did it before we did it and announced in Lancashire that they were going to do it, the press would be on them like flies on hotcakes. So, all we're doing is giving people inspiration to do protests against violence in a nonviolent way. All the marches get front-page news about violence and the police or from the crowd or whatever, and violence begets violence, and we're saying the obvious: you got to get it peacefully.

QUESTION: I think most people think you can find something else to do.

JOHN: What's more peaceful than that? We'd like to meet with the president and give him some acorns to plant as a symbol for world peace. Acorn trees grow, and acorns are simply seeds, and that's a very symbolic thing. It's also a positive move towards peace, and there need be no discussions about what size table or field to plant it in: just plant it, and that's a positive public move. Besides just saying, "I'd like to start talking about it, talking about it, talking about it."

QUESTION: The last time the president tried to plant a tree, he ended up straining his back.

JOHN: Well, I think it's worth it for world peace.

QUESTION: Tell me about the acorns.

JOHN: That originated from a piece of sculpture at the Coventry Exhibition at Coventry Church, which was a heavy piece of metal. And we came up with the idea to seize it as a living sculpture, and we did that, and then we resurrected it for world peace, you know.

QUESTION: When you got back from Amsterdam, you said something about mailing acorns.

JOHN: We'll mail them as well, but we thought that by taking them we would make sure they got it. If we get into the States we'll mail from the U.N., where everybody is in one pile. Except for China—they stay outside it. The acorns are waiting for us in parcels with everyone's name on them, but we thought if we could give them personally to one or two world leaders and then post them to the other people, then they'd have more effect than having one shot in the paper of us posting acorns, which might get lost or unacknowledged. Think of it like a big pop song, and you got to have a great catch phrase, and the catch phrase is "acorns for peace," and we're keeping the beat, and there is people catching on.

QUESTION: So that's what you plan to do if you get to see the president?

JOHN: Yeah, and get him to plant them for peace—that's our main intention of getting into the States. Everything else will be a sideline.

QUESTION: That and getting access to the public newspapers and communication people over there.

JOHN: We can get them from the Bahamas—it shouldn't take long to get down. I did *Help* down there, a Beatles film, and they were there, weren't they?

QUESTION: Maybe what you want to do is to have some guy hire a boat to run you there and back again.

JOHN: No, that's too risky. I don't want to do anything illegal.

QUESTION: Do you see this becoming a world movement, this lying for peace?

JOHN: We could get them thinking, get them thinking of other ways. If they don't think of anything, then lie in for peace. If they think of something to top it, then that will be our competition of other peace gimmicks. Then the others can just use the word "peace."

*A rare, previously unpublished shot of John at home in Liverpool
before setting off to conquer the world, 1964.*

Mimi's comfortable front room in "Mendips," the suburban semi-detached home on Menlove Avenue where John grew up.

Alfred Lennon, John's unpredictable, seafaring dad, 1965.

John's beloved stepsisters, Julia and Jacqui.

Julia Stanley Lennon holds her last child, Jacqui Dykins.

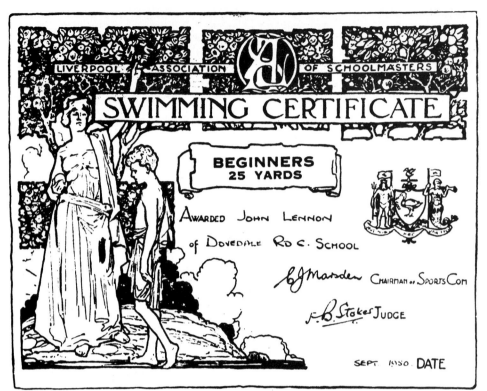

LIVERPOOL ASSOCIATION OF SCHOOLMASTERS

SWIMMING CERTIFICATE

BEGINNERS
25 YARDS

AWARDED JOHN LENNON

of DOVEDALE RD C. SCHOOL

C.J Marsden CHAIRMAN of SPORTS COM

F.B. Stokes JUDGE

SEPT 1950 DATE

*John becomes a qualified swimmer
at the ripe age of 10.*

*In the beginning,
1964.*

*Pete Best after being
unceremoniously sacked
from the group.*

An early British television appearance.

The Beatles pose with "My Guy" singer Mary Wells.

John with his trusty Rickenbacher in hand.

Performing in Hong Kong in 1964 with Beatles' replacement drummer Jimmy Nichols.

Arriving in America.

*Ripping it up
on the road.*

*Fun with the Fabs in the
comfort and privacy of
your own home!*

Another silly Fab Four photo op.

A rare shot of John at the keyboards.

The Fabs play in sunny LA.

Visiting with a long-lost relative in New Zealand.

The Beatles meet the press yet again.

Classic Lennon on stage with the Beatles.

John and Cyn happy, together on holiday in the mid-sixties.

John as the happy washroom attendant in the BBC television special, "Not Only But Also," starring Peter Cook and Dudley Moore.

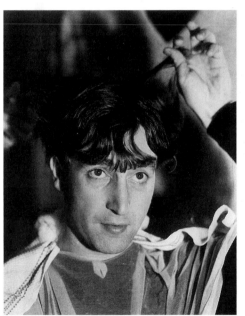

John's spiffy new haircut for How I Won the War, 1966.

Lennon as Musketeer Gripweed in How I Won the War.

*John presides over a mock wedding at a London costume party
during the Summer of Love.*

With his Holiness The Maharishi Mahesh Yogi, London 1967. Although he and John had an initial falling-out, the giggly guru's teachings remained a source of inspiration for Lennon throughout his life.

The best of friends, at the press reception for Sgt. Pepper, 1967.

Psychedelic John at an art show opening

The Beatles attend the gala premiere of How I Won the War, *London 1967.*

The Beatles following their performance of "All You Need Is Love" at the world's first live global satellite broadcast, "Our World," circa 1967.

Sharing a laugh during the filming of Magical Mystery Tour.

John and Cynthia in 1968, as reports grow in London that their marriage is on the rocks.

A paparazzi shot of Lennon and Yoko, circa 1968.

Lennon on The David Frost Show *performing "Hey Jude," 1968.*

John Lennon and Yoko Ono

PRESS CONFERENCE #1

London, 1969

QUESTION: Recently, all the things you've done seem to be very public.

JOHN LENNON: You're in a fishbowl, so make use of it, man. Instead of all the cameras on the outside looking in, we got cameras on the inside looking out. It's no good working for money, and there's nothing else to do but work. So working for peace is now our objective.

QUESTION: This is a new development—you haven't actively pursued this in the past.

JOHN: We were sneaky peaceniks. We always came out anti-Vietnam, but now it's all positive. Now, if we put out *Sgt. Pepper's Lonely Hearts Club*, "for Peace" gets stuck on the end. I can't speak for all of the Beatles, but everything I do is for that.

QUESTION: As I remember, John, you were pained about the reaction to your Jesus statements. How do you feel about public reaction these days?

JOHN: Well, it varies. I'm still human. I get hurt and I'm pleased, depending on the remarks.

QUESTION: How would you say your relationship with Yoko has affected your personal outlook?

JOHN: She released me, and I'm me again. I got lost in the Beatles, and now it's John Lennon again. That's what she's done. It was coming. It was happening slowly. We stopped touring for all the reasons we had taken a couple years off and sold ourselves out. We just got lost, and now I've found myself happily married.

QUESTION: How has it affected your relationship with the other Beatles?

JOHN: Like most close friends, they were a bit puzzled at first, but they got over it. It appeared I had freaked out. I left home and moved in with a girl nobody knew anything about, who hadn't been on the scene. It all happened overnight for them.

QUESTION: How has it affected you creatively?

JOHN: Very positively. She's encouraged all the other talents I possess. We released each other. She was in an art bag and I was in a pop bag. So what we did for each other was to get ourselves out of the bag we were in. We got out of art and pop in that way. I mean we are in the same bag, but we got out spiritually.

103

QUESTION: Can you give me an example of how this release has specifically affected your work?

JOHN: I'm making these albums with Yoko. *Two Virgins* is the next one, and the other one is already in the can.*

QUESTION: What did you do on the *Rock 'n' Roll Circus?*

JOHN: Well, I did a track from a Beatles LP called "Yer Blues." Then Yoko came on and sang while we gigged a twelve-bar. There was also a violist trying to play, but he lost out.

QUESTION: In one of the interviews I read, you said that you were "waiting for this kind of woman." Was that an accurate quote?

JOHN: I'd always dreamed of this woman I'd be physically attracted to and had a brain, but I was beginning to think she didn't exist. So she's one in a million, and a tough one, because she had to make it on her own in the art world, which is as snide as show business, if not more. It's a tough world and she's a tough woman, like I'm a tough guy, but I'm also not tough. It's both black and white, one completely weak and one strong. So if one of us is strong and the other is feeling weak, one can carry the other. It was like the Beatles used to do for each other. So we do that for each other, and when we're both strong, we're very strong. When we're both weak, we hide.

QUESTION: Inevitably this is going to weaken your psychic ties to the other Beatles, because you are going to be getting the same input you used to rely on the others for.

JOHN: Yeah—you see, they're growing up too. We all still want the Beatles, because it's a big power, and we've no intention of splitting, none of us.

QUESTION: But your relationship has a different shape to it now.

JOHN: I can't be specific, but obviously if I'm deeply involved with Yoko, I may be less reliant on the others. It goes for the others too, as we are all branching out. We nip out and do some work and nip back.

QUESTION: So the stories of strife and conflict are exaggerated?

JOHN: Yeah. George and Paul have an argument, and it came out in all the papers George and I had a fistfight. Sure, we have arguments—we never said we didn't. We used to bitch like hell on those tours. We had only each other to bitch at. You've got to release it somehow, and that's how we got so close—

---

* *Two Virgins*, which featured John and Yoko nude on the front and back covers, was released on November 22, 1968. The other album John makes reference to is the similarly avant-garde *Unfinished Music Number 2/Life with the Lions*, issued May 9, 1969.

because we were tied in a room together. Just like those films you see where a group of people are stuck in the Amazon because their plane crashed, and they've got to work it out. We've been through that, the old army buddies bit. That's how we got so close, by being together all the time.

QUESTION: Recently there has been some discussion about whether there's going to be another Beatles tour.

JOHN: It's a possibility, but Ringo says it isn't so, that's what it is.

QUESTION: Have you talked it over with him?

JOHN: Not specifically. There was somebody interviewing him at the time, asking if there had been any talks, but we haven't talked at all. I've been speaking to Paul about possibly going on tour and how we'd do it. Then someone asked me, and it just so happened both quotes came out at the same time. So I said, "Yeah, there's a possibility," and then Ringo says, "No tour." I saw Ringo and said, "So what is it?" and he said, "I don't know. I don't fancy it." And I said, "Well, I do under certain circumstances." And he said, "It would be the same." I said, "Well, it wouldn't be the same." And that's where it is. I'm not that keen on it, but it wouldn't harm us.

QUESTION: How would it be different?

JOHN: Well, for a start, we wouldn't do it every night, jumping plane to plane. We'd do it to suit us and not the promoter. With all that's going on with the reshaping of Northern Songs, it's almost impossible to talk about what the Beatles are going to do as Beatles. The thing we can do, however, is record. Nothing seems to affect that.

QUESTION: Is the new album going to be a double album?

JOHN: No, a single. It's caught live, it was recording while we were filming. So no gimmicks. If we did a bum take, after ten times we just picked the best one. It's *Nashville Skyline*, backwards.* We went in, sang them, and came out. We were really just rehearsing for this show we were going to do but never did. The album is a rehearsal for the show that was never us.

QUESTION: What is the style going to be? There has been a lot of talk about the change from *Sgt. Pepper* to the latest double album.

JOHN: The basic styles never change. Some tunes are slow with an offbeat, some tunes fast with an offbeat.

QUESTION: The style was not different from *Sgt. Pepper?*

---

* Bob Dylan's breakaway country album, released following his near-fatal motorcycle accident near his home in Woodstock, New York, in which he broke his neck.

JOHN: The *presentation* was different. I mean, "Sgt. Pepper," the actual song, was a rock tune. It was just songs, some fast and some slow. But the packaging and overall image was the difference, and the linking of the tracks. It still didn't make the songs any different. If people recorded them individually, somebody didn't record "Getting Better" from the opera *Sgt. Peppers Lonely Hearts Club Band*—it would be "Getting Better" as a pop song.

QUESTION: You don't claim any special significance for the *Sgt. Pepper* album?

JOHN: Well, *Sgt. Pepper* was significant in our lives. Our LPs reflect where we are at the moment, and *Pepper* reflected the changes we were going through and what we looked forward to. It was significant, I'm not putting it down, but it wasn't an opera. Any one of the numbers could stand individually. It's like a box of chocolates, and with *Sgt. Pepper* we wrapped the chocolates up in nice paper or wrapped two together. All we had, in fact, was still a box with chocolates.

QUESTION: People have said *Sgt. Pepper* wasn't just the packaging, it was the lyrics and overall symbolism.

JOHN: There is just as much symbolism in *Rubber Soul* or *Revolver. Sgt. Pepper* was more important because it was the best album to date. That symbolism, however, only exists in people's minds—therefore it's right. If an intellectual sees intellectual shit in it, it's there. And if a drug addict sees drug shit in it, it's there. Like the incident with "Lucy in the Sky with Diamonds"—it wasn't LSD. My son really said "Lucy in the sky with diamonds" about a picture. He didn't say, "LSD." And the other song which was supposedly drug oriented, but wasn't at all, was "Mr. Kite." "Mr. H. will demonstrate"—everyone thought it was heroin, but it wasn't. It was me trying to say "Mr. Henderson will demonstrate," but I couldn't get "Henderson" to fit, so I called him "Mr. H."

QUESTION: It doesn't stop there. They're talking about the line "Get it under your skin" as symbolism for heroin.

JOHN: You get used to it, believe me.

QUESTION: And "Happiness Is a Warm Gun."

JOHN: That was the greatest, because it was so far from anything! I know that "I need a fix" means that in a way, but it also means anything else you need a fix of. "Happiness Is a Warm Gun" I got from a gun book, the latest monthly. It said, "Happiness is a warm gun," and I couldn't believe it. And the rest were bits of songs stuck in, joined up to make one song. It really sounded like a trip through rock 'n' roll to me.*

---

* Interestingly, it was at this time in his life that John was regularly using heroin.

QUESTION: "I Am the Walrus" has been called a Hindu mantra.

JOHN: *All music is mantra.* Everything is mantra. Like writing, mantras are a repeat or vibration. Pop music is like the people's mantra, and the offbeat keeps it steady.

QUESTION: What was the thing with "I am he as you are . . ."?

JOHN: Well, that's just a statement saying, "We're all one."

QUESTION: It didn't relate to your experience at the time?

JOHN: It relates to me in as much as I was the person going through that at the time. What you write is influenced by everything. I didn't think, "I've learned meditation, so I will put mantra into this song as a specific format." It just happened, but everything that happens rubs off on me, and I'm influenced by everyone and everything. So it's no deeper than that.

QUESTION: How about on "Hey Jude"—the ending makes it seven minutes long.

JOHN: Well, the ending was so good, we just kept on going. When we got into it, we just couldn't stop. That's a mantra at the end.

QUESTION: So you liked the ending a lot and simply decided to make it long?

JOHN: Yeah, that happens a lot, but we never got to seven minutes.

QUESTION: In your *Rolling Stone* interview you said, "What we are trying to do is rock 'n' roll with less philoso-rock, because rock is what we are."

JOHN: Philoso-rock is all the psychedelia everybody went through. It's valid because it was the experience we went through. Now we sing "Get Back" instead of "Get Back Monkey." Most of the lyrics on the new album are pretty straight: "I love you, you love me, and we are all together." I'm fed up with that shit, and everybody's going through it. Nobody's sitting down planning the next move. Everybody's had enough of it, and everybody wants to "kick out the jams," as I believe they're saying over there.

QUESTION: I don't think that's a saying over there.

JOHN: Yes, it is. The MC5, one of your motherfucking baby-kicking groups!

QUESTION: Have you heard Judy Collins's version of "In My Life"? You really ought to listen to it—it's fabulous. It's on an album titled *In My Life.*

JOHN: Okay, I'll get it. I've only heard Jose Feliciano's, which was beautiful.

John Lennon and Yoko Ono

Press Conference #2
•••••••••••••••••••••
London, 1969

QUESTION: I'm going to reverse the usual rules and say something and see if you agree with me. I was dismayed and appalled by what you did in sending back your MBE. You didn't appreciate the award, fine. You didn't care about having it, and you were going to send it back anyway in 1970. So you used huge, cata-strophic events of unspeakable horror as a convenient reason. You might just as well have got up and said, "I had a sinus headache this morning."

JOHN LENNON: Convenient reason for what?

QUESTION: Sending back the MBE. Did you really send it back to protest the "Nigeria-Biafra thing"?

JOHN: I'll tell you the answer . . .

QUESTION: You say you didn't want it and weren't going to use it when you got it?

JOHN: When do I get a go? I wanted to send it back maybe a year ago and was thinking about doing it privately. If I had sent it back privately, it would have got-ten back to the press anyway. I can't do things like that privately. If you accept that, I have two choices: send it back privately and it gets out anyway, or make a point of sending it back publicly and make some use out of sending it back.

QUESTION: But you didn't make any use of sending it back.

JOHN: I could disagree. It's a matter of personal opinion whether it's of any good or not. The Biafran public relations people said it was of great use. Burton Russell thought it was of great use, so it's a matter of opinion.

QUESTION: It just struck me that it diminishes you, sending back something that was worthless, calling an award so grotesque and horrible . . .

JOHN: Okay, it's worthless.

QUESTION: It won't work.

YOKO ONO: But people are getting killed every minute.

QUESTION: What I'm saying is, you are no better for what you did, so why did you diminish yourself? People thought you just did it as a gag.

JOHN: But people thought we also did the bag event for a gag, but we changed their minds.

QUESTION: Did you! Did you!

JOHN: What the hell! The Biafran public relations people thought it was good for their cause, and I'd accept their opinion over yours any day. I'm not worried about what other people think I should be doing. The people of Biafra thanked me for doing that event, and that's enough. They want all the publicity they can get. All they want is publicity.

QUESTION: It's the same thing as saying I'm ordering lunch and I'm not ordering apple pie, because I don't like apple pie anyway.

JOHN: If it gets on the front page of the paper that I don't like apple pie for peace.

QUESTION: Is that all you care about!

JOHN: Listen! Listen! Listen! If I'm going to get myself on the front page, I might as well get myself there with the word "peace" . . .

QUESTION: You're a fake.

JOHN: Okay, that's your opinion . . .

QUESTION: There are people who know that a protest movement doesn't involve chauffeured cars and sending back medals you despised in the first place.

YOKO: You're embarrassing him.

JOHN: Do you despise advertising?

QUESTION: I have nothing to do with it.

JOHN: You don't like it, is that what it is?

QUESTION: I don't consider it.

JOHN: Well, we use advertising . . .

QUESTION: You're an advertisement.

JOHN: Will you shut up a minute!

QUESTION: I'll try.

JOHN: We use advertising. Everybody in this century uses advertising, including politicians, the Biafrans, the Vietnamese, everybody. I use advertising to promote what I think. And I think "peace." So I promote it by using the technique called advertising . . .

QUESTION: Why don't you go to Biafra, or give money?

JOHN: I don't want to get killed. The publicity the Biafran publicity department got was worth about a quarter of a million pounds. If I gave every penny I've got, then I've got nothing and I've got to start again. Those people need money for advertisements to bring the attention of the public to the problem. They don't care how you do it, as long as you get them some attention, and that's what it's all about.

QUESTION: We're not having a discussion because you're saying, "The Republic of Biafra mission in London thanked me, and you don't see the point at all?"

YOKO: That's a good point, because those are the people in trouble, and those are the ones we're trying to help. They're the ones who need help, and we gave help to them . . .

QUESTION: It's just a huge joke, the whole thing.

YOKO: It may not be meaningful to you, but you're not the one who is going to die.

QUESTION: Well, I know a great deal more about Biafra than you, and you say because the Biafran public relations thanked you . . .

JOHN: And Burton Russell, who knows a damned eye more about protest than you, as you're claiming absolute knowledge of protest movements. We don't know much about protest movements. We know some of them go wrong and some go right. He's like, "king of the protests," man, isn't he? He didn't say anything to us about the bed event. He obviously didn't think much of it or think it was effective, but the MBE event affected him, and that's his generation. We got a telegram from him this morning, and he's the daddy of the protests as far as I'm concerned. We're just beginners in this protest bit. All we were mainly doing for Biafra was because I began to feel ashamed I was British. I've learned from being in the public eye that if the castle falls, it falls from within. We were doing this naturally. Yoko was telling me how this ancient Chinese book advises how to fight a battle. You never close all the doors, because the enemy will attack in vast concentration, but if you leave one open, you know where the enemy is going to come in. We leave many doors open, like irrelevant comments about "Cold Turkey," long hair, and nakedness. While people are so busy attacking we can go on protesting for peace, because that's what we do. And while they're bothering with how long my hair is or the irrelevancy of "Cold Turkey" or how dare you insult the queen and how Auntie was upset by handing it back. That's the purpose of leaving the door open. I'm personally too frightened to go to Biafra. I'm a nervous type, and I don't want to be a dead saint. People prefer dead saints to live freaks, and we intend to stay live freaks as long as we can.

John Lennon and Yoko Ono
PRESS CONFERENCE #3
London, 1969

QUESTION: Tell me about *Get Back*.

JOHN LENNON: It's a straight documentary, but there's a few things being added to the version you've heard.

QUESTION: I don't know whether it's true, but I've heard a copy has already been sent to the States.

JOHN: Yeah, it was on the air, but now it's a different album from that. It's been changed a bit. Now there's "Across the Universe" on it, which we recorded in 1967, but I sing it in the film, so they're putting it in, at last! I gave it to Spike Milligan for some wildlife thing, and it's been two years. On the film, it's just us starting off to do a TV show and ends up a TV show.*

QUESTION: Is there a row with George in it?

JOHN: George didn't have a row with me. I think he had a bit of a barney with Paul, but you don't see that. You just see that one day George isn't there and it's just the three of us playing. He said, "I'm leaving," and we carried on playing.

QUESTION: And Ringo, I gather, at one time left? "It's just not fun any more" was his quote.

JOHN: Yeah, yeah.

QUESTION: But you always come back in the end. When you think about it, there's no reason the Beatles can't function together while we all function as individuals.

JOHN: It's just that if it's happy, we do it, and if it's not, we don't.

QUESTION: Is there anything you'd like people to know at this point?

JOHN: I'd like them to know the Plastic Ono LP is coming out on December twelfth, so get your copy now. By the way, bed events and MBEs and other people doing things has made people like Nixon have to adjust. I'm not saying it's a *direct* consequence of what we do, but it's part of the overall pattern of people

---

* *Get Back*, eventually entitled *Let It Be*, was the Beatles' cinematic swan song, released in theatres worldwide on May 13, 1970. The intimate and, at times, disturbing documentary exposed the already widespread dry rot inherent in the group.

like us and our friends around the world. It's making him very nervous. People should realize any little bit helps, that's all I want to tell you.

QUESTION: I sometimes wonder if you have some kind of kinky wish to be hated.

JOHN: I'd prefer to be loved. I'd prefer the whole world to be loved—that's the game. You've got to love me, even if I'm a hunchbacked Negro with one leg and a transvestite.

QUESTION: Jewish?

JOHN: Okay, a hunchbacked Jewish Negro with one leg who's a transvestite. I want to be loved for myself and not a kind of image. I'm not painting myself white to be loved. That's the whole game—prejudice and fear. Most journalists write about how my Auntie felt about my MBE rather than peace in Biafra, because they don't want to be conned. They're frightened of committing themselves, and rather than being conned by the entertainer, they'd sooner divert their attention to something irrelevant.

QUESTION: Let's not be so cynical for a moment. Maybe it could have been a strictly human thing.

JOHN: But what's important? The MBE, Biafra, Vietnam, or Aunt Mimi's feelings?

QUESTION: Yes, in that order, fine.

JOHN: And so, folks, the Plastic Ono Band comes out December twelfth with a nice picture of the sky and a fab calendar of yearly events by John and Yoko with lots of poetry and fun. It's a live performance from the Toronto Rock 'n' Roll Freakout! Price, I don't know. Ask EMI. Depends on who's paying for the calendar.

QUESTION: The Rock 'n' Roll Revival in Toronto, was this a big nostalgic trip?

JOHN: Well, when I heard that Little Richard and Chuck Berry were going to be on, I thought, "Right, lets go." Of course, I was so busy being sick backstage I never saw them. I was crapping meself, because I haven't performed for twenty years or something. I mean, I'd done "Cambridge '69" with Yoko, but that was a small place where I just sort of went with me guitar.* But this time I said, "How does this go?" to the band, because I couldn't rehearse them.

QUESTION: I noticed you are doing an appearance at the Lyceum.

JOHN: We're not. They keep saying that. It's not definite.

YOKO ONO: Only you [the media] said it was definite.

---

* This improvisational piece was later released on the album *Life with the Lions, Unfinished Music Number 2*.

JOHN: The way they conned the public, we're going to get the finger pointed at us. I think we might help them, because it's a good UNICEF gig. But that's what they've done. They say we're coming. Whether or not someone in the office gave them a hint or something, we never said anything. I came home from holiday and read I was performing at the Lyceum Ballroom. So there's been a lot of stick about that.*

QUESTION: How does Yoko feel about playing live in front of thousands of people? Does it give you any emotions?

YOKO: I've been appearing before in smaller circles. But to me, whenever I get on stage it's a different kind of high, and it doesn't matter if there are twenty thousand or twenty. Well, twenty is a bit depressing, depending on the hall. But in the end, it really doesn't matter.

---

* The Lennons did perform at the star-studded event. Several of the tracks were subsequently released on John and Yoko's *Sometime in NYC* LP.

John Lennon and Yoko Ono
PRESS CONFERENCE #4
London, 1969

QUESTION: When you think of the word "parents," what comes into your mind?

JOHN LENNON: Wedding Album.*

QUESTION: Think of the word "hatred."

YOKO ONO: Love.

QUESTION: The word "insecurity."

JOHN: Fear.

QUESTION: Maybe I haven't explained it correctly. I don't want you to give me one-word associations.

JOHN: I thought it was like a game.

QUESTION: And I thought this was famous Lennon wit. What I meant was, if I say a word, just tell me your thoughts. Are you with me? If you don't have a thought . . .

JOHN: Well, I'll always have a thought!

QUESTION: Let's start again. Think of the word "children."

JOHN: Missing. I'm thinking one word, and that's it. You see, our children are missing from our lives, folks.†

QUESTION: The word "police"?

JOHN: Just men in uniform! I don't have a feeling in general towards them. It might just be human beings in uniforms. They all have very short hair.

QUESTION: The word "work."

JOHN: Play. I mean, work for me and my dear wife is play.

QUESTION: Explain.

---

* *The Wedding Album* was the Lennons' third album of so-called unfinished music, released on November 7, 1969. It was perhaps the first boxed set containing not only an LP but an assortment of memorabilia relating to the Lennons' recent nuptials in Gibraltar.

† Here Lennon refers to the fact that his and Yoko's recent divorces temporarily kept the couple from spending time with their two young children, Julian and Kyoko.

JOHN: Well, we just went on a two-week holiday to Greece for a few days, and then we went to India, and all the time we were trying to get through to the office to find out what's going on, you see. So, we spent the whole two weeks trying to get through from India. We prefer work to anything else. Work is life.

QUESTION: Think about the word "money."

JOHN: Paper, as the song goes, and power or protection from our insecurities and fear, constable.

YOKO: It's very, very tricky. Everybody thinks it's so tangible. When you feel like it's tangible, that's when it traps you.

QUESTION: "Insecurity."

JOHN: Just fear. I can't think of anything else except fear. We all have it. Money doesn't solve it and work doesn't solve it, but work is the best cure for anything, really. You've no time to be insecure if you're doing something productive.

YOKO: Work is divine.

JOHN: Yeah, so when we're not working, we get depressed. But people think, "What's work to you is all gimmicks and events," but events and gimmicks are work. It hides insecurity—in fact, it makes you secure when you're working. There's nothing like, after a full day's work, sitting and thinking, "That was good, that was bad, I'll do that tomorrow."

QUESTION: Tell me about the word "Christmas."

JOHN: I don't know. I've only got the child's image of Christmas.

QUESTION: Tell me about the image.

JOHN: Well, the child's Christmas image is just snow and red scarves, getting mouth organs, and things like that. That's Christmas. To me, Christmas now is, "What kind of event can we do for Christmas, what kind of scene?"

QUESTION: "Love."

JOHN: Well, it means Yoko to me, God and people. I think love is a gift. You can't just sit on your back with it—you have to nurture it like a rare flower or something. You have to water it, make sure the flies don't get to it, don't let the dog crap on it. You have to work on it to help it grow. It's a full-time occupation, being in love. It does come out of the sky, but so does rain. If you want to make use of it, you have got to do something with it.

QUESTION: "Hate."

JOHN: Hate is like fear and insecurity.

QUESTION: Do you hate anything?

JOHN: I have moments of hate and insecurity, but I have no permanent hate object. I hate fear and hate.

QUESTION: "Death."

JOHN: Death *is*. I hope we both die together. One of our greatest fears is one dying before the other, even three minutes. We'd like to die together—that's the last trip.

YOKO: We're not afraid of death.

JOHN: It's like being born.

QUESTION: "Failure."

JOHN: I don't know what it is. I think failure is only a state of mind. It's like people saying our film *Magical Mystery Tour* failed. But it didn't fail for me.

QUESTION: How did you feel when everybody said you failed?

JOHN: I just thought, "It was on at the wrong time, and it should have been in color." The movie itself will stand the test of time. They called giving away all the clothes at the Apple shop a failure, but it wasn't.* It was a grand event, like giving the MBE away. So failure is how you look at it.

QUESTION: "Royalty."

JOHN: Royalty. It's something on strings—I mean velvet. Royalty has its name on biscuits and tea, that's what it means to me.

QUESTION: "Fans."

JOHN: All the young kids I think of. There is a difference between fans and someone who just digs you. There's different ways of digging people. I think fans worship. It's something you do when you're eighteen to twenty-one, and you often don't grow out of it. You either continue in a different kind of relationship with the object or you become a fan of somebody else, if you want to remain a fan all your life. I was a fan of Elvis, Little Richard, Chuck Berry, Carl Perkins, and Gene Vincent, but now I couldn't be termed a fan, so I have another relationship with them. That's what I think a fan is—it's a kind of relationship.

QUESTION: Devote your minds to thinking about the word "privacy."

JOHN: That's a state of mind as well. The kind of physical privacy, like John and Yoko being at home alone, you enjoy. Privacy is just me and Yoko being alone, and part of that's a state of mind, alone in a crowd. So that's privacy.

---

* On July 31, 1968, the Beatles closed down their boutique on Baker Street, London, by giving away the entire contents of the store.

QUESTION: "Childhood."

JOHN: Nice—lots of summers, family holidays, and parks.

YOKO: I wouldn't want to go through it again.

JOHN: Oh, no. I don't miss anything. The memories are nice—of all the good times, mainly.

QUESTION: "London."

JOHN: Nice, and they're cleaning it up, which I like. It smells nice. I miss it when I'm not there, and that's London.

QUESTION: What does Christmas mean to you, Yoko?

YOKO: It's the same. The Japanese are catching on to the ways of other nations—it's also very nostalgic.

QUESTION: How do they celebrate it?

YOKO: It's the same. Even when I was five, there were discussions among the adults about whether to tell me Santa Claus really existed. I really didn't learn Santa didn't exist for a long time—they were playing that game, you know.

QUESTION: What do they call Santa Claus?

YOKO: Santa Claus.

JOHN: They're just Americans in drag.

YOKO: I mean, if you go to Japan and say that Santa Claus is purely a Western thing, they might be offended.

JOHN: They have a perfect clockwork imitation of Santa there, born on Mt. Fuji.

QUESTION: How do you react to the word "criticism?"

JOHN: It's part of the game—it's still communication, whichever way the criticism goes. And communication is what it's all about, folks, for us and you, too.

YOKO: Even if they criticize you badly, you know someone's going to think it's all right. It's always fifty-fifty.

QUESTION: "War?"

JOHN: It's a game that goes too far and you actually get hurt. The whole world seems to be playing that game, and we've all gone too far, and everybody is so into it. They've forgotten. It needn't be like that at all. So that's what our game is—to remind people that it's a game that has gone too far and we can stop it.

QUESTION: "Religion?"

JOHN: Established money and buildings. I can never remember what the real word means. It doesn't mean that much to me.

YOKO: Religion is all right as long as they're only telling us the rules. What people want is a father figure—they think in terms of Buddha, Christ, or Mohammed, whatever. They want to rely on their father. It's not just learning the rules, which is very crude—it's adoration. There's no difference between that and adoring Hitler. It's a very dangerous game to play.

JOHN: I think they'll always want the Big Father—I don't think they'll ever lose that.

QUESTION: "Laughter?"

JOHN: Our next LP, which we are going to make this evening, is going to be an LP of laughter.

QUESTION: How are you going to do that?

JOHN: We're going to get a few friends together and have a laugh. That will be Yoko and me; Mal, the engineer; Jack, the A&R man; Malcolm, our road manager; and a guy we've heard has a great laugh. A few funny noses, a bottle of wine, and off we go. Laughter is good news.

QUESTION: "Happiness?"

YOKO: Being together.

JOHN: There's no permanent state of happiness, unless it's when you go to heaven. It's something you only get a *bit* of here on earth. It's like you have roast lamb on Sunday—you can't have it every day.

QUESTION: "Poverty?"

JOHN: I'm not sure. I don't think I've ever been poverty-stricken, so I don't really know what it is. It's probably a pretty tough scene. It depends on the people though, I suppose.

YOKO: There must be a line where it becomes masochism. I'm sure there is a way of getting out of poverty, and there's a point whether you either decide to get out or not.

QUESTION: A lot of people don't control their own destiny.

JOHN: We're hardly allowed to, the way things are set up.

YOKO: I find this in many people who are poor—it's a state of mind. They have a certain kind of pride that's almost incomprehensive.

JOHN: Well, there's probably as much happiness among poor people as anywhere else. I don't know about people who are literally starving on the streets of India. Even that will have some angle to it—the universe seems to be built like that.

YOKO: It's like saying, "I'm starving, but I've never been a whore," so that means she prefers to starve rather than being a whore. There are certain kinds of rules they have that makes them stay in that position.

QUESTION: Okay, the last one: "fear."

JOHN: We keep having this one, though.

QUESTION: Did we?

JOHN: We had "insecurity," and then we had "fear." You obviously have got some fear in you!

John Lennon and Yoko Ono
BAG EVENT
Vienna, Austria, 1969

QUESTION: Will you come out?*

JOHN LENNON: No.

QUESTION: Why not?

JOHN: Because this is a Bag Event—total communication.

QUESTION: Don't you think it's a little out of fashion, what you do?

JOHN: You think it's a fashion to stay in a bag?

QUESTION: What is total communication—an invention of John Lennon and Yoko Ono?

JOHN: No. It already exists, and we're simply showing you one example.

QUESTION: Are there holes in the bag?

JOHN: There's a hole to get in and out.

QUESTION: Have you got a bag with you?

JOHN: It depends what language you're speaking.

QUESTION: Cockney, in this case.

JOHN: Cockney, I see. I don't think so.

QUESTION: Don't you feel warm?

JOHN: It's not too hot, thank you.

QUESTION: Would you like a drink?

JOHN: No, thank you.

QUESTION: If you could change two things about your face, what would they be?

JOHN: I have no idea. I've never thought of that.

QUESTION: Do you think you're beautiful?

---

* During this entire press conference, John and Yoko were hidden inside a very large white cloth bag. The press was, not surprisingly, quite consistently astounded.

John: I'm quite content.

Question: What about your wife?

John: I think she's very beautiful.

Question: Have you conceived a baby?

John: I've no idea.

Question: What are you going to name your child?

John: I don't want to speculate on a name, really. The "Amsterdam" idea was a joke, you know.

Question: Perhaps you could change the name to "Vienna" if it happens here.

John: Yes, certainly. This is another peace protest, by the way, folks.

Question: For peace or against?

John: *For.*

Question: Are you aware you're in the City of Love?

John: Are we? That's beautiful.

Question: They used to rent this place to the Hapsburgs.

John: Really? Well, we're highly honored.

Question: This is where the Hapsburgs used to live.

John: Did they? Well, good luck to them.

Question: But not in a bag.

Question: Somebody said they didn't know whether to pull up the drawbridge or lay out a red carpet.

John: For us or the Hapsburgs?

Question: What was your reason for coming to Vienna?

John: Well, we have a film on TV tonight, and we thought we'd plug that a bit and also plug peace from this here bag.

Yoko Ono: This is our first announcement of Bagism to the world, and we decided to do it in Vienna.

Question: By God, why?

John: Because when we were in Amsterdam doing Bed Peace, we realized we needed to make it easier to recognize what we're doing, so we are calling it

Bagism. If we, or anybody, has something to say, they can communicate from one room to another and not confuse you with what color their skin is, how long their hair's grown, or how many pimples they've got.

QUESTION: How long is your hair?

JOHN: You'll have to guess. It's not important—it's only what I *say* we're here for.

QUESTION: But you're not really saying very much, are you?

JOHN: Well, if the questions are going to be banal, you'll get banal answers.

QUESTION: Are you in that bag to hide your pimples?

JOHN: I don't have any, actually.

QUESTION: Can you prove that to me, please?

JOHN: Take my word for it.

QUESTION: Can you give us a recipe against pimples?

JOHN: I have no idea, you know. Eat good food.

QUESTION: Can you prove you're John Lennon?

JOHN: I don't have to. I'm here just to talk about peace. It doesn't matter who I am.

QUESTION: Are you the ghost of John Lennon?

JOHN: Could be.

QUESTION: Would you come out if we gave you a gold record?

JOHN: We're not coming out for the conference, but we'll be out for chocolate cake later.

QUESTION: Do you have any statement about your film on Austrian television tonight?

YOKO: I think the film will explain itself. It's very important we are communicating verbally. We are making total communication without thinking about what sort of face you have or your taste in clothes, etc. Those things usually block the minds of people, and they can't communicate.

QUESTION: If you could send anybody in show business to hell, who would it be?

JOHN: I wouldn't send anyone there willingly. I really wouldn't wish it on anybody.

QUESTION: Is there any music you especially dislike?

JOHN: I like practically all music, but there's some I definitely prefer.

QUESTION: Have you heard Viennese music?

JOHN: I've heard the waltzes, you know. I don't think anybody hasn't.

QUESTION: I didn't know you frequented places where they played waltzes.

JOHN: I don't have to. There was a thing called radio invented a few years back.

QUESTION: It brought people like you into the world.

JOHN: And it brought you into the room!

QUESTION: How about the statement Ringo Starr recently made that you'll never play in public again?

JOHN: All of the Beatles said that two years ago. Personally, I'd prefer them to come out of their box, or bag, and do another tour. But I'll have to talk to Ringo and see how he feels. It was probably when Ringo was making the film,* when George, Paul, and I were in discussing whether to go out on the road again. We were inclined to if we could get a groovy show together. Maybe take Apple on the road or something. I think perhaps it was a lack of communication between us and Ringo.

QUESTION: Perhaps it's Ringo, then, that suffers from a lack of total communication?

JOHN: No, we were just remixing the tracks we'd done† and were chatting, so when the press talked to Ringo, he wasn't even aware of the chat we'd had.

QUESTION: Is it true you once said you would appear free in concert in Vienna if it were in the opera house?

JOHN: I never said I would appear free *anywhere*.

QUESTION: Is money so important?

JOHN: I didn't say that. The Beatles have done many charity shows. I even appeared free in the Amsterdam Hotel for peace for seven full days.

QUESTION: But there was only peace in the room, not outside.

JOHN: Uh, the peace was in our minds, really. We donated one week of our two-week holiday for world peace. Now, some cynics have said, "Oh, it's easy to sit in bed for seven days," but I'd like them to try it. All we're saying is, give peace a chance.

QUESTION: Would you give me an example of anything you've changed with this action?

---

* The dark comedy *The Magic Christian*, starring the late Peter Sellers.

† Lennon is referring to the infamous and extended *Let It Be* sessions at Twickenham and Apple Studios, London.

JOHN: I couldn't give a concrete example, except for a few good cartoons that came out of it and a few interesting reactions from readers in England. One old woman claimed she had the best laugh of her life. If all we do is give someone a laugh, we're willing to be the world's clowns, because we think it's a bit serious at the moment, and intellectual. That's the least we can do, because everybody's talking about peace, but nobody does anything about *it in a peaceful way*. If you donate your holiday instead of just sleeping with your wife and giggling, you might actually do something. I'm sure the local press would be just as interested in you as they are in us.

QUESTION: Fortunately, they can't see me in a bag.

JOHN: Well, we weren't in a bag in Amsterdam. This is a sort of compressed seven days. The Hilton Hotel was a bag, in a way.

QUESTION: How were the beds?

JOHN: The typical Hilton bed, you know.

QUESTION: I guess money's not really important when you don't have to work, is it?

JOHN: I'm in a position to have money—I'm fortunate. I think the ones with real freedom, though, are people with a lot of money and people without. It's the in-between ones that have a hard time.

QUESTION: Do you ever share your money?

JOHN: I've shared a lot of my money with the poor. That's why I'm going to try and get the Beatles on the road again.

QUESTION: What's the next step for Bagism?

JOHN: I have no idea. We'll just wait for an idea to come and then go with it.

QUESTION: What do you think about the queen?

JOHN: I don't often think about her, frankly. It's a hard life she has, and her way of communication is shaking hands, as is the president's and premier's way. I don't think it's very effective, because the public knows less about the queen and the presidents than they do about us by staying in bed for seven days.

QUESTION: Maybe the queen should do that also.

JOHN: If she's interested in peace, I think she should do something positive about it.

QUESTION: Are you going to watch your movie, *Rape*, in bed tonight?

JOHN: We'll probably watch it with Hans, the guy that set everything up for us over here.

QUESTION: Did you ever betray your wife?

JOHN: No, because I love her totally and I don't want to destroy what we have together.

QUESTION: Do you think it will last forever?

JOHN: I hope so, but I can't speculate on tomorrow.

QUESTION: Would you defend your wife if it meant breaking the peace?

JOHN: Yeah, sure, but I prefer peace. I'm as violent as the next man, but I prefer myself in a peaceful state. I think violence is probably necessary in some form, but it could be channeled. I just don't want violence to interfere with my way of life. I don't see why I should be involved with other people's madness.

QUESTION: You were married only eleven days ago and you seem to have some very original ideas. Why do you rely on such a normal institution like marriage?

JOHN: We went through the whole bag about marriage. Intellectually, we know some man just gave us a piece of paper after we'd already lived together a year. Some Establishment games do happen to have a basic truth, and I think marriage is one of them. For us it was a very emotional, romantic thing to do. It's intellectual snobbery to dismiss everything that comes from the Establishment, or any other quarter, is pure crap.

QUESTION: What do you think about the Maharishi today?

JOHN: He taught me meditation, which I still do, and he also taught me—in a roundabout way—we're all our own guru.

QUESTION: What do you think about people that say he's a gangster?

JOHN: I don't think he's a gangster, personally, and if he really was a money conner, the press are not that stupid and they'd be able to find out where he's got it. What do you think he can do, cut off his beard and wear an Italian suit for the rest of his life in South America? You guys could catch him if he really was a gangster. I don't believe he is.

QUESTION: What do you think about the life you're living?

JOHN: I have various thoughts about it, but my most happy moments are since I met Yoko.

QUESTION: What about your Aunt Mimi?

JOHN: Well, Mimi reacts like all mothers. She still says, "What are you doing with your hair?" That's just the way she is, you know.

QUESTION: I hear she wants to move to London.

JOHN: Yes, well I'll help her if she really wants to. She's always the same, you know. "What are you doing with that long hair, and what's all this I read about in the press?" She'll never change.

QUESTION: Do you still remember Timothy?

JOHN: Oh, yeah, Tim the cat.* Mimi tells that story very often. It's a he, a very old tom. He does well. I think animals are generally in a better state of communication than humans.

QUESTION: What do you think about the Catholic Church?

JOHN: I think it's about as far from the truth as any other religious establishment. I think that Christianity, Buddhism, Hinduism, and Communism all have a basic truth which is very similar, if not the same, but the message has been lost.

QUESTION: If you could send one gift to the pope, what would it be?

JOHN: Peace.

QUESTION: What is the last book you read?

JOHN: Actually, I don't read much. There's no time for reading. I read papers— they're the novels of today. Newspapers are the best form of written communication. I think I read *Wuthering Heights* last year, actually.

QUESTION: You worked on your last film in Austria for about three or four weeks. What impression did you get of Austria?

JOHN: When we made *Help*,† you mean? It was beautiful, you know, just a fantastic place. We'd like to come again sometime and see it out of the bag, but this time it's the bag, you know.

QUESTION: What would you do if you woke up one morning impotent?

JOHN: Masturbate! I heard from a close friend it's not too bad.

QUESTION: Is it true you're making a film about all this?

JOHN: Yes, we're making a film of the Bag Event. We'll put it out as soon as we can get it together.

QUESTION: Do you know the title yet?

JOHN: It'll probably be *Bagism Baby*.

---

* Lennon's cat as a teen, at his home, Mendips, in Woolton, just outside Liverpool.
† The Beatles' second feature, released on August 11, 1965.

QUESTION: John, are you going to go to the States to accept this offer of four million dollars for the Beatles to play?

JOHN: I'm not going to accept that offer particularly. I mean, Mr. Bernstein makes offers every year, and he'll probably get a surprise one year and we'll accept it, but I think he wanted TV rights and all. I mean, I wouldn't do that for four million dollars.

QUESTION: Do you often wear clothes?

JOHN: Of course, yes. We have to walk down the lobby, you know.

QUESTION: Do you wear your wife's clothes?

JOHN: Oh, that's a secret, you know. We're wearing a white bag at the moment.

QUESTION: Pretty warm in there, isn't it?

JOHN: It's getting hotter, yes.

QUESTION: You don't like to change?

JOHN: No. You know, people get to saying, "Are you coming out of bed yet?" Well, we didn't come out of bed until the time was up, and we'll come out of this when the time is up.

QUESTION: Where are you going to show this new [Bagism] movie?

JOHN: Everywhere we can. I'm sure we'll show it in every country that will accept it.

QUESTION: For money or for charity?

JOHN: Sure, for money! We've got to pay for the cost of the film, man. I'm not a walking charity.

QUESTION: Would you have liked to stay some days in Vienna?

JOHN: We would have liked to stay some days in Vienna, but we came here on the run, as it were. Hans Prynor rang us up and said, "How are you? Why don't you come over?" and we said, "Okay." But I have to be in London to finish off the Beatles LP.

QUESTION: Why did you accept the offer from Austrian television?

JOHN: Because even being a Beatle, it's hard to get films you want to personally make distributed, especially on TV. So Austrian TV kindly gave us an hour and a half to play with, and we played with it.

YOKO: And we believe that TV communication is very important.

John: Oh, I think it might be the most.

Question: Mr. Lennon, are you looking forward to being de-bagged?

John: I'm looking forward to it, yes.

Question: Who's the ugliest person you've ever seen in your life?

John: I have no idea. I try not to judge people by their appearances and beauty.

Question: What do you think about the Mothers of Invention?

John: I think they're very good, and I'm sure Frank Zappa would dig this event.

Question: Do you know what he said about you?

John: He said a lot about me. But I've said a lot about him, too.

Question: He said your music is amusing. Would you accept that?

John: I would accept that, of course. I think records are a good example of total communication, because there's no bias. People just hear it, and they're not worried about how the person looks or what he's wearing.

Question: Couldn't you sing us a song, John?

John: " 'Those were the days, my friend, I'd thought they'd never end' . . ." that's all I know " . . . 'da, 'da . . .'"

Question: And now Yoko.

Yoko: (*Yoko sings a Japanese song.*)

John: The singing bag, olé!

Question: Could you translate this into Chinese now?

John: Very funny, very satirical.

Question: What are you doing now?

John: We're just wriggling about.

Yoko: We're bagging!

Question: Yoko, how many languages are you speaking?

Yoko: Uh, two.

Question: Do you intend to go out of the hotel after the show or just stay in your room?

John: We'll probably stay in, because we'll be pretty tired after this event, you know. I'd prefer to sleep and then just travel on.

QUESTION: Are you interested in the reactions of the TV public on your show?

JOHN: Of course I am. I'll hear it all from Hans if I'm not here to see it myself.

QUESTION: Do you intend to go out on the street and ask people tomorrow morning how they liked it?

JOHN: I have no time, you know. I must get back to London quickly.

QUESTION: Which kind of music do you like to listen to?

JOHN: Uh, when I have time I listen to rock 'n' roll, you know. Or John and Yoko music.

QUESTION: Who?

JOHN: Elizabeth and Richard* music.

QUESTION: I believe Yoko made a public appearance as a singer in Cambridge and the critics said it was very bad?

JOHN: By the time the critics catch on, we've moved on.

QUESTION: Are the Beatles still a group?

JOHN: I should say so. They still sell a lot of records, so that makes them popular—pop stands for popular.

QUESTION: Yoko, if you will have a baby, do you want to have a boy or a girl?

YOKO: Either way is fine.

QUESTION: Do you think Apple was a good idea?

JOHN: Yes, the *idea* was terrific.

QUESTION: And what came out of them?

JOHN: Some very good things. The only trouble was, the Beatles couldn't handle the business and be the producers and the artists all at the same time, but now we have a good guy to look after it who will handle the business for us.

QUESTION: And how about your next Beatles film—any plans?

JOHN: There's been talk, but as you know, it's pretty difficult to find a film for four people that isn't *Help* or *A Hard Day's Night*. We've been looking for two or three years, and there are one or two things in the air, but it's still nothing definite.

QUESTION: And how do you like the film Hans did for you?

---

* A sly reference to Elizabeth Taylor and Richard Burton, at the time the "other" front-page showbiz couple.

JOHN: What was that?

QUESTION: *Yellow Submarine.*

JOHN: Oh yes, that was beautiful. I think he's a beautiful artist, and he did wonderful things with it.

QUESTION: Are you going to put all your apples in one bag?

JOHN: I think they are, actually.

QUESTION: I read somewhere where some television people bought most of the shares of your company.

JOHN: Somebody bought all of the shares that were owned by Dick James, not by me. Paul and I still own exactly the same amount of shares as we did before.

QUESTION: What kind of comments did you receive about your naked body?*

JOHN: The usual narrow-minded stupidity.

QUESTION: What do you think about journalists?

JOHN: I think journalists are a functional, communicational media and they're as necessary . . . what?

QUESTION: As good records?

JOHN: I think they're better than records, because they come out every day. If I could get a record out as fast as a newspaper, I'd be very happy.

QUESTION: Why don't you publish a newspaper?

JOHN: It takes a lot more money than I've got.

QUESTION: How much money do you have?

JOHN: Very little, you know.

QUESTION: Can I lend you some?

JOHN: You may, yes—no interest, if you don't mind.

QUESTION: Do you take sugar?

JOHN: I take anything. All donations are welcome at the foot of the table.

QUESTION: Care for any drinks?

JOHN: No, thank you.

---

* The journalist is referring to John and Yoko's appearance nude on the album cover for *Two Virgins.*

JOHN: Well, that sounds like the end of it to me.

QUESTION: Are you coming down the stairs?

YOKO: No . . .

JOHN: No, we'll wait for you to go and then we'll come out the back.

QUESTION: With the bag on?

JOHN: Yep, with the bag on. Only the feet will freeze.

John Lennon

Press Conference
● ● ● ● ● ● ● ● ● ● ● ● ● ● ● ● ● ●

London, July 1970

Question: In terms of the music right now, rock is getting down to whether you're going to go with Led Zeppelin, this incredibly intellectual sound, or Bonnie and Delaney and so forth. "Let It Be" is in the swamp-music mainstream more than . . .

John Lennon: We don't think in terms of "schools" of music—it's all rock. Either slow rock or fast, you know. It's still down to that.

Question: Do you think of popular music in terms of emotional reaction, as opposed to actually saying something?

John: It's either something I like, don't like, or it's heavy or light. I like heavy music, but I still call it rock. I like Zeppelin, although I've only heard a couple of things, but they're okay. I also like Bonnie and Delaney. I like the record they made with George and Eric. There's nobody who I like *all* their stuff, including me or the Beatles. I just like bits and pieces. I don't like the intellectual school of music the same as I don't like classical or modern jazz. I don't dislike modern jazz or classical music in general, but rather the people that surround it. Name some of the intellectual bands, and then we'll know what we're talking about.

Question: Take the Doors or Iron Butterfly—they need to say something very complex.

John: They're trying to say something universal, only they're just heavy writers. It's just like some journalists can write like people read, and some journalists can't. Personally, I go for writers that say it like the *Daily Mirror*, because that's the language we're talking. Everybody can read the *Daily Mirror*, but not everybody can read the *Times*. So I go for the *Mirror*, you know.

Question: What has happened in the U.S. over the last couple of years is that a young audience has developed that would rather read the *Times* and listen to the Doors than dance to Otis Redding and read the *Mirror*.

John: In the old days, they would have probably listened to some kind of intellectual jazz or something. It's not really important.

Question: Probably the initial audience you will hit in terms of saying you want to have a peace festival or a Year One A.P. [After Peace], or whatever.

JOHN: Yeah, if they're getting into that they'll notice we talk in terms of "Give peace a chance" or "year one." We talk in promos: *Daily Mirror* headlines—or even *Times* headlines—with jingles. We sing and talk in jingles. It's not anti-intellectualism. It's just functional to communicate like that. That's the way I talk naturally, and the way I think. I've met more people who think in those terms than in other terms. There are more of us than them, so we must use a common language. It doesn't matter if people want to go home and embroider things, but when you're down to it, there's no time for long speech.

QUESTION: In terms of your peace movement, what's the major audience you want to reach? My parents, eventually, or me?

JOHN: I don't really care what age they are, but I suspect more young people will be able to understand what we're saying than anybody else, but that's only because they haven't got an identification hang-up. The only difference is the older generation will have an identification hang-up. But that's our problem, not theirs. We're the hip ones, so let's see what we can do with them.

QUESTION: Do you see any point in infiltrating society to help spread your philosophy?

JOHN: Yeah, I think we should work like the Commies. I mean, if we're really seriously trying to change things, let's get in there and change it. I believe in 'drop in.'

QUESTION: Become president of the company and then go from there?

JOHN: Sure, but you don't have to sell your soul to do it. There will be one or two human beings in amongst all those companies somewhere. The thing is to make contact. You know what John and Yoko have been doing round the world is making contact with people from different countries on all levels. That's all we're doing. But you'd be surprised where they are. They could be in Blackburn—they're not all "where it's happenin', man." There's as much junk in the underground as anywhere—perhaps more so. I think the underground are guilty of inverted snobbism. They just make me sick. It's just as bad there as in the *Daily Express*. Wherever we are, what I call the *real* underground could be any-where—in the Welsh hills, in India, Australia, or anywhere. The thing is to just show your colors and it happens.

QUESTION: The only cultural revolution was the underground, and yet, when they got through, they turned out to be even worse than the men on Wall Street.

JOHN: It's just like flower power. The message was right—"Make love, not war"—but it got lost in the hype, and so did the underground. But it'll resurrect itself. Whoever were the instigators of certain ideas will come up with something new. It's like all the businessmen are wearing Beatle hair cuts. Nobody but old guys have got Beatle haircuts these days. Most of the people who are the underground have moved on somewhere else. It's always like that. Everybody can't get turned on in the same second, and that's the drag, you know. Until we think of something, I suppose.

QUESTION: Would you accept some gimmick so that you could get everyone to join your underground?

JOHN: Oh, yeah. That process seems natural. If we make peace trendy for six months, that'll give us enough energy to carry on. It's like the original flower-power people are still saying the same thing. The original underground are still saying the same thing. That problem isn't over, the race problem isn't over. What *Look Back In Anger*, the film, did in Britain isn't over. It got lost, but it isn't over. The problems aren't solved, and all those messages have to be regurgitated, you know. Nothing has really changed that much.

QUESTION: Let me ask you one question about your music in terms of the Plastic Ono Band. Collecting musicians together as you've done for Plastic Ono, do you see this as what is going to be happening? That people will express their own music in relation to other people instead of forming traditional bands?

JOHN: It is happening. I'm not forming a Plastic Ono Band. I mean, the original idea was that *you* are the Plastic Ono Band. I've used two people on practically every session—Klaus [Voorman] and Alan [White]—but there's a chance I won't, you know. They're not permanent, and *the audience is the band*. Like in one film we made, *Smile*, the instructions at the beginning were to make your own music—the music was *them*, you know. And if Yoko and I went on with the so-called Plastic Ono Band and instead of the audience just sitting there or waiting for us to perform like seals (because everybody wants to be a star, you know), let them be a star. Let's all groove together. When we performed with George, Eric, and Bonnie and Delaney, and everybody at the Lyceum, I didn't care what the pop press said, it was a funky show. Some of the audience right there with us were sky high—it was an amazing high. A seventeen-piece band. It's great with four musicians groovin', but when you got seventeen, it's somethin' else! And when you got the audience as well. The day we go on the audience is the rhythm section, then we're really groovin'—that's what I want. So it wouldn't matter whether I was on the stage or if I got fed up and went down in the audience for a bit too. Let's take turns being the big superstar, you know.

QUESTION: Do you think being in the news is the best medium you have available, as opposed to, say, making an album or perhaps a film?

JOHN: We're doing it all. We try and sustain newsworthy peace gimmicks, and we haven't slowed up production of our music or films, so we're doing it all. It's just like we were saying: "Grow your hair for peace." Well, now chop it off for peace or cut your teeth for peace, you know, just to set up that mantra. In the old days they used to say, "Workin' for God and bless the food." Well, let's call God "peace" and do it that way. It's not like we have the answer—there *isn't* one. What we do is worldwide. We meet people like Tim Leary, Dick Gregory, or the guy who opens the door for us, and we compare notes and years of experience, or whatever highs we've had, or exchange energy, whatever your gig is, and then we move on with this new knowledge. And if we open the door with music, a film or something, all we're doing is saying, "Hey, this is what we just discovered, anybody digging it? Does it mean anything to you?" And somebody will say, "Yeah," and they'll make a comparable record or sort of answer it. Then suddenly you hear a record and you know that they've just been through the same door as you have, or they're just one door ahead, or back, or whichever way it is. We're all just comparing credentials all the time. And that's the way it is, folks.

QUESTION: And leaving the door open when you go through as well . . .

JOHN: It seems to be the law of the universe that as you move forward, you must move something back. The "do unto others" bit. And whatever you've found out, you've got to pass it on to your next of kin to make your next move up.

John Lennon
PRESS CONFERENCE
London, 1970

QUESTION: Isn't there room today for the Beatles as a contemporary band? You're surely now far more aware as people. Must it always now be that the Beatles made "yesterday's music"? Or is it you're too egocentric to be able to work together fully, even if you tried?

JOHN LENNON: We always were egocentric. But look, George is on half my new album playing guitar. The only reason Ringo wasn't on it was because he was abroad making his movie.* So the three of us would have been on, but then it wouldn't have been the Beatles. It would have been Plastic Ono, because only I would have had the final say. There would be no decision making by George or Ringo. Which is what happened with the Beatles, but then it was a bit more diplomatic. Yes, it's quite possible about the Beatles as a working unit, because I might just play on George's and Ringo's projects if they wanted my style of playing. But imagine how we've flowered since then. George is suddenly the biggest seller of us. I think my music's improved a millionfold, lyrically and everything. And Ringo's coming out and writing "It Don't Come Easy," and now he's going to write the title for this cowboy thing he's in, where he's playing a really tough guy and all that. It's really beautiful. The fact is, the Beatles have left school and had to get a job. That's made us really work harder. I think we're much better than we ever were when we were together. I'd sooner have *Ram*, *John Lennon Plastic Ono Band*, George's album, and Ringo's single and the movies than *Let It Be* or *Abbey Road*.

QUESTION: Do you resent journalists talking about the past?

JOHN: No. I'm always doing it myself. It's only human. Something funny happened the other day. I went into Apple, and they said, "Jesus, you look like a Beatle again." And you know, just for a second, I'd forgotten what a Beatle really was. It was because I'd just got back from New York and I hadn't been a Beatle at all.

QUESTION: Are you totally cleansed of any hang-ups of the past?

JOHN: Oh no. I just know myself better, that's all. I can handle myself better. That Janov thing, the primal scream and so on, it does affect you, because you recognize yourself in there. The difference between us and Janov, as Yoko puts it, is that the past we remember is the past we create now because of the neces-

---

* The obscure spaghetti western *Blindman*, produced by Beatles manager Allen Klein.

sity of the present. I wouldn't have missed it, though. It was very good for me, I'm still "primal," and it still works.

QUESTION: What is your philosophy of life? Many of your comments on society have been construed as extreme left wing or even Communist.

JOHN: They knock me for saying "Power to the people" and say no one section should have the power. Rubbish. The people aren't a *section*. "The people" means everyone. I think everyone should own everything equally, and people should own part of the factories, and they should have some say in who's the boss and who does what. Students should be able to select teachers. There is no real Communist state in the world if Russia isn't. It's a fascist state. The socialism I talk about is British socialism, not the way some daft Russian might do it or the Chinese might do it, that might suit them. Us, we'd have a nice socialism here, a British socialism.

QUESTION: Don't you both spend a great deal of your time filming yourselves and having yourselves filmed?

JOHN: Why not? It's home movies. And the ultimate movie is a home movie. Luc Goddard, or whatever his name is, is now making eight-millimeter films. Home movies is where it's at. Poetry's done at home—why shouldn't movies be the same way?

In our film *Apotheosis,* you see us for only two seconds. In *Fly,* Yoko's film, she's not even in it. In *Rape,* there was a Hungarian girl. In *Erection,* the one I've just made about a hotel, it was all done from still photographs over a year and a half. There's only a couple with us in, so that whole thing is a lie.

QUESTION: Yoko's work seems to me to exclude appreciation of the more established works of art—the Mona Lisa and so on.

JOHN: Not necessarily. Her art is the very opposite of making a saint out of the Mona Lisa.

QUESTION: Are you still even remotely interested in singles or chart success?

JOHN: Sure. I get all the musical dailies. I get my world chart thing and *Billboard* and *Cashbox,* and I mark off the Apple records all round the world. The Beatles are blasting the world up—we've got records everywhere, and two or three in every chart. I get a kick out of it, because I'm getting through to all those people and because I'm doing it on my own or with Yoko. I like singles and not LPs. I like the idea of saying everything in three minutes.

QUESTION: Did you listen to Paul McCartney's *Ram* album?

JOHN: Of course I did. The first time I heard it, I thought it was awful, and then the second time, ahem, I fixed the record player a bit, and it sounded better. I enjoyed a couple, like "My Dog It's Got Three Legs" or something and the intro to "Ram On" and the intro to "Uncle Albert." In general, I think the other album he did was better, in a way.* At least there were some songs on it. I don't like all this dribbling pop-opera-jazz. I like pop records that are pop records.

QUESTIONS: Is there a song on your album *Imagine* that refers to Paul—lines about a pretty face and the sound of Muzak?

JOHN: Well, there's a song which *could* be a statement about Paul. But then it could be about an old chick I'd known as well.

QUESTION: What do you think of your own album?

JOHN: It's the best thing I've ever done. This will show them. It's not a personal thing like the last album, but I've learned a lot. This is better in every way. It's lighter too—I was feeling very happy. There's a guy called George Harrison on it, and he does some mother solos. George used to be with the Bubbles or somebody. Then there's a guy called Nicky Hopkins; Jim Gordon on drums; Alan White, drums; Jim Keltner, drums, and they're all fantastic! Yoko's on whip, and that's very good. Whip and mirror, actually. Then we had John Barnham on a few things,† and King Curtis is on sax. The Flux Fiddlers are on violins. Eighty percent of it was recorded in Britain in seven days. I took them, remixed them, and took it to America, like they used to do in the old days. It took me nine days to make this album and ten to make the other before. So I'm getting faster.

---

* *Red Rose Speedway.*
† John Barnham is a topnotch arranger who has worked extensively on Apple projects, including the *Radha Krishna Temple* LP, produced by George.

John Lennon
PRESS CONFERENCE
● ● ● ● ● ● ● ● ● ● ● ● ● ● ● ● ● ●
London, July 1971

QUESTION: Your latest record* and your recent public statements suggest your views are becoming increasingly radical and political.

JOHN LENNON: I've always been politically minded and against the status quo. It's pretty basic when you're brought up like I was, to hate and fear the police as a natural enemy and despise the army as something that takes everybody away and leaves them dead somewhere. I mean, it's just a basic working-class thing, though it begins to wear off when you get older, get a family, and get swallowed up in the system. In my case I've never *not* been political, though religion tended to overshadow it in my acid days, around 1965 or '66. That religion was directly the result of all that superstar shit. Religion was an outlet for my repression. I thought, "Well, there's something else to life, isn't there? This isn't it, surely?"

I was always political, in a way. In the two books I wrote, even though they were written in a sort of Joycean gobbledegook, there's many knocks at religion and there is a play about a worker and a capitalist. I've been satirizing the system since childhood. I used to write magazines in school and hand them around. I was very conscious of class, they would say, with a chip on my shoulder, because I knew what happened to me, and I knew about the class repression coming down on us. It was a fucking fact, but in the hurricane Beatle world it got left out, I got farther away from reality for a time. When it comes to the nitty gritty, they won't let the people have any power. They'll perform to and dance for them, but no real power.

QUESTION: The danger is that once a revolutionary state has been created, a new conservative bureaucracy tends to form around it.

JOHN: Once the new power has taken over, they have to establish a new status quo just to keep the factories and trains running. We all have bourgeois instincts within us, we all get tired and feel the need to relax a bit. How do you keep everything going and keep up the revolutionary fervor after you've achieved what you set out to achieve? Of course, Mao has kept it up in China, but what happens after Mao goes? Also, he uses a personality cult. Perhaps that's necessary— like I said, everybody seems to need a father figure. But I've been reading *Khrushchev Remembers*. I know he's a bit of a lad himself, but he seemed to

---

* *John Lennon/Plastic Ono Band*, released on Apple Records on December 11, 1970.

think that making a religion out of an individual was bad, that it doesn't seem to be part of the basic Communist ideal. Still, people are people, that's the difficulty. If we took over Britain, then we'd have the job of cleaning up the bourgeoisie and keeping people in a revolutionary state of mind.

QUESTION: How do you think we can destroy the capitalist system here in Britain?

JOHN: By making the workers aware of the really unhappy position they are in. Breaking the dream they are surrounded by. They think they are in a wonderful, free-speaking country. They've got cars and tellies, and they don't want to think there's anything more to life. They are prepared to let the bosses run them, to see their children fucked up in school. They're dreaming someone else's dream—it's not even their own. They should realize the blacks and the Irish are being harassed and repressed and that they will be next. As soon as they start being aware of all that, we can really begin to do something. The workers can start to take over. Like Marx said, "To each according to his need." I think that would work well here. But we'd also have to infiltrate the army too, because they are well trained to kill us all. We've got to start all this from where we ourselves are oppressed. It's false, shallow, to be giving to others when your own need is great. The idea is not to comfort people, not to make them feel better, but to make them feel worse, to constantly put before them the degradations and humiliations to earn what they call a living wage.

John Lennon

INTERVIEW
• • • • • • • • • •

New York, 1976

RADIO CALLER: Hello?

JOHN LENNON: (*German accent*) This is WFBI, playing all your favorite tunes.

CALLER: Hello?

JOHN: This is Edgar Hoover here, and I'd like to do your room.

CALLER: What color would you like to paint it?

JOHN: No, no. I'm going to *Hoover* it, ha, ha, haw! *Mother!*

John Lennon and Yoko Ono

INTERVIEW

●●●●●●●●●●●

New York, December 6, 1980

QUESTION: Let's talk about the single "(Just Like) Starting Over." Was that an obvious choice for the both of you, as a single? Were you happy with that?

JOHN LENNON: Yeah, because it was . . .

YOKO ONO: It's the message.

JOHN: It was really called "Starting Over," but while we were making it, people kept putting things out with the title. There was a country-and-western hit called "Starting Over," so I added "Just Like" at the last minute. It was obvious, because it was the one where the musicians got very loose—because it was such simple rock 'n' roll, there was no problem. They really relaxed, and they'd all be like that after it. Even though I don't think it's the strongest track, perhaps some of the other tracks are stronger. Like "Losing You" might be a stronger piece of material, but "Starting Over" was the best way to start over. To me, it was like going back to fifteen and singing à la Presley. All the time I was referring to John [Smith], the engineer, here in the room, I was referring to Elvis Orbison. It's kinda "I Want You," "Only the Lonely," you know—a kind of parody but not really parody.

QUESTION: A little tongue-in-cheek?

YOKO: Oh, very.

JOHN: A little! When I was doing it, I was cracking up.

QUESTION: You relieve me greatly, because we still do *Round Table*, the review show, and I was one of the guests the night the new Lennon single arrived in the studio, and there was absolute pandemonium, and it was on the turntable, and the man who hosts the show, Adrian Love, said to me, "What do you think?" And I said, "Terrific, but a little tongue-in-cheek."

JOHN: Right, exactly. Some people took it seriously, you know, saying, "What's he trying to do?" and all that, but they forget . . .

YOKO: He was winking, you know, with that one.

JOHN: I've had tongue in cheek all along. "I Am the Walrus," all of them had tongue in cheek, you know. Just because other people see depths of whatever in it, what does it really mean, "I am the eggman"? It could have been the pudding basin for all I cared. It was just tongue-in-cheek, it's not that serious.

142

QUESTION: Do you, and did you, get fed up with people ostracizing your lyrics and trying to read marvelously intellectual interpretations into them? Both of you, this must apply to?

JOHN: Sometimes it's fun, but then it gets to be stupid. That's why I started from the *Mother* album [*John Lennon/Plastic Ono Band*] onwards trying to shave off all imagery, pretensions of poetry, illusions of grandeur. What I call à la Dylan— Dylanesque, you know. I didn't write any of that. Just say what it is, simple English, make it rhyme, put a backbeat on it, and express yourself as simply as possible, straightforwardly as possible. As they say, Northern people are blunt, right, so I was trying to write like I am. I enjoy the poetic side, and I'll probably do a little dabble later, because Yoko's lyrics are so poetic. I get, "Well, maybe I should do some of that," and the track you were talking about, "Walking on Thin Ice," was one of the extra tracks. We cut twenty-two tracks in ten days—it was just like we had diarrhea of rock here. We just zapped out these twenty-two tracks and then got it down to fourteen, and one I played you before was "Walking on Thin Ice," which was one of Yoko's tracks that we didn't put on for many, many reasons. Some were selected, some not.

QUESTION: Which is a marvelous dance track, I must hastily add.

JOHN: Well, then "Kiss Kiss Kiss," which is the other side of "Starting Over," is getting a lot of rock-club, new-wave, whatever you call it, disco exposure. So we made a special kind of disc for them, and Yoko came up with the idea, "Why don't we give them something they don't have?" And we made a kind of dis-coesque long six-minutes version of "Walking on Thin Ice" which will go out. There's a separate disco or rock-club mix, and it'll go out to them.

YOKO: And we threw in "Open Your Box," which is one that was banned.

JOHN: We've thrown in "Open Your Box" for old times' sake.

QUESTION: Tell me about "Kiss Kiss Kiss," Yoko.

JOHN: Tell them how you recorded it in the pitch dark, hidden behind these big walls here.

YOKO: I started to do it, and then I suddenly looked and all these engineers were all looking, and I thought, "I can't do that." So I said, "Well, turn off all the lights and put the screen around me." And so they put the screen around me, and I did it that way.

JOHN: We were all sitting there saying, "What's she doing?" She was having an orgasm and nobody was there. I was saying, "Well . . ."

YOKO: It's called acting, you know.

JOHN: Oh, very good, dear, very good, yes, Ziggy Stardust!

QUESTION: Do you get embarrassed in the studio, Yoko? Doing something like that?

JOHN: Sorry to interrupt, but there was John—me—Jack, and Lee, the engineer, and a few people. We were all in there.

YOKO: I'm glad I didn't know that. I mean, "Kiss Kiss Kiss" is what it is, and the song itself will explain. And if you listen to it, you will get whatever you want to get out of it, probably. But it's mainly sort of a feminine and Asian vulnerability that women are not scared of exposing now. It's all right to show vulnerability and in a way it's saying, "Well this is woman."

QUESTION: From what you've just said, the most interesting statement to me is that you, the person listening, would derive what they wish out of it. Do you deliberately produce songs like that? It's rather like the movie business, isn't it? You can go and see an adaptation of something, and it sticks in your mind as being *the* adaptation you might remember for the whole of your life. If you write a song and people can derive what they want from it, it's a very personal thing, isn't it? And that's a special way of communicating.

YOKO: Oh yes, I think most of my songs—well, I can't help doing, so I'm not saying I do it intentionally, but I have these visions, visual things, you know, and that comes out. So that it's a visual, almost. You can interpret a vision in any way you like, in a way.

QUESTION: Do you feel now, at this stage, here we are in December 1980, that the theme and the ease of writing is now back with you?

JOHN: Yes.

QUESTION: And that you're going to be extremely prolific in the months and years to come?

JOHN: Yes, I think it's going to be the one period they say, "Those two will do anything for publicity, for Christ's sake. Get them off the front pages, oh get them off." You know, people are bitching at us because we were always doing something, and then they were bitching at us because we weren't doing anything. And I have a funny feeling that it's going to be the other way round again, because we're talking and talking and talking. There are all sorts of plans and ideas we have in our heads—it's just a matter of getting it done, you know? We already got half the next album, and we'll probably go in just after Christmas and do that. We're already talking about what the ideas for the third album are—I can't wait. So it's a matter of just getting it done, and I'm sorry about you people that get fed up of hearing about us, but you know, we like to do it, so it's too bad.

QUESTION: The problem is, of course, there's always the time gap between finishing the recording and people like myself being allowed to sit and talk to you. That worries me somewhat, because it's past history to you—as you've just said a moment ago, you're already two albums ahead of me as we sit here now.

JOHN: Right. We're already on the third in our minds, but the second physically, as it were, beginning to think about it. But you can't do it at the same time, you see. You can't be discussing it while you're making it. Or you don't even know what you're doing. You're kind of making it and you're so into it, you cannot be objective about it. Even some of the records I made, when you talk about them, at the time I wasn't consciously knowing what I'm doing, in a way. And it's only when you look back at it, you "Oh, I see what I was feeling at that time." Even though one tried to express it in the music, you're not conscious of what you're expressing, and it's sometimes about two or three years later when I've realized what we made then. But *Double Fantasy* I can talk all night about, but it'll be two years before I can see it really for what it is. How can we talk to you and make it at the same time? It's impossible. It's like inviting you to the rehearsal of a play, you know, and then . . .

QUESTION: Changing it the night afterwards?

JOHN: Right. Even the opening night it can change, the night after, right? So you can't. It's too bad. Too bad.

YOKO: You do need tremendous luck. Tremendous amount of luck probably made us finish that album. I mean, the fact that it's a man and woman, and that we were able to work together, that the songs came to us at the same time almost as a dialogue, etc.—these are just pure, in a way. It's been given to us, almost, hasn't it?

JOHN: And the fact we can work together and express it in many different ways, starting out with "Kiss Kiss Kiss." I mean, the difference is obvious in the sound and everything, but we can both be part of both.

QUESTION: "Beautiful Boy," John, a song about Sean?

JOHN: Yeah. Well, you know, Stevie Wonder wrote about his kid, didn't he? "Isn't He Lovely?"

QUESTION: That was recorded here, wasn't it? He did *Songs in the Key of Life* in this studio, I think I'm right in saying.

JOHN: In the Hit Factory, New York, New York. Yeah. Very near Times Square, folks. You come out of here after a session and there's strange women standing on the street. You know, I mean, it's really cooking, it never stops.

QUESTION: Yeah.

John: Funnily enough, for the first time I was with Sean in the kitchen with the bread, and you know, all I kept thinking, "Well, I ought to be inspired to write about Sean. I mean, I ought to." I was going through a bit of that, and when I finally gave up on thinking about writing a song about him, of course, the song came to me. When he was four, four and a half, or five, it was just coming up to October when I suddenly got the song about him.

Question: Is he developing an interest in music?

John: Oh, he's very musical. Absolutely. I noticed something in the hospital. This is—maybe you don't need this—but when the black nurses come in, they put on WBLS, which is an R&B disco station. When the white nurses would come in, they put on the country-and-western station. When the black nurses fed the babies, they picked them up and held them on their hip and danced round the room with the bottle. When the white nurses came in, they just sit still and jam the bottle down his throat and not move. So I thought, "Ahh . . . ha, I want him to have natural rhythm, you know." I mean, seriously, I noticed the different attitude . . . not only was it warmer, with more contact, there was constant movement. Officially, they weren't allowed to put the radio on. But when the head nurse's away they put it on all the time, because people don't want their children not being able to sleep without music. Long story short: which I didn't. I did the same with Sean till he could walk. Whenever I fed him, I put the rock 'n' roll on or the R&B and I danced with him. He can dance like nothing on earth. He's perfect pitch in key. He's into "Hound Dog" now, because I said that in an interview, so he thinks it's about hunting. And "Bee-Bop-a-Lula," he knows backwards.

Moving Mountains/ Press Releases, Etc.

TRADE AD—THE BEATLES CAMPAIGN

On Monday, December 30, a two-page spread will appear in *Billboard* (it may be in *Cashbox,* too, on that day or it will run a week later). We have ordered large quantities of soft-sheet reprints of that ad. Each B/D will have these reprints in bulk. Make sure that all important radio station personnel and retail account personnel have their own personal copy of this ad. It's a good one, and will do the job of introducing them to the Beatles.

We have also ordered easel-backed reprints of this ad in large quantity. All B.Ds will have enough so that one should be on the counter of all of your important accounts. The copy on the easel-back has been changed to make the ad interesting to consumers. Put it where they'll see it, where they'll be compelled to buy both the Beatles single and LP.

We've asked that both of these items arrive at BDs no later than January 2, so you can start off the *Year of the Beatles* on the right foot.

• • •

"BE A BEATLE BOOSTER" BUTTONS

Shortly after the first of the year, you'll have bulk quantities of a unique see-through plastic pin-on button. Inserted in each button is a shot of the Beatles, with each boy identified. What to do with the buttons? First, have all of your sales staff wear one. Second, offer them to clerks and jocks. Third, arrange for radio station give-aways of the buttons. Fourth,

keep some in reserve for the requirement which will be listed below under "Tabloid."

• • •

BEATLE WIGS

Again shortly after the first, you'll have bulk quantities of a Beatle hair-do wig. As soon as they arrive—and until further notice—you and each of your sales and promotion staff are to wear the wig during the business day! Next, see how many of the retail clerks in your area have a sense of humor. Then, try your jocks, especially those who hold hops. Then, offer some to jocks and stores for promotions. Get these Beatle wigs around properly, and you'll find you're helping to start the Beatle Hair-Do Craze that should be sweeping the country soon!

• • •

"THE BEATLES ARE COMING" STICKERS

As soon as possible after the first, you'll have fantastic quantities of these two-inch by three-inch teaser stickers. Now, what are you going to do with these huge amounts of stickers? Put them up anywhere and everywhere they can be seen, that's what. It may sound funny, but we literally want your salesmen to be plastering these stickers on any friendly surface as they walk down the street or as they call on radio or retail accounts. That probably won't get rid of them all, however. Make arrangements with some local high school students to spread the stickers around town. Involve you friends and relatives. Remember the "Kilroy Was Here" cartoons that appeared everywhere about 10 years ago? Well now it's going to be "Beatles Are Coming" stickers that are everywhere you look.

• • •

NATIONAL RECORD NEWS—BEATLE ISSUE

Publicity Director Fred Martin has concocted a simply marvelous vehicle for spreading the Beatles story. It's a four-page tabloid newspaper which looks deceptively legitimate, but of course it's our doing, and all it contains is picture after picture and story after story on the Beatles.

You'll be getting huge quantities of this tabloid. How to exploit it? Send bulk copies to all major retailers for distribution to consumers. Offer bulks to jocks for give-away. But most important, make arrangements with local high schoolers to distribute them to fellow students after school. The idea is to get as many copies of this tabloid as possible into the hands of potential Beatle buyers. Don't, under any circumstance, end up with any large quantities of this tabloid sitting in your back room. They won't help there!

Important note for Sales Office Managers: Because of limited storage space, make immediate arrangements to send some of the tabloids out to your salesmen's homes, while you send others right out to retailers. Just keep on hand that quantity you'll distribute through the high school students.

• • •

BEATLE PROMO LPs AND DIE-CUT JACKETS

On or before release date (looks like mid-January at the latest) you'll have exceptionally large quantities of both promo albums and jackets. With each copy of the LP that you give to jocks, make sure to include a copy of the Tabloid. You'll have enough promo to allow you to set up contests with your jocks with the album as prizes.

We've sent you the largest quantity of die-cut jackets in history. Get them displayed . . . everywhere!

• • •

BEATLE MOTION DISPLAY

Along about the first week in February, you'll receive bulks on an extremely exciting motion display. Sorry it will take us so long, but you'll agree it was worth the wait when you see it. About mid-January, you can begin telling your accounts about the display and arranging for windows.

That about does it. Please get this message to your salesmen, and please follow the directions included in this memo. If you have any questions, contact George Gerkin immediately.

1964

• • •

CAPITOL RECORDS DISTRIBUTING CORP.

Dear Reviewer:

In the past few days, you may have received an advance promotional copy of The Beatles' new album, *The Beatles Yesterday and Today*. In accordance with the following statement from Alan V. Livingston, President, Capitol Records, Inc., the original album cover is being discarded and a new jacket being prepared:

> "The original cover, created in England, was intended as 'pop art' satire. However, a sampling of public opinion in the United States indicates that the cover design is subject to misinterpretation. For this reason, and to avoid any possible controversy or undeserved damage to The Beatles' image or reputation, Capitol has chosen to withdraw the LP and substitute a more generally acceptable design."

All consumer copies of The Beatles' album will be packaged in the new cover, which will be available within the next week to 10 days. As soon as they are, we will forward you a copy. In the meantime, we would appreciate your disregarding the promotional album and, if at all possible, returning it, C.O.D., to Capitol Records, 1750 N. Vine Street, Hollywood, Calif. 90028.

Thank you in advance for your cooperation.

Sincerely,

Ron Tipper
  Manager
  Press & Information Services.
  RT:s

JUNE 14, 1966

• • •

WORDS FROM APPLE

Beatles to introduce **Zapple**, new label and recording concept.

On May 1, just two weeks short of the first anniversary of the formation of Apple Corps Ltd. and its Apple Records division, the Beatles company will introduce a new label and recording concept.

The label will be called **Zapple** and it will emphasize a series of 'spoken word' albums and some music releases of a more wide-ranging and esoteric nature. Price of the Zapple albums will generally be $1.98 or $4.98 depending on the type of release.

Zapple will be a division of Apple Records, which is headed by Ron Kass, who is also chief executive for all Apple music activities. Supervising the Zapple program will be Barry Miles, a British writer-intellectual in his late 20's.

The first three releases on the Zapple label are now being pressed and include:

1. A new John Lennon—Yoko Ono album titled: *Unfinished Music Number 2—Life with the Lions;*
2. A George Harrison composed-produced electronic music album which was recorded with a Moog;
3. A spoken-word album recorded by poet-writer Richard Brautigan.*

Other well-known writer-poets already committed to Zapple releases include: Laurence Ferlinghetti—

---

* This album, while completely finished, was never released by Zapple/Apple.

America's best selling 'serious' poet; poet-playwright Michael McClure; veteran literary figures Kenneth Patchen and Charles Olson and poet-essayist Allen Ginsberg. Additionally, Zapple will release one of the late Lenny Bruce's last concerts as an album.

It is the hope of Apple Corps Ltd. that the new label will help pioneer a new area for the recording industry equivalent to what the paperback revolution did to book publishing.

The company is now studying new market ideas for the label, which it hopes to eventually retail in outlets where paperback books and magazines are sold, University and College outlets will also be emphasized in Zapple's distribution plans.

Discussions are now in progress with several world figures as well as leaders in the various arts and sciences to record their works and thoughts for the label. The Beatles plan to tape several discussion sessions amongst themselves as an album release—probably for the fall. It is assumed Zapple will have little difficulty attracting these people, who might not normally record albums, because of the general educational tone of the project.

In the U.S., Zapple will operate out of Apple Records Company Headquarters in Hollywood. Its world-wide headquarters will be in the Apple Building, London.

FEBRUARY 3, 1968

• • •

FROM APPLE CORPS LTD.

John Lennon and Paul McCartney of the Beatles are in New York for three days to conduct business conferences regarding the development and expansion of their corporate structure. Mr. McCartney and Mr. Lennon are accompanied by six members of their executive team. Neil Aspinall, Brian Lewis, Denis O'Dell, Ron Kass, Mal Evans and Derek Taylor.

Beatles Ltd. has undergone a transformation to Apple Corps Ltd., a world-wide group of companies held equally by Messers. John Lennon, Paul McCartney, George Harrison and Ringo Starr, which marks a new concept in business organizations. The Establishment of Apple Corps Ltd. is intended to give other artists much wider creative latitude than they have ever enjoyed in the past.

Apple Corps Ltd., which has been established in Canada, West Germany, Italy, France, Switzerland, Sweden, Netherlands, Great Britain and now the United States, encompasses four divisions: films, electronics, music and merchandising.

The film division includes the creation, development and production of feature films, animated films, television programming and television commercials.

O'Dell and Lewis are also announcing plans for two television specials, details of which have not been finalized.

The Beatles' next movie will be an Apple production. There are no specifics to be announced at this time but on July 18, at the London Pavillion, *Yellow Submarine*, an animated feature film using Beatle songs and animated representations of John, Paul, George and Ringo, will have its world premiere. *Yellow Submarine* is produced by a Beatle-owned forerunner to Apple Films in association with King Features.

MAY 14, 1968

• • •

The Beatles have asked Mr. Allen Klein of New York to look into all their affairs and he has agreed to do so, it was announced from their headquarters at Apple, 3 Savile Row, London W1, today Monday, February 3, 1969.

• • •

On behalf of Apple Corps and associated companies Apple spokesman Derek Taylor today said, "Allen Klein, who one month ago signed a business contract with the Beatles and their company Apple Corps, Ltd., is not, as was reported in *Variety*, July 2, in any way terminating his relationship with the Beatles or with their associated companies. It is not true as suggested in *Variety* that his representation of the Rolling Stones and Donovan has impaired his relationship with the Beatles. The New York firm of Eastman and Eastman, said by *Variety* to be taking a more active role in managing the Beatles' business affairs, in fact, acts solely as representatives of Beatle Paul McCartney as an individual. Eastman and Eastman does not act as general counsel for the Beatles or any of their companies. Apple, Beatles, Eastman and Klein have over the past few months established a warm, workable relationship which is to their benefit.

• • •

Apple announced today, September 30, that John and Yoko are resting comfortably at Tittenhurst Park after their completion of mixing and recording with the Plastic Ono Band their single, "Cold Turkey."

• • •

Yoko Ono Lennon lost the baby she was expecting today at King's College Hospital, Denmark Hill, London. Mrs. Lennon is resting comfortably.

• • •

John and Yoko Lennon today announced from their Apple Headquarters, 3 Savile Row, London, W1, that they plan to make a film about James Hanratty, the convicted A6 murderer. After discussion with Hanratty's parents the Lennons, convinced that James Hanratty was innocent of the crime for which he was hanged, said they are going to make a film that will insist that a new public inquiry be held and they themselves plan to reveal startling new facts about the case.

DECEMBER 9, 1969

• • •

NEWSWECANALLDOWITHOUT

Although John and Yoko and George, and George and Ringo, had played together often, it was the first time the three ex-Beauties had played together since, well, since they last played together. As usual, an awful lot of rumors, if not downright lies, were going on, including the possibility of impresario Allen De Klein of ABCKO playing bass for the other three in an as-yet-untitled album called *I Was a Teenage Fat Cat*. Producer Richard Perry, who planned to take the tapes along to sell them to Paul McCartney, told a friend: "I'll take the tapes to Paul McCartney."

The extreme humility that existed between John and Paul seems to have evaporated. "They've spoken to each other on the telephone, and in English, that's a change," said a McCartney associate. "If only everything were as simple and unaffected as McCartney's new single, 'My Love,' then maybe Dean Martin and Jerry Lewis would be reunited with the Marx Bros. and *Newsweek* could get a job," said an East African official.

YOURS UP TO THE TEETH,
JOHN LENNON AND YOKO ONO, 1973

•   •   •

FROM THE DESK OF JOHN LENNON

To: Harold Wilson
25th September 1969

Dear Harold

I am returning this MBE in protest against Britain's involvement in the Nigeria-Biafra thing, against our support of Americans in Vietnam and against COLD TURKEY slipping down the charts.

With love

John Lennon of Bag

•   •   •

I told Sean what happened. I showed him the picture of his father on the cover of the paper and explained the situation. I took Sean to the spot where John lay after he was shot. Sean wanted to know why the person shot John if he liked John. I explained that he was probably a confused person. Sean said we should find out if he was confused or if he really had meant to kill John. I said that was up to the courts. He asked what court—a tennis court or a basketball court? That's how Sean used to talk with his father. They were buddies. John would have been proud of Sean if he had heard this. Sean cried later. He also said "Now Daddy is part of God. I guess when you die you become much more bigger because you're part of everything."

I don't have much more to add to Sean's statement. The Silent Vigil will take place December 14th at 2 P.M. for ten minutes.

Our thoughts will be with you.

Love,

Yoko & Sean
Dec. 10 '80
N.Y.C.

SPIRIT FOUNDATION PRESS RELEASE

I think of John's death as a war casualty. It is the war between the sane and the insane. All his life, John had fought the insanity within us, and of the world. Ironically, he was killed by an insane act at the time he was enjoying the sanest moment of his life. Through the warm letters I received after John's death I have learned that there are many beautiful people in the world leading good lives and enjoying good thoughts and good deeds. Though they are not mentioned in the press for their quiet contributions, they are the true silent heroes holding the sky up through these turbulent times.

The Spirit Foundation received many gifts from such people. One person sent a $10,000 check anonymously; another sent a large tip, five dollars, that she received waiting on tables. To date $285,829 has been received by the Spirit Foundation this year . . .

The support we have received for the Spirit Foundation has given me great hope for the future. Think globally and act locally is our motto. Let's not waste John's death. Please let John's death become a springboard for finally bringing sanity and peace to the world, for ourselves and our children.

Thank you and a merry Christmas and a very, very happy new year from Sean and I.

YOKO ONO, 1981

Colliding Circles/ Lennon on the End of the Beatles

Don't you think the Beatles gave every sodding thing they got? That took our whole life, a whole section of our youth. When everybody else was just goofing off, we were working twenty-four hours a day.

1969

• • •

After Brian died, Apple was full of hustlers and spongers. The staff came and went as they pleased and were lavish with our money and hospitality. We have since discovered that two of Apple's cars completely disappeared, and we owned a house which no one can remember buying.

People were robbing us and living on us to the tune of eighteen or twenty thousand pounds a week. It was rolling out of Apple, and nobody was doing anything about it. All our buddies that worked for us for fifty years were living, drinking, and eating like fuckin' Rome. I suddenly realized it and said we're losing money at such a rate that we would soon have been broke, really broke. We didn't have anything in the bank, really, none of us did. Paul and I could have probably floated, but we were sinking fast. It was just hell, and it had to stop.

1970

• • •

By the time we got to *Let It Be*, we couldn't play the game anymore. We could see through each other, and therefore we felt uncomfortable, because up until then we really believed intensely in what we were

doing. Suddenly, we didn't believe: it'd come to a point where it was no longer creating magic.

1970

• • •

One has to completely humiliate oneself to be what the Beatles were, and that's what I resent. I mean, I did it, but I didn't know, I didn't foresee. It just happened bit by bit, until gradually this complete craziness is surrounding you, and you're doing exactly what you don't want with people you can't stand, the people you hated when you were ten. Fuckin' big bastards, that's what the Beatles were. You have to be a bastard to make it, and that's a fact. And the Beatles were the biggest bastards on earth!

1970

• • •

After the Beatles' last tour, which was the one where the Ku Klux Klan was burning Beatle records and I was held up as a Satanist or something, we decided no more touring. So I said yes to Dick Lester that I would make this movie with him.

1970

• • •

Someday they're gonna look back at the Beatles and the Stones and all those guys as relics. The days when bands were all just men will be on the newsreels, you know. They will be showing pictures of the guy with lipstick wriggling his ass and the four guys with the evil black makeup on their eyes trying to look raunchy. That's gonna be the in-joke of the future. It's tribal, it's gang, and it's fine. But when it continues and you're still doing it when you're forty, that means you're still only sixteen in the head.

1980

Things We Said Today/
The Interviews
Part Two

Yoko Ono
INTERVIEW
•••••••••
New York, January 1983

GEOFFREY: John and Yoko are legion in Toronto. I recently ran across thirty-two photographs of you and John at the Science Center, where you gave your press conference in 1969. You had the big black floppy hat on and everything. Do you remember that day?

YOKO ONO: Oh sure, I remember. We often thought of Canada—it's very lovely, and we did the Bed-in there. John liked the Skidoos so much we just went on riding until very dark. I was a bit scared, of course—it's a bit rough, isn't it?

ALLEN LYSAGHT: Did John really love England?

YOKO: Oh, well, he's an Englishman.

ALLEN: But he liked New York so much, that's why I asked.

YOKO: Well, New York is more like Liverpool, I think. It's home. But he was always an Englishman at heart, shall we say.

GEOFFREY: John always said it's the Englishman's inalienable right to live any damn place he wants to.

YOKO: Well, God is an Englishman, I understand. It's a book I saw when we browsed through a shop. I spotted it: "Well, we'd better get this for you, John." That was the attitude, I suppose, for a long time.

GEOFFREY: Did you like England?

YOKO: Oh yes, until even *after* I met John, until after a very long courtship we were finally together. People are very nice there.

GEOFFREY: I met a man in London and he said, "Yoko Ono lived in the same building as I, and I had a little stepladder that I used to get into my apartment with . . ."

YOKO: Oh it's that, I remember.

GEOFFREY: ". . . You know, I went there one day and it was gone, and I found a little note under the door that said, 'Please come see your stepladder at the Indica Gallery,' so I went, and it was painted white." Did you do that, did you steal someone's stepladder?

YOKO: No—well, we didn't steal. We *borrowed* his stepladder.

GEOFFREY: Was that for the Indica Gallery [where John and Yoko first met in 1966]?

YOKO: Yes. I think some of the gallery people said, "Well, we can pay for this, it's just a ladder, isn't it? Aren't you pleased it's in an art exhibition?" But he wasn't very happy about that. He was saying, "No, I would like it back, and I don't like it white," and all that, you know. We paid for it, but it was very strange. I think the gallery people thought he'd be delighted that suddenly his ladder was an art piece.

ALLEN: Yoko, the first thing we want to ask you, obviously, is your last album.

YOKO: Thank you very much. Let's see . . . it's called *It's Alright* and *I See Rainbows*. In fact, you know, I'm getting all these little postcards and letters from people saying, "I see rainbows too." Which is very nice, there's lots of little rainbows coming to me now.

GEOFFREY: John did a song which was not released called "Watching Rainbows." Did you know that?

YOKO: No.

GEOFFREY: I have a copy of it. He's talking about sitting in his garden watching rainbows, and he says, "If you don't have a rainbow, go out and make you one."

YOKO: Amazing. Well, you see, that confirms in a way, "It's Alright" as a kind of title I would never put out myself. "Season of Glass" is more like me. I like an artistic title. So I was thinking, "Should it be 'Speck of Dust,' should it be . . ." whatever, and I thought, "No, that's not the right attitude." This is to say, "It's all right, I want to hold your hand!" "It's Alright" was a title I subconsciously had chosen. Then, later, when I was talking to some DJs on the phone, a friend of mine called and said, "Oh, the DJ plugged your record, and right before that, he played "Whatever Gets You Through the Night." He turned up the place that says, "It's all right, it's all right," then said, "By the way, there's a record from Yoko called *It's Alright*." I thought it's so strange—it sounds awfully like John, doesn't it?

GEOFFREY: Yeah.

YOKO: So of course, I put it together. I didn't realize he was saying "It's all right" in "Whatever Gets You Through the Night." If I had noticed it, my artistic ego might have changed the title, but somehow he slipped it in. That was beautiful.

GEOFFREY: He said that in "Revolution," too. No, he said, "It's *gonna be* all right." (*The sounds of children playing in a nearby hall filter into the room.*) Excuse me just a second, shall we let these people go somewhere else?

GEOFFREY: Is that young Master Lennon?

YOKO: Yes. Sean. Sean!

SEAN: What?

YOKO: Would you mind coming here?

GEOFFREY: Well, he snaps to the whip, doesn't he? A well-trained boy.

YOKO: He's thinking about it. (*Sean enters.*) Hi. You're back now. He was just at a country place called "Iron Gate." So how was it?

SEAN: Yeah, it was wonderful. I went sledding every day.

YOKO: Oh, I see. That's very nice. (*Sean exits.*) In hindsight, yes, it suddenly dawned on me how John was saying those things. If it had dawned on me before I made that album, then probably I would have avoided it. These days I am resigned: "All right, all right, so we were a couple for how many years, how many decades?" So when he was alive, I used to always try to keep my independence, because he was such a strong, powerful energy. With the whole world behind him as well, by the way. So if I didn't keep my independence, I would have been swallowed up. Whenever somebody calls me "Mrs. Lennon," I used to say, "Mrs. Lennon? I'm Yoko Ono, thank you."

ALLEN: It would have been very easy to be swallowed up.

YOKO: Yes, and I was a bit careful about it.

ALLEN: You were an established artist before you ever met John.

YOKO: John also encouraged that, in the sense that it was good I was independent so we could have a dialogue. Then, after John died, somehow when people called me Mrs. Lennon, I felt good about it. People write to me saying, "We grieved over John's death and just wanted to know how his widow was doing." That would have maybe made me feel a bit strange two years ago, but now I'm grateful people are writing because they love John and are concerned about his family. Whenever I do something now, I feel my first concern is, "Do you think John is liking this?" I don't want to do anything that would shame his name or embarrass him. When I'm doing something and I know John would have approved, I feel better. Let's say all this has mellowed me in a way. As Yoko Ono, I am very mellowed, to the point that "Yes, it's all right, I am Mrs. Lennon." So that independence thing is rapidly disappearing, and if John was the one who thought of "It's Alright" and that's why I slapped it on my album, that's fine, thank you very much, John, that's the feeling. Also, hearing about this, what is it, "Let's Make a Wish"?

GEOFFREY: "Watching Rainbows."

YOKO: "Watching Rainbows." Sounds beautiful. So we're together again, you know. It's a nice feeling.

ALLEN: Your attitude seems so positive.

YOKO: Well, I was a kind of cynic in a way, part of me. When I'm making music, I didn't really care so much about how people were going to take it. This time around, it was really in my mind I was carrying on what John and I did together. So I didn't have a partner who was taking care of the mass media side. In those days I thought, "Okay, he can take care of that side and I'll just do my own thing, thank you." But it wasn't like that this time. I was really talking to his fans as well. Because they were the ones who were really concerned about us and sent us their love and prayers, which really helped us get through the hard times. That's another new discovery—I didn't really think that would happen.

GEOFFREY: You're talking to us about how you've grown through the whole damn thing.

YOKO: Oh yes, it's really amazing. Initially, when my assistants showed me piles of letters and telegrams, I said, "Oh, too bad that John's not here," meaning I automatically thought they were sent for him. And they said, "No, no, these are for you." I actually checked all those envelopes to see who they were addressed to, and they all said "Yoko Something," you know? And that was the start. From then on, there was a nice dialogue going on.

GEOFFREY: I heard that you actually read a good bit of that mail.

YOKO: Yes, I do.

GEOFFREY: Do you ever answer any? Once in a while you send out a letter from you and Sean to everyone.

YOKO: Yes. That was an attempt to say "Thank you, and by the way, hello." It's hard to send a reply to each letter. When I made that attempt, of course, a lot of people were happy about it and thanked me for it. Also, some people were upset it was just a set letter to all of us. It wasn't an individual reply, and some people were saddened by that. They just have to understand that with so many letters and telegrams, I just couldn't answer each one of them.

ALLEN: You took out a full-page ad in the *New York Times* to thank people after John died.

YOKO: Yes. That's true.

ALLEN: I see *It's Alright* as a much more positive album. I associate some sadness with *Season of Glass*.

At the London premiere of
Yellow Submarine, *1968.*

*George and Pattie, 1968. Lennon always
had a thing for the gorgeous Mrs. Harrison,
a fact not unknown to George.*

Lennon in his fashionable "Hur" coat made entirely of human hair.

Arriving in Holland for the now infamous "Bed-In," March 1969.

In bed for peace at the Amsterdam Hilton.

Plugging peace at the Montreal "Bed-In," May 27, 1969.

John holds his latest invention, the "Bag o' Peace," Canada 1969

"Mr. and Mrs. Love and Peace" spreading the word.

At the Ontario Science Center, Toronto, the site of John and Yoko's now historic Peace Conference.

A pensive John meets the press in Toronto.

John and Yoko return to London following a harrowing car crash in Scotland, July 1969.

The Lennons calmly face the media, 1969.

Sending out a strong message from Ronnie Hawkins's rural farmhouse in the company of Avant-Garde *magazine publisher Ralph Ginsberg.*

Yoko, Julian, and John at "The Rolling Stones Rock'n'Roll Circus."

Relaxing at the Windsor Arms Hotel, Toronto.

Arriving in London with Yoko's daughter Kyoko, 1969.

*John and Yoko on location in rural Suffolk while shooting
one of their many avant-garde films together.*

Playing in the snow in Mississauga, Ontario, December 1969.

A rare public speaking engagement in the early seventies.

Smooching at London's Heathrow Airport on their way to the Cannes film festival to premiere several of their avant-garde films, May 1971.

John's thirty-first birthday in Syracuse, New York, October 9, 1971.

Arriving in London in July 1971 to launch Yoko's new book, Grapefruit.

Heading back from a holiday in Spain in the early seventies.

The Lennons hold forth during a lively press conference at the Everson Museum of Art, Syracuse, New York.

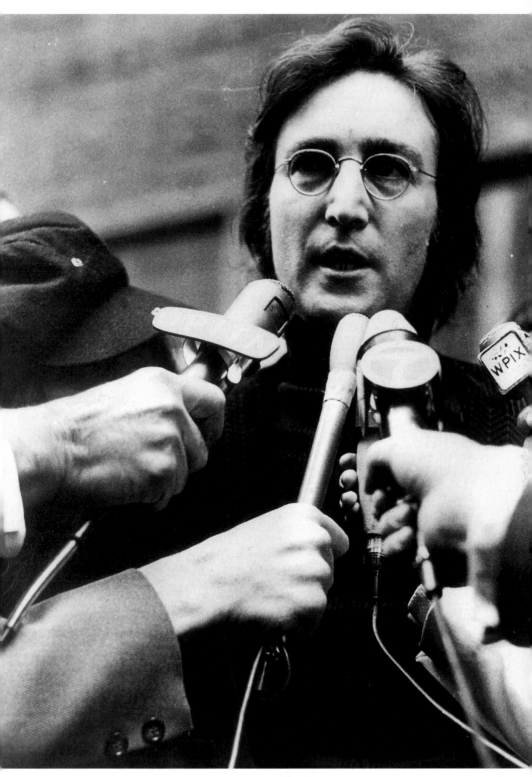

John and Yoko face the press following the extended immigration proceedings they were forced to endure, 1973.

Lennon partying during his infamous "Lost Weekend" in Los Angeles in the mid-seventies. Left to right: John Lennon, Anne Murray, Harry Nilsson, Alice Cooper, and Mickey Dolenz.

Arriving at Jimmy Carter's Inaugural Ball. James Taylor is at the extreme right.

Julia and Jacqui during the lost years, when they seldom heard from their famous big brother in New York.

Backstage at the Grammy Awards in the late seventies.

A pensive John, 1977.

The Lennons arrive at the Hit Factory in New York for their final sessions together, August 12, 1980.

In New York in 1980.

The swank Dakota in New York where John Lennon lived and died.

John leaving the Dakota during the last few weeks of his eventful, turbulent life.

John's uncle, Charles Lennon, Liverpool 1985.

Yoko, Sean, and the author at the Dakota.

YOKO: You have the right to. It was a sad period. Nobody could expect anything other than that from me at the time. I was just being myself, just sort of blabbing off. It's like a primal scream, you know.

GEOFFREY: "Approximately Infinite Universe," the song, is fantastic. Did you ever think of re-releasing anything?

YOKO: Probably one day. When I'm not making a new record, you know.

ALLEN: On "Never Say Goodbye," is there a little bit from the *Wedding Album* in the middle?

YOKO: I didn't think about that. What? What did we do?

ALLEN: Calling out "John!" and "Yoko!"

YOKO: Oh, yes, well, John was always saying "Yoko." I remember him like that. He was a very direct person, open—well, there was the other side, too, very shy and not open—a complex person. But that side is what woke me up, in a way. I was like most end-of-the-fifties crowd, getting more and more complex, becoming a little bit out of touch with your own body, shall we say. That sort of bag. And here comes this man, who is doing very simple chords most of the time and saying, "What do you really mean? Don't give me all this roundabout tiptoeing." "Oh, I see, okay, well, uh, what I meant was, probably, well, I love you." You know, we never say "I love you," we always say, "Well, spring is here and it was very beautiful outside, and somehow it made me feel good," or whatever. That's what he did for me, and now Sean is doing the same kind of thing. Again, I was into my bag of being shy and not communicating, or if I do communicate, communicating with a little symbolism, and here comes Sean saying, "Wake up! Come on, wake!"

ALLEN: The child is the father of the man.

YOKO: I don't know whether it was him, or whether it was him *and* John, together.

GEOFFREY: You showed a lot of people, my wife and I, for example, that I can be yin sometimes and she can be yang, and we can go back and forth like that. That's a very nice thing that John and Yoko gave to a lot of people growing up around you.

YOKO: It has a lot to do with John, too. I mean, if he didn't have the material, I couldn't have worked on it, you know? As I said before, John was an Englishman, and you can imagine an english couple, the strong-headed woman, independent, but caring . . .

GEOFFREY: Like Auntie Mimi, right?

YOKO: Yes, you know, saying, "It's time to get some milk for the cats, dear," or whatever, and the men tending the garden. That's how it was, in a way, and that's all right. John had that side of him. Making tea was very natural for him to do, so he'll make the tea for me, it was very nice . . .

GEOFFREY: And bake bread!

YOKO: Yes. So there was nothing new about that, really. But we were trying to state that, yes, we can do that, too, if we want to. He had a very vulnerable side, and I had the tough side, I suppose, as well, just as much as the vulnerable side. So we can all exchange roles once in a while, and that was very natural for us.

ALLEN: But you said the same thing in "Kiss, Kiss, Kiss."

YOKO: I suppose all the songs in *Double Fantasy*, like "I'm Moving On," had this little edge to it . . .

GEOFFREY: "Walking on Thin Ice," too, had a bite to it.

YOKO: Maybe because of how I dealt with the situation after John died, people think I'm a very strong woman and therefore I am different, so they say, "It's all right for you, you're especially strong!" No, nothing like that. I consider myself just normal. If somebody says something nasty about me, I get hurt and think about it for the whole day. And the way I coped with the situation was almost a miracle! Part of me was . . . well, part of me is *still* in shock . . . and the other side of me was like a little baby. I felt like I was five years old, saying, "Oh, why did this happen?" And "I need a big teddy bear," or whatever. So when I look back on what I did last year—the videos, or the album, and the announcements—that's when I think, "Wow, how did I do that?" So there are several people in me, and they somehow organized it, you know? That put me in a situation, and I just coped with it. If you were in that situation, you would've done the same, or maybe even better, I don't know . . .

GEOFFREY: There was a lot of talk when the eighties came around that they were going to be far out, like the sixties. Then this thing happened with John, and people said, "Oh shit, there goes the decade." But now I see the work that you're doing—and we're all trying to do it—is to make that thing happen. You're getting on with your work to help make the eighties the thing that John wanted, so that the "crazy man" up in Washington doesn't have his way. We're just getting on with life and making that promise of the decade come alive, right?

YOKO: You mentioned "the crazy man," so I will say this: each time there's a president, we tend to say, "He's not good enough, let's wait for the next election." I think that when you really look into the system, it has an automatic operation that stops anyone who's there, regardless of his personality, from going too far afield from what the people want. Now, it's our responsibility to give him a definite sign of what we want, and a unified opinion. Even in a man/woman relationship, we know that we are giving many conflicting signals to each other, and that's made it very difficult. We are getting wise on an individual level, so why don't we get wise about communication with the government? Now, if we do have a unified opinion, *he* has the responsibility to carry it out. The problem is that we don't have a unified opinion, or we're not expressing it. We have to be very thankful we have a system like that. In a dictatorship, they don't have to care about people's opinion. So since we do *have* to, we should use that.

ALLEN: I congratulate you on your optimism . . . but I think it is expressed. I think in '69 and '70, when you were having the Bed-ins, people agreed . . .

YOKO: No, no, wait a second, that's not true necessarily, because the Bed-in was ridiculed in some ways—even the liberals were saying, "What's this? It's too naive." There were a lot of comments . . . not surprisingly, but from *our* camp, more so than the other camp, which was trying to ignore or suppress it. What I think is that this time around, we have to really voice it. When I say "express it," I don't mean a million in Central Park, so that they can say, "It was five hundred thousand, and by the way, there were . . ."

GEOFFREY: "Several arrests for drunkenness and marijuana."

YOKO: Well, "It was minority," and they're right to say it's a minority, because a million people *is* a minority . . . though we can say, "A million represents ten million," or whatever. So this time around it has to be all three hundred million of us, really giving the vote. And I'm suggesting a "peace poll." Done on the congressional level. Every city, every town in the United States, all the states, do a "peace poll."

GEOFFREY: That's not a new idea for John and Yoko, either—there was your "Peace Vote" of 1969 . . .

YOKO: Yes, but this time we should do it on a level that would be understood by the people who we want to communicate with. The point is, they may feel we're not communicating with them yet, you see. "When in Rome"—it's that one. You go to Japan, you try to talk in Japanese, not English. That's how it is. So we have to talk in their language, which is the congressional vote. We have to put it there.

GEOFFREY: Work through the system, then?

YOKO: Yes. Because the system is still usable—it's a very good system, actually, if it's used right—but we have to know how to use it.

GEOFFREY: One of the things I liked about what you and John said in one of his last interviews was, "What's all this 'Star Wars,'" projecting war in space with lasers? Don't you understand that all these mind projections add up? They calculate karmically or whatever . . . so let's just project a positive image. We can create other things to entertain our children with than lasers and *Star Wars* and all that! It's very important that everything we do has this consciousness, to project this peace principle.

YOKO: Yes. Since John died, too, in the past two years there were many things that happened in my life I just never expected—very cruel, heartbreaking things—and it was an experience, I just had to learn another lesson. Because I thought when that happened in 1980, the rest of my life, just coping with that emotion was almost . . . big enough for me. But then there were many unexpected incidents. I thought, "How am I going to deal with this?" What happens usually is that the good people usually confront these negative attacks, and then they start to get busy just coping with that, trying to fight the negative. And they spend the rest of their lives fighting with a negative. Instead of doing that, let's *ignore* the negative—just forget it. It's hard, but just forget it, and meanwhile create positive things. While we're fighting with a negative, we're going to be on the same level as them, and nothing positive will happen while we're doing that. So don't put your energy or attention into negative matters.

GEOFFREY: Just leave it alone, and it will go away?

YOKO: It'll go away when the positive becomes large enough. Now, there's no chance of the positive becoming large if we don't *do* anything, you know, and we're just fighting them. So that's the trap we fall into.

GEOFFREY: At least we're still alive. We thought we might be blown up by now, didn't we?

YOKO: Yes, that's true too, therefore I'm saying it's going to be all right. One day we can all laugh about it, I suppose.

GEOFFREY: Yoko, do you believe in God?

YOKO: God or Goddess? No, it's just a joke. Well, look, I do believe there's some kind of big power that is beyond us . . . and in us, right? But you can explain it in a way that agnostics could understand—it's like a mass dream, a human race dream. We had a dream that we realized: we always wanted to fly, and for centuries people tried to jump off the . . . whatever, and finally, yes, we have airplanes. And of course, this is not quite the way we were thinking of flying. We were thinking of flying without anything, but . . . still, we're flying. There was always talk in poetry about what would it be like to be on the moon. We always talked about the moon. So we went to the moon. So there's always a collective dream that we have as the human race. And this time around, I think there's another dream we've always had, which is to survive. That's a very strong one. There are three things we all want, which are to love and be loved, to be happy, and to survive. There's nobody in the world who doesn't want that. Even the people who are saying, "I want to commit suicide"—it's a kind of reverse expression of happiness—and wanting happiness, wanting love, wanting to survive in that way. And anybody who thinks they can somehow con us into thinking otherwise, *they're* the dreamers. We are the realists. Because there are billions of us thinking the same thing, and that is our collective dream. That's what I call the "great design" that is above us.

GEOFFREY: On the back of *Approximately Infinite Universe,* you said, "The dream we dream alone . . ."

YOKO: " . . . is only a dream. But the dream we dream together is reality." In the sixties, we waved flags and everything. [In] the eighties, however, it's a bit dangerous to even go on the street, even. And most of us—it's not just me, it's not just old ladies on Amsterdam Ave. Even the kids—they're sort of frightened of going out. They're basically all sitting at home watching TV or something. So I thought, "What can we do now?" Because the eighties has its own way of doing things, we can't do in the way we did in the sixties. It's not gathering at Woodstock, because to go to Woodstock on the subway might be dangerous.

GEOFFREY: Besides, there's no good bands anymore either, no one to listen to.

YOKO: Oh, there might be music, but it's impractical, because oil is expensive, and you don't want to travel that far, you know.

GEOFFREY: And we all live in suburbia now and wear ties all day. No one would show up anyway.

YOKO: So where could we connect, where could we gather all together and make this thing big enough that it would actually change the world? Dream power!

GEOFFREY: I got a bootleg the other day of "What a Shame Mary Jane Had a Pain at the Party." It's the funniest thing I've ever heard, and you're in there. I heard Magic Alex was at that session and John wanted to release the song on Apple.

YOKO: Yes.

GEOFFREY: Is it the same as "It's the New Mary Jane"?

YOKO: Yes. I don't know how to tell you, it was just one of those . . .

GEOFFREY: Do you remember who was there?

YOKO: The usual crowd. I don't think Paul was there. I think probably George was . . . I don't particularly remember that. I do remember we did it, but I don't particularly remember it as a very great time.

GEOFFREY: John said he'd like to be remembered as a great peacenik. How do you think the world can find peace today?

YOKO: We'll do it. We just have to do it step by step and it will happen.

GEOFFREY: I don't think the bomb's going to go off, do you?

YOKO: No. But that's not the problem. The problem is more in the way we think. It's not good that the economic situation is so bad and there's a lot of people suffering, which is making the world very tense and violent. That sort of thing can be solved rather easily through the political system we have. It's no longer true to say that war is economically viable.

GEOFFREY: "Let's have a war and get the economy going."

YOKO: That one. There's that sort of feeling still in some of us, and that's why there's only a million people in the peace march rather than ten million—some people are still not quite sure. We have to understand the reality of that.

GEOFFREY: "We'd like to be peaceful, but the Russians will never be peaceful with us, so we'd better keep up this macho image . . . "

YOKO: But that's what the Russians are saying too!

GEOFFREY: If only we could get together and say, "Game over, let's just be peaceful," but to do it is tough.

YOKO: Well, no, it's not really that tough, and there are ways of doing it. As you say, it's obvious that everybody wants peace, but it has to be voiced. And not just voiced through a few hippies, or whatever.

GEOFFREY: Will you continue to voice it for us in a way, and with us?

YOKO: I'll be doing my share, whatever that is.

GEOFFREY: But we need leaders, don't we?

YOKO: No . . . I think each of us is very important in that sense. Naturally, because of the particular environment I'm in I have my share of doing, I suppose . . .

GEOFFREY: We can trust you, I think . . .

YOKO: Well, you can trust me as what I am, whatever *that* is, you know. It's coming to a point that the thing is so important, and we don't have much time. And to make the real turn around, the most important people are really just *people*.

Numbers count now. Maybe they can conveniently hide one spokesman. If it's one spokesman, it's easy to deal with.

GEOFFREY: I heard that you and John were going to a march with Cesar Chavez near that terrible time in 1980, weren't you?

YOKO: The plan was, we were going to go to San Francisco that Thursday to join a march the next day for equal pay for Oriental people in San Francisco. It was announced, we sent a statement there, and John was very happy to do this, because John had a son who was half Oriental. So he was envisioning carrying Sean and saying, "Here's . . . "

GEOFFREY: "Living proof of the harmony."

YOKO: Yes . . . that was one of the things we were going to do. And that probably indicated we were going to do a few things in that direction.

GEOFFREY: May I ask, do you still own your cows?

YOKO: Yes, I do. Or rather, the cows are still with us.

GEOFFREY: Are you vegetarian? I heard you don't kill any cows.

YOKO: No.

GEOFFREY: When they get old and don't give milk, you don't cut them up for meat do you?

YOKO: No, of course not. That's not why I got them. It just was suggested to us as one of those business situations. But since then, we've had so much involvement with that area . . . and the cow's sacred in India—there may be something going on there that we didn't know! And somehow the cows were saying, "Well, look, we'd like to be with people who won't kill us!"

GEOFFREY: A Gallup poll recently said that four out of five people believe in reincarnation. Do you?

YOKO: Well . . . I think we have many lives, probably. I hate to label myself, so I don't even want to say I'm a vegetarian. I eat fish and things like that, too, and occasionally I might just go off and eat chocolate or whatever. But generally speaking I do keep a vegetarian diet, just because it's good for my health. But it may not be for others.

QUESTION: You don't want to dictate behavior.

YOKO: No, because each person has their own karma. I don't even know what *my* karma is, so.

QUESTION: You're finding out—we all are.

YOKO: Right. Gradually finding out, yes.

GEOFFREY: I was reading in some book that you and John actually lived with the founder of the Hare Krishna Movement, Srila Prabhupada.

YOKO: Yes, he was with us.

GEOFFREY: Tell me about that.

YOKO: He was in one of the cottages we had at Tittenhurst.

GEOFFREY: How did you find him? Because everyone says, "They're a cult, they're going to rob you and take your mind—zombies," but they didn't seem . . . they were at your "Give Peace a Chance" Bed-in, they banged the drum and all that.

YOKO: Well, I think each person has his or her own karma. So I'm not the one to say which one is which. People gather where it's naturally important for themselves. In my view, all religion is the same, in a way. If somebody understands it this way better, then they should go there, you know?

GEOFFREY: Elliot Mintz said that in John's famous "God"—which, by the way, is a great song . . .

YOKO: I was just saying that this morning! Somebody was saying, "What songs do you like of John's?" and of course I said that "Imagine" is probably one of the most important songs he put out, but "God" is one that I like very much.

GEOFFREY: John said, "I don't believe in Jesus, Krishna, Gita," etc., but Elliot said John *did* believe in all that. Because when he went with you to Japan, he visited the temples of Buddha . . .

YOKO: Oh, sure. He believed in all that, because it's just a variation. All this is just another way of expressing the same thing. He believed in the "root," which is the big power, and any expression of that he had respect for. I do, too. But what he did in "God," that very powerful song, is like a declaration of independence. "Let me be me now, and let's start from here!"

GEOFFREY: No more daddies.

YOKO: Yeah, right, so it was a beautiful statement—I really like that song. Also, the myth is "the Beatles—and Yoko," or whatever. I'd like to say that until I met John, I didn't really know what the Beatles were about. I suppose I heard about them, like most people in those days—not as fans, but as a social phenomenon. Elvis Presley was another phenomenon I wasn't involved with, but just sort of knew about it. Since I got involved with Paul, I now know what he has done . . . and it's a beautiful thing he did. After all, he's one of the Beatles, and that's what John did as well, and John being Sean's father, etc., so I'm part of it! I feel a family pride in what they did. It's beautiful. As opposed to—not to knock them or anything—but certain groups making their career out of only saying negative things. What the Beatles were about was just simple love and "I want to hold your hand"—that's the gist of it. It's a beautiful thing, and no wonder it was so popular. It changed the whole world. Working-class was something to be ashamed of before that, especially in Britain. But now, even the shopkeepers know that if a young guy comes in who's speaking with an accent, you're not supposed to be impolite to them just because they're young and not from an aristocratic family. It changed everybody's consciousness. If you can make it when you're young, that's fine. Being young and rich doesn't mean that you were born into a good family.

GEOFFREY: You performed with the Beatles on "Bungalow Bill." Actually, you're on a few Beatle cuts.

YOKO: But that doesn't mean anything—it just could've been some girls outside. When they needed a chorus, they used to say, "Let's get some girls in here." So it doesn't mean anything, but I would say I was definitely there when John and I started to do *our* thing. A lot of things we did together were not a waste—it was something that spoke and will probably speak much later, too.

GEOFFREY: We talk about John and Yoko's contribution to music all the time, but I remember Box of Smiles, Acorns for Peace . . .

YOKO: Mmmm, those things.

GEOFFREY: . . . your video for "Cold Turkey," your conceptual films . . . what about Yoko Ono's other artwork?

YOKO: Well, it was natural for John and I to meet. I was in Trafalgar Square standing in a bag, saying this was my peace statement. One day John and I were lying together—as usual—saying, "What about this and that, and what about the working class?" He was bringing up the working class a lot, saying sort of, "Let them eat cake. What did you do for peace?" What was I doing? "Standing in Trafalgar Square." "Oh, I see, that's what you were doing, okay, well look— why don't we stand in Trafalgar Square together, in a bag?" "Well, okay, if you want to." "Well, no, that's a bit too much, why don't we go in a Rolls and bring out all this beautiful picnic stuff and just have a picnic in Trafalgar Square?" That's more our style. I said, "Well, all right." He said, "No, why don't we just sit in bed?" Well, it's easier, isn't it? as we're sitting in bed then. "So what're we gonna do?" "Invite the reporters, tell them we're just sitting in bed for peace." "But then all these reporters will be climbing up the windows and everything, it'll be terrible." "No, we won't do that." So eventually, "Let's go to a hotel and do it." What I'm saying is that I was doing things on my own, and he was doing it with the Beatles, in the sense of "All you need is love," etc. So when we got together, we had nothing to disagree on. That was basically the way it was. That was our meeting.

GEOFFREY: The question is, will you make more things, more films, maybe show us what you've made in the past again . . . what else?

YOKO: Well, the future's an open book. I don't know what's going to happen. I never know. Every time I turn around there's some big surprise, so I wouldn't know. The things I did before were pertinent then and not now. So I don't feel like going back to any of the things I did. It's something that's still there, and I don't have to duplicate it. So it's there, and other than that, I just go on.

GEOFFREY: Someone tried to sell me one of your original Acorns for Peace for five hundred dollars the other day. I just thought you'd like to know.

YOKO: It's so funny.

GEOFFREY: Can you say anything about the night John died?

YOKO: I was still shaking in bed, so to speak, and the bedroom was the old one that John and I used to sleep in, which is on the Seventy-second Street side. All night these people were chanting or playing John's records, so that I heard John's voice, which at the time was a bit too much. What I learned was that I don't have much control over my destiny or fate—anything. Seems like it's all out there, somehow, and certain things I'm not supposed to know. John and I thought we knew all about enlightenment, so there was that arrogant side of us. And this was like a big hammer from above saying, "Well just remember you don't know it all, there's a lot more to learn."

ALLEN: I want to ask you about "Walking on Thin Ice."

YOKO: I was in Cold Spring Harbor, I was in this limousine, and it just came to me. I didn't have anything to write with, so I asked the driver, "Quick, quick, do you have a pencil and paper?" He gave me this small piece of paper, and I just wrote it down. I was waiting for us to come back here, I just ran into my studio downstairs and played it on the piano and put it down. It was like a little scribbling, actually.

ALLEN: And the guitar that John puts in.

YOKO: Oh, that's superb, isn't it?

GEOFFREY: You said it was indicative of the way his music would've gone.

YOKO: He was sort of saying, "Let's forget all the others and go on from here." It might have gone that way very easily . . .

GEOFFREY: The video for "Walking on Thin Ice" was fantastic, and very surprising!

Yoko: You like that, huh?

Geoffrey: Sexy! [The video showed scenes of John and Yoko making love.]

Yoko: There's that part of John and me, but it's only shot from up here . . . That was taken about a week before he died. In the gallery. John was saying, "Let's show them," because people have a feeling that somebody who's married for ten years . . .

Geoffrey: Won't get into it anymore.

Yoko: Some old middle-aged couple, what are they doing—watching TV or something?

Allen: You've taken a lot of classical piano training, and one of the most beautiful Beatle songs is "Because"—and the story we heard is that you were playing some Beethoven . . .

Yoko: *Moonlight* Sonata, yeah.

Allen: Could you tell me that story?

Yoko: Piano has been my security blanket all my life, and whenever I'm nervous or something, I tend to go to the piano. I was playing [the] *Moonlight* Sonata, and John said, "Oh it's beautiful—could we just hear the chords, and play it from this end, backwards," and he used a chord progression from the back on, and it worked. In classical music, chords are nothing, really . . . well, we know all the chords, let's put it that way—but in rock, knowing a chord progression means a lot. So that's what I learned—"You mean, you don't know all the chords?!" It's very interesting—John knew a lot . . .

Allen: He knew it intuitively, somehow.

Yoko: Not only that, but you see, when I did *Double Fantasy* with him, I had to realize yet again how much he knew. He was like a living dictionary about all the little licks and this and that, just *everything*. It was amazing.

Allen: But he didn't read music?

Yoko: No, no.

Allen: Could you explain what you had in mind with Strawberry Fields, of nations sending stones and plants and things?

Yoko: Oh, sure. It's getting to be very beautiful. It's strange that the easiest part was getting the participation of all the countries. It seemed like they were very agreeable. Also, I didn't have any trouble with New York City, in the sense that they're very happy about this international garden that will come to life and be beautiful. It's just the paperwork, also some bureaucratic things I have to go through, that's taking time. Many people are sending money to me, saying, "Will you please use this for Strawberry Fields?" All the monies that are coming to me I directly put into Spirit Foundation, which is something John and I founded together. The unique part of that is that all the administration of the foundation is taken care of by us, and so there's no administrative expense, so that any money that's sent is directly used for whatever purpose we feel is important.

ALLEN: John once summed things up by saying, "I don't regret a thing, you know. Especially since meeting Yoko. That's made everything worthwhile." Does that sum it up for you? (*At this point Yoko becomes somewhat emotional, softly weeping.*)

YOKO: Well . . . that sums it up for me, I suppose. I feel that now John is helping me through Sean.

GEOFFREY: Same birthday.

YOKO: Mmmm. You could ask his statement, because the last time some British radio people came in they said, "Could we ask Sean to make a statement?" I was sort of worried then, though. "Look, these guys are very nice guys, they'll edit whatever. So don't worry about it, it's for the girls and boys in Britain." He was thinking so long, I thought, "He's stuck, he's stuck, oh it's not gonna work," and he just said, "Keep having fun, because it's worth it." I thought that was like John. John used to tell me about his salmon fishing. One of his aunties lived in Scotland, and she had married a Scottish man, so whenever John visited them, he went salmon fishing. This man really liked fishing, and he did it by himself, usually, but sometimes John was allowed to join him. Salmon was a big thing to him. John used to say, "Scottish salmon, there's nothing like it." When I visited this auntie with him I did get to eat the salmon, and it was very fresh. Here, we used to get smoked salmon, but most of it that I get here is sort of salty, and the salmon we got in Scotland were really good. I don't know why they don't export that one. Salmon was one of the things we enjoyed eating.

GEOFFREY: How profound!

YOKO: Yeah, right!

Yoko Ono
STRAWBERRY FIELDS DEDICATION PRESS CONFERENCE
New York, Mid-1980s

YOKO ONO: Last April, in memory of my husband, John Lennon, New York City designated a beautiful triangular island in Central Park as "Strawberry Fields." Since then, I have made a public request to all heads of state in the world to send a tree or a stone from their countries to make this island into a garden of love—an island in which all nations can grow together in harmony. To the people of the world: You are my family, this is your garden. It is a gift from John to you, to the city, to the country, and to you. Enjoy its beauty and its growth. Your love is what makes a garden grow. Listen to the trees and the stones—they will tell us of the countries they come from and give their spirits and roots to our children. I've received thousands of letters from people of all nations asking what they can do to help. Some sent money without being asked: thank you. Some offered their services. Some simply wrote to say that the project was in their prayers.

Julian Lennon
INTERVIEW
· · · · · · · · · · ·
Toronto, October 1984

GEOFFREY: Julian, on your first album, *Valotte*, I noticed you did some recording in Muscle Shoals Studios, in Alabama. Now, on several of your father's albums, there's been a credit to a Muscle Shoals horn section. I was wondering if they are the same people?

JULIAN LENNON: Well, I don't know, but I wasn't hooked up with the horn players. It was just the keyboard, bass, and drum guys.

GEOFFREY: Did you, many years ago, bring home a drawing of a little girl named Lucy?

JULIAN: Yes, well, I came up the drive from school. I'd just been dropped off and was waddling along up to the house with this big picture in my hand which was all watery and blurry. I mean, how well can you paint at five? It was just a school friend, "Lucy," that I'd drawn. It had green grass at the bottom, a dark-blue sky at the top with very rough-looking stars, and these long, curly golden locks of hair on my school girlfriend, Lucy. Dad just said, "Well, what's that?" So I said, "That's Lucy in the sky with diamonds." I guess the song just got worked up from that.

GEOFFREY: Does the drawing exist anywhere, or is it long gone?

JULIAN: I'm sure it's long gone by now.

GEOFFREY: They'd love it at Sotheby's, wouldn't they?

JULIAN: You're not kidding!

GEOFFREY: And what ever happened to Lucy?

JULIAN: Who knows?

GEOFFREY: That's an "om" earring you have on at the moment?

JULIAN: Yep. I used to see Maureen Starkey a lot, and she's into the "om" thing. I was just walking down Portobello Road looking for a new earring, and this took my fancy.

GEOFFREY: Ringo's son Zak is about your age now, and he's a terrific drummer. Have you ever considered working with him?

Julian: He's a fantastic drummer. I mean, incredible, *but* . . .

Geoffrey: "Son of Beatles" might be a bit too much?

Julian: Yes, but also our musical attitudes aren't really quite the same.

Geoffrey: How do you avoid falling into the trap of artists like, say, Frank Sinatra, Jr.? How are you going to find your own identity, both as a performer and a person?

Julian: Well, hopefully everything will just fall into place, but I really don't know. I think it's really just a question of working at it, but who knows when?

Geoffrey: Do you like Beatles music, Julian?

Julian: Oh, yes—I mean, that was one of my influences as well.

Geoffrey: On this album?

Julian: Oh yes, pretty much so. There are a couple of tracks on there that really reflect the Beatles' style.

Geoffrey: Were you always into their music, or did you all of a sudden become a teenager and realize, "Hey, wait a minute, there's all this great music around!" It wasn't played around the house much, was it?

Julian: No, no, but the corny thing is, whenever I walk into a shop or something, it always comes on the bloody radio, you know, *always*. Of course, I did get into it a bit later, or more so than I had originally.

Geoffrey: What are your favorite Beatle tunes?

Julian: I haven't really got a favorite. I do like "A Day in the Life" and stuff like that.

Geoffrey: Your bio suggests that you're interested in acting. It seems like a good idea to me.

Julian: No, that was years ago. Well, a couple of years ago, anyway. I don't really like the idea of mixing media too much. I want to continue with one career. If I'm going to do music, I'm going to stick to that, you know. Being silly once in a while on video is okay, but I think one career is really enough for me.

Geoffrey: Sam Peckinpah directed the video for *Valotte,* and everyone expected something to blow up or machine guns to go off because of his wonderful reputation! But actually, it was a very laid-back, nontheatrical video, wasn't it?

Julian: Originally we weren't even going to do a video, but it does help to get the music across. I mean, if you're going to have to do it, the simplest way is to just throw somebody in the studio and tape it there.

GEOFFREY: There was a story in the press recently that you had one of John's tapes and that you were going to be recording some of your dad's work. What was the story on that?

JULIAN: Yeah, this guy that used to work for my dad in New York [Frederick Seaman] apparently stole some stuff and gave me this tape of dad's, you see. The tape was great. There were some really wonderful old songs on there, just a guitar-in-front-of-a-microphone-type stuff. So he sent along a guitar of dad's with it. Anyway, I thanked Yoko for it all, and she said, "What are you talking about?" She then found out the whole plot and that things had been stolen, so off they went, back to America.

GEOFFREY: So you have no plans, then, to record any of John's unreleased material?

JULIAN: Oh, no chance, no.

GEOFFREY: Steve Holly's a buddy of mine—how did you feel about recording with him?

JULIAN: He's great, absolutely fantastic.

GEOFFREY: Do you remember seeing this? It's the Beatles' 1968 Fan Club promo forty-five given to club members, and you are credited on the back as contributing to the sleeve design! Did you know it existed?

JULIAN: No, I didn't, incredible!

GEOFFREY: It's very rare these days. Your dad did the front cover, the collage, and you did another of your famous drawings on the back.

Tell me, why did you decide to dedicate *Valotte* to your father?

JULIAN: We were always in touch. I'd go and see him during my holidays, and we used to call each other frequently, just to keep in touch. It's been written that I only saw him in 1977, but that's not true. In fact, we lost touch for only a few years. Since 1974, we've had regular visits. I was with my mother and he was with Yoko, but we still used to see each other.

GEOFFREY: You also dedicated the album to your mother for "all she's had to cope with."

JULIAN: In the beginning, the Beatle thing was really crazy—too many people and a lot of tension. I only have dim recollections, like the shooting of *Magical Mystery Tour*. I was there. It's not easy to keep a family together under those conditions. My mother had some very difficult moments.

GEOFFREY: You've composed for years now. Why did you wait so long to record?

JULIAN: It was my friends who liked the songs and got me to record. So I finally just figured, "Why not?"

GEOFFREY: Do you think of yourself as a musician primarily, or a songwriter?

JULIAN: Both. I love to write, especially at the piano. But I also play bass, drums, and guitar as well.

GEOFFREY: What exactly are you trying to say in your lyrics?

JULIAN: I write about the situations people live in and the relationships they have.

GEOFFREY: Why didn't you print the lyrics on the album sleeve?

JULIAN: I don't know, maybe I'm embarrassed or something. I'm not really sure that they're perfect. I would like to say, though, that there is no use looking for any hidden meanings in them. It'd be a waste of time.

GEOFFREY: It's difficult not to when you call a song "Let Me Be"!

JULIAN: Maybe there is something behind that one, but it's certainly not deliberate or intentional. I don't play with clichés, and if someone thinks I do, then that's their problem.

GEOFFREY: *Valotte* doesn't really sound like something from the eighties, do you think?

JULIAN: I don't really listen to a lot of things from today, except U2, for example. I think the music today lacks a lot of emotion. I have older influences.

GEOFFREY: Like the Beatles?

JULIAN: Of course. But Steely Dan too, and, of course, Keith Jarrett is one of my favorite musicians. I also like the Police, and I listen to Kate Bush a lot.

GEOFFREY: Do you ever see Paul, George, or Ringo these days?

JULIAN: I didn't for years, but I saw George about four years ago. He's a fantastic guy, very warm. With Paul, we met for the first time in ten years recently. We talked about the past. Before he left, I told him how much I loved his new single, and he told me he dug my single very much, too. Coming from him, that really meant a lot.

GEOFFREY: Well, *Valotte* is a big success already. It's a wonderful album, and we wish you all the best of luck with it.

Charlie Lennon*

Interview
· · · · · · · · · ·
Liverpool, 1986

GEOFFREY: What do you remember about John being born?

CHARLIE LENNON: Actually, John was born while I was away. I didn't see him until he was two and a half years of age. I met John while the family was living at 9 New Castle Road. I was on leave, and John's dad[†] had just come home from sea. He said to me, "Would you come up and do a bit of painting for me?" So I went, and we went out for a drink afterwards, later that night. Anyway, Alfred said to me, "I'm sure there's something going on in that house, but I can't put my finger on it." So I said, "Have you tried any [sexual] relationships of any sort?" He said, "In fact, I haven't. I'd been away at sea, been sunk a couple of times. I thought perhaps I wasn't capable." So I said, "Well, my advice is to try tonight." The next day he comes rushing down to me, saying, "I rang up Auntie Mimi and was told there was nothing wrong." You see, Julia rang Alfred while he was on the ship in Southhampton, collecting troops from Canada or America and then fetching them over to England. Judy[‡] rang Alfred on the ship, and the captain said, "Well, look, is there anybody you can ring?" Alfred said, "Yes, there's a sister, Mary—Mimi, they call her. Anyway, I'm going off ship." The captain said, "You step off this ship and I'll slap you in irons, because we're sailing on the tide. You'll phone up from ship to shore." So Alfred rings Auntie Mimi, and she said, "Oh, take no notice of Judy, nothing's wrong." Now, she must have known there was something going on. Men were coming in and out of that house all the time—soldiers, civilians—which was happening.

GEOFFREY: Tell me what you remember about John as a little boy. What kind of a child was he?

CHARLIE: The first night of my stay, when I went to do the painting, we went out together the next day for a walk round. I took John into a shop and bought him a big tin bus! Well, he got himself a Donald Duck and walked out of the shop, and I had to go and pay for the Donald Duck as well as the bus! I'd only seen him a few times in his youth. His mother never came near our home.

GEOFFREY: After the Beatles became famous, did you see John very much?

---

* Charlie Lennon is John's paternal uncle. A retired seaman, he currently resides in suburban Liverpool.
† Alfred "Freddie" Lennon.
‡ Julia Stanley Lennon, John's mother. "Judy" was a family nickname for the vivacious redhead.

CHARLIE: He did invite me up to his home to celebrate my birthday in 1967, and I went up from Birmingham. He got on the phone and said, "Uncle Charlie, it's your birthday this weekend, isn't it? Are you coming up?" I said, "Look, John, how can I come up, because Saturday's my busy weekend? Though it is my birthday, I'm still at work." He said, "Forget it. Get up here and we'll have a do." Of course, I had to go in and see my manager. The boss said, "Look, if your nephew wants you there, you're going." John was out until the evening. The Beatles were doing that *Magical Mystery Tour* picture. You realize I had written a stinking letter to John, telling him off over slamming the door in his dad's face over a record Alfred had made.* His dad had gone off to see John to find out why Brian Epstein had killed his record. It was going up in the charts as well. It was called "That's My Life," backed by "The Next Time You Feel Important." Anyway, his dad rang me up and said, "John slammed the door in me face. He wouldn't have done it, but Tony Cartwright happened to be with me." He was acting as Alfred's manager, you see. John didn't like this Tony Cartwright, and when he saw this guy, that's when he slammed the door.

GEOFFREY: Did you talk to John about this when you saw him that weekend?

CHARLIE: No, I never mentioned anything. I didn't even say, "Did you get my letter, John?" I thought he might punch me in the gut or something. Actually, he was quite talkative and jovial about it, saying how great his dad was. That's all he was wrapped up in. "I think my dad's great—I don't care what anybody else says, not even you. I think my dad's great, and that's all that matters." I said, "I've thought otherwise."

GEOFFREY: What did his father feel about his success?

CHARLIE: He was quite proud of him. He said, "Well, he's another typical Lennon, isn't he? The talent's in the Lennon family. Look at my dad." There's a talent from Jack [father of Alfred, Charlie, and Sidney] to me. Though my eldest brother was a canon in the local Church of England, he was also a singer. He said, "It's all in the family." My mother used to say many years ago, "If, in their day, they could have afforded a piano, somebody would have definitely been a pianist!"

GEOFFREY: Tell me about Fred getting married to Pauline Stone.†

CHARLIE: I was really shocked when he rang me up and said, "I'm getting married." I said, "What? Isn't one fallen marriage enough for you? Do you have to do the same thing again, and with a younger girl at that?" He said, "Well, it's John that's pushing me. He said he wants to see me happy."

---

* "That's My Life, My Love and My Home," backed by "The Next Time You Feel Important," and released on Pye Records in 1967.

† Fred Lennon's second wife and the author of the little-known memoir *Daddy Come Home: The True Story of John Lennon and His Father.*

Dr. Leila Harvey* and Julia Baird†
INTERVIEW
• • • • • • • • • •
Manchester, 1986

GEOFFREY: Tell me a bit about John's mum.

DR. LEILA HARVEY: John was Julia's only son, and his pictures were put up all around the kitchen. He was never, *ever* separated from his mother. It was an extended family of five sisters and seven children. We could be in anybody's house, and so could John. His mother lived only about ten minutes away from Mimi, so we could always go and spend the weekend with Judy [Julia].

GEOFFREY: Although Julia was untrained, could she sing?

LEILA: Yes. She played the banjo and sang beautifully. Me being prejudiced, I would say she was even more gifted than John. Judy had personality, she was a little darling. She was offered professional work by Mater's [Judy's sister Elizabeth] husband, but she refused. She was too lighthearted. Judy wasn't serious enough to sing or be an entertainer, but she could catch anyone's heart.

GEOFFREY: Julia [Baird] says that had she lived, Judy would have been right up there onstage with the Beatles.

LEILA: She would. Right up front, and everybody would have loved her. I guarantee you won't find one person who would say a bad word against Judy, apart from people writing silly books who don't know anything about her. She was lovely to everybody. Anybody who stopped by would have a cup of tea. The main thing about her was that she was always very, very witty.

GEOFFREY: Do you remember anything particularly charming about John's childhood?

LEILA: At about fourteen or fifteen, John could pick up any instrument and play it—the mouth organ, the accordion. He was very affectionate and sweet natured. We'd sit watching television, and he'd always put his head on my lap.

GEOFFREY: There's another view of John, you know—that he was a bit of a neighborhood bully.

LEILA: Aren't all fifteen-year-olds trying to be a bit macho? He was very sweet and soft. And quite serious about things—what's right and wrong. John would

---

* Dr. Leila Harvey is Lennon's first cousin on his mother's side. As children, she and John were exceptionally close.
  † Julia Baird is John's maternal half-sister. She works as a French teacher in Chester, England.

often talk to me about what he should do. He was a very serious little lad some-times. Still, I only knew him until the age of fifteen.

GEOFFREY: What are your first memories of the Beatles? Did you go and see them when they were in Germany?

LEILA: I didn't, no. I was working day and night. I did buy their first four records, and then I thought, "Well, four, that's enough. He's going to go on doing this forever, so I'm going to buy a bit of classical music now."

GEOFFREY: Did John ever ring you or anything?

LEILA: I had no contact with him. The next time we connected was when the Beatles were beginning to break up, in 1969. The family said he was on this terri-ble diet and looked very ill. When I saw him, I was shocked. It was at Apple, and he looked a hundred. He was eating his three lentils and two grains of rice a day. He looked really ill. I visited him once at Weybridge. There was no security—I just walked right into his office. I visited him there because that was the last time I could see him, as I was back at work and had three children to look after.

GEOFFREY: Life does go on, doesn't it?

LEILA: Families do separate to that extent, yes. I was with John totally from the age of two to fifteen. Our whole childhood, all our Christmases, Easters, all our summers were spent together. After that, hardly at all.

GEOFFREY: What did you think when you saw John in this condition?

LEILA: I was very upset at the state of his health and worried about him.

GEOFFREY: Did you say that to him?

LEILA: It wasn't easy to get a word in edgewise with the lady there [Yoko]. We had a good old chat at Weybridge, though. At that point, John was very sepa-rated from his family.

GEOFFREY: Had he gotten too big for his boots?

LEILA: No, I don't think so, but he was weighed down and engrossed. Fame is a very big thing to be plunged into like that, with the whole world looking at you.

GEOFFREY: Did you just turn up at Apple unannounced?

LEILA: No. Mimi took me there. We had lunch, but it was very difficult to speak to him because I think they [John and Yoko] were still courting, and she was very hot on the idea. So I didn't say much. But a couple of weeks later I went out to Weybridge, because I knew I wouldn't be able to visit him again, really. We had a little chat about old times. I think he got married the next day. That nasty little boy didn't even tell me. I should have boxed his ears for that. There was really no more contact after that. When my mother died, though, he wrote, because he felt guilty.

GEOFFREY: We've been talking around it, but obviously you weren't very impressed by Yoko. Do you think she had a positive influence over him?

LEILA: No, I wouldn't say that. I think Yoko provided John with what he needed *at the time*. I think his life would have been more in balance if he hadn't gone so far out. We didn't like the vulgarity. It's not our style, and really, it's not John's style. John was a healthy, normal male. We didn't like the exhibitionism.

GEOFFREY: Are you referring to their *Two Virgins* nude album cover?

LEILA: The nude photographs, yes.

JULIA BAIRD: All of that sort of nonsense.

GEOFFREY: Why do you think he did it?

LEILA: John was not really an exhibitionist. John had a musical talent. His body was nothing to write home about. As Mimi said at Apple, "It would have been all right, John, but you're both so ugly. Why don't you get somebody attractive on the cover if you've got to have somebody naked?" It was just silly. It was childish exhibitionism. It's like, "We've done everything else, now what can we do? Take our clothes off!" That's what children do at the beach. I've had a recent argument with Yoko concerning the sale of my letters from John. She was rather rude on the phone, telling me off about it. And I don't consider that she is in any position to criticize my morals. I said, "Look here, you were only married to John, but he was *our* blood." That really annoyed her. She said a rude word, which I'm not going to repeat, because that would be bitchy. She stopped sending her little Christmas gifts after that, so she's obviously annoyed. She rang my brother, David, and thought I would apologize. She has no right to ring me up and criticize my morals. If I wish to sell John's letters—and I didn't, actually. I wanted to wait until I was dead.

GEOFFREY: No one ever made any more money off John Lennon than Yoko Ono!

LEILA: Well, I certainly haven't made any, but my daughter did. I could have had anything I wanted from John when he was alive, but it would have hurt him if I asked, so I didn't. I've never been short of money. But my daughter is just starting off in life, and she wanted something. So she sold them and she got the money. She shared it with her brothers, and I never touched it. I think Yoko feels the family might try and take away a bit of her fun. But we're not interested in publicity. We have our normal lives and our families. That's *her* life. She thinks we're muscling in on her turf, but we're not. She was afraid that my daughter selling those letters might somehow affect the attendance at her concerts.

GEOFFREY: The only thing that affected her concerts was her complete, innate inability to sing on key and people not wanting to buy tickets to hear her crucify John's songs.

LEILA: I was never rude to her. The only thing I said which really annoyed her was, "Look, Yoko, John was our blood, you were only married to him," which I think is a fair comment.

GEOFFREY: What do you think about Julian and his entrance into show business?

LEILA: I've never met Julian. John asked me to visit him, and I thought, "What is Julian going to say?" An auntie coming into his life when he's eighteen, whom he's never seen. It wouldn't mean a thing to him. John should have really kept his children in his family. He shouldn't have neglected that side of things. Julian *should* know his family. But I don't really think it can be meaningful to him at this stage. Still, I think he's a very nice lad, and good luck to him. I'd love to have met him, but we never did.

GEOFFREY: I guess because of this gap between Yoko and the family, you'll never have the chance to know Sean either.

LEILA: I wrote Sean a very long letter, mostly about Judy.

GEOFFREY: Was this recently?

LEILA: No, about two or three years ago, because she sent the little Christmas gifts, so I wrote him about three or four letters. There was no reply, so I don't think Yoko ever passed them along. I don't think she wants Sean to know about John's family, but that's all right. It's her son. We always look on children as very special in our family, every one of them. All the children used to go to Mater's for summer holidays. She was really lovely with children. That's why we're all so good natured. That's why John was so nice. To Mater, every child was a very important person. That's how we feel about Sean, but Yoko thinks that's wrong.

JULIA: It's Sean and Julian, really, that have been deprived of that special feeling we share.

GEOFFREY: I spoke to one person that had some dealings with John, and he said that he never wanted to hurt anybody's feelings.

LEILA: He was a big softy, John. A complete softy.

GEOFFREY: Even when people were taking him for a ride and he knew it, he still didn't want to hurt their feelings.

JULIA: He was brought up like that.

LEILA: Liverpool people are pretty soft.

GEOFFREY: When your contact with him was finally re-established near the end of his life, did he just send you a letter out of the blue?

LEILA: He wrote me because my mother had died. He was feeling guilty, and I wrote him a nice letter saying it was all right. He used to say, "Call collect," but I wouldn't. I paid for any calls I made to John.

GEOFFREY: Did you ever have any problem getting through to him?

LEILA: No. Yoko always put me through. I would have been extremely angry if she hadn't given me that much respect.

GEOFFREY: What were your conversations like?

LEILA: There were some personal things I wanted John to do for me, which he did. I could always ask him to do things like that. It would be about a once-a-year letter and a once-a-year phone call. Yoko kept saying, "He's going to come home," when he couldn't, because of the drug thing. If he left [the United States], he wouldn't have been able to get back in.

GEOFFREY: There seems to be a dichotomy between the fact that John Lennon was externally so concerned about people, and yet charity naturally begins at home. It doesn't seem as though he was doing much for you folks at all.

LEILA: I think to some extent John was quite weak. He was easily dominated, and I think he *was* dominated. Everybody in the family felt in the early Beatle years he was quite normal with us all. When John started this new phase of his life with Yoko, however, it was a bit way-out for us. That's when I think he drifted out of touch.

GEOFFREY: I mean, no one in the family got a job at Apple, and he commanded a very big organization. Why didn't someone at least get a good job?

LEILA: I don't know. I think that was a weakness in John. Weakness is weakness. You don't excuse it. If we had asked John for anything, we'd have gotten it.

GEOFFREY: Why did you say it would have hurt John [for you] to ask for anything?

LEILA: Because he would think you were only contacting him for that. So many people did. He was surrounded by people who wanted something from him.

GEOFFREY: Pete Shotton, John's school friend, was set up for life by John. He bought him a supermarket, a betting shop, and today the guy is rich.

LEILA: And he wasn't even one of his closest friends. His best friend was Ivan [Vaughn].

GEOFFREY: He's got Parkinson's disease today.

LEILA: I saw Ivan on television—lovely boy. They were best friends, Ivan and John. In the back garden, they'd have their own special whistle.

GEOFFREY: What do you mean?

LEILA: When they were going out to play, they would whistle. Off they would go, and I would have to play boy's games with them because there were no girls, so I had to climb trees and be the Indian when they were the cowboys.

GEOFFREY: Was John often the leader in your childhood games?

LEILA: John was the baby. Stanley was seven years older, so he made all the games up. John was a little boy, so he couldn't be a leader, with me four years older and Stanley yet another four years older on top.

GEOFFREY: Let me ask you about Uncle George [Mimi's husband], because they say he was a real sweetheart.

LEILA: He was lovely. The most inoffensive, kind, nice fellow. He worshipped John and shared many little secrets with him.

GEOFFREY: How did John react to George?

LEILA: There was never a cross word. George was very easygoing. You could never quarrel with him. He was a big fellow with silver hair, very tall, over six foot.

JULIA: I remember he was always hitting the top of the doors as he walked out. John use to always give him "squeakers," or kisses, before he put him to bed. No wonder he was such a softy when he grew up—completely ruined.

GEOFFREY: Have you gotten into John's music very much?

LEILA: I wrote him about his record "Imagine" and told him it was lovely. He was very pleased. As he said in a letter to Mimi, "I didn't have talent. I was struck lucky," and he was quite pleased to have it. My son plays music and thinks John's the tops. John's talent was that he had a perfect ear and a very nice nature from being so adored. Everybody adored him all his life—five women. And his oldest cousin loved him very much as well.

GEOFFREY: Was he spoiled?

LEILA: No, he wasn't spoiled, because Mimi was always quite strict, but he was loved.

GEOFFREY: When he was in seclusion as a househusband and then re-emerged with that last album [*Double Fantasy*], were you excited to hear that John was back on the charts?

LEILA: That was right before he died. When Sean was born I wrote him and said, "I hope this child inherits more than your money and your genes." I think he took that a bit to heart, because he really did give that child a lot more attention. He didn't treat Julian right.

GEOFFREY: I've interviewed Julian, and he said to me, "My father said I was born out of a bottle on a Saturday night. But I don't care, I love him, and he's my father."

LEILA: I've criticized John profoundly for not treating his two sons equally. When he was doing his will, he had two sons, and he shouldn't have given it all to Sean. That's crucifying Julian. Julian has a right.

GEOFFREY: Not only that, but Julian had one of John's guitars, and Yoko sent someone from New York to get it back. What can you say about someone like that?

LEILA: It's amazing that the boy's as well balanced as he is.

JULIA: It is.

LEILA: Although Mimi says sometimes things are going on that I don't know about. As I see Julian, he's fairly well balanced, and it's quite amazing, because he had a rough life. John, on the other hand, had a lovely childhood until he was fifteen. Then his mother died [when he was] sixteen. That was terrible, because she was still in her prime, she was lovely. Many's the time Judy's cheered me up. If I had a quarrel at home, I'd go and sit in her house. I'd watch television, and she'd give me an apple. She wouldn't say anything—she knew I was in a bad mood. I'd have my apple, and as soon as I felt better, I'd go in the kitchen and she'd cheer me up. She'd have you laughing in no time. When John died, I thought, "Well, Judy, you've got him back now." You get over the immediate shock, but it's never natural when someone young passes.

GEOFFREY: John was a nice man.

LEILA: I didn't know him as a man, but he was certainly lovely as a boy. He was normal, which he didn't appear to be later on.

GEOFFREY: The drugs do change you, and he had a lot of drugs. I had a lot of drugs, and many people in our generation had a lot of drugs.

LEILA: I wrote him and said that taking drugs is a sign of a weak character. Now I'm insulting you!

GEOFFREY: No, our entire generation did it. Those were the days, my friend.
　　Were you upset when the Beatles' music got very psychedelic? "Strawberry Fields" you must know by heart.

LEILA: Well, I think it's all right, but I don't know it by heart. It's not too painful on the ear. "Strawberry Fields" reminds me of the place we used to walk past at Easter. We use to eat our Easter eggs and amble past the old children's home.

GEOFFREY: How do you look back on it all?

LEILA: Wishing I hadn't been so busy I didn't go box his ears a few more times.

JULIA: Because you think people are going to be there forever. You assume that when you're ready, they'll be there.

LEILA: On the other hand, there's the actual business of life you have to get on with. You've got to be fit to work the next day.

GEOFFREY: What about when he was going to bed for peace and getting into bags with Yoko?

LEILA: I thought it was silly.

GEOFFREY: Inconsequential and silly.

LEILA: Silly, *not* inconsequential.

JULIA: It had great consequence.

LEILA: If he wanted to do that, all right, but I personally think it was silly. He would have been better sticking to the character he had.

GEOFFREY: Did you ever meet any of the other Beatles?

LEILA: Very briefly. I met George Harrison when I visited his house. You must understand, the Beatles aren't really a very big issue in our lives. John's work was his profession. We didn't want to interfere with his public image.

JULIA: That's right. He's singing, you're doctoring, I'm teaching.

LEILA: He didn't come and interfere with my patients, saying, "She did this and that when she was a child," telling all my secrets on me. And I'm not going to do that to him. The only thing that really annoys me is when people say he was aggressive, which he wasn't. He was a lovely, competent boy.

GEOFFREY: What did you think when John got on heroin?

LEILA: I don't think John took heroin.

GEOFFREY: He said he sniffed a bit.

LEILA: I don't see that it matters at all. He wrote some lovely tunes, and if people want to write this garbage, he didn't care. He was no angel. No one's trying to say that John was ever an angel.

Norman Birch*
INTERVIEW
Liverpool, 1986

GEOFFREY: I understand John used to visit here. Who'd he come with, Yoko?

NORMAN BIRCH: Yes, he's been here with Yoko, on the way to Scotland, when he had the car accident.

GEOFFREY: Nineteen sixty-nine. On the way to see Aunt Mater.

NORMAN: That's it. You know better than I do. Yoko did all the cooking, if you want to call it that.

GEOFFREY: What did she cook?

NORMAN: Fish . . .

GEOFFREY: Do you like Yoko?

NORMAN: I don't dislike Yoko. I don't really know her.

GEOFFREY: She's a kind of matriarchal person herself. She's sort of a Stanley in the way she runs everything, isn't she?

NORMAN: No, she's a hard-nosed businessperson. John obviously wasn't. If you ask me, from what he told my wife, Harrie, it's a toss-up whether he ever really loved her at all. I know that towards the end of his life he was thinking of filing for divorce.

GEOFFREY: You're not impressed by John's celebrity, are you?

NORMAN: Not at all, no. Don't forget, I knew Lennon when he was still in short pants. He was an engaging little fellow, I will say that. I remember he had these great gooseberry eyes. He used to come over to visit as a lad and play safari with my old riding crop and hat. The ones hanging there in the hall.

GEOFFREY: How long did John and Yoko stay when they came here?

NORMAN: Only a few days. If you want to know the truth, except for tea they pretty much kept to themselves up in that back bedroom upstairs. What they got up to, I've no idea.

GEOFFREY: Did the neighbors realize John and Yoko were here?

---

* Norman Birch was married to John's maternal aunt Harriet. He died recently in a tragic hit-and-run accident outside his home in suburban Liverpool.

194

NORMAN: Next door never did. The son, though, had a group or something and gave me his tape for John. Nobody comes around here—it's not like Mimi's. Mimi looks after all the media. I'm surprised you even found me.

GEOFFREY: Does she like to meet people and talk about the old days?

NORMAN: She's ill at the moment. She's very ill.

GEOFFREY: When John lived in New York did he ever ring you? Did you ever chat with him?

NORMAN: My wife, Harrie, spoke to him fairly often. She always felt very close to John, I think. Harrie used to get in touch with him as well. John was very isolated in those final days, if you ask me.

GEOFFREY: Did he send Christmas cards and things?

NORMAN: Yes, very often. Letters, birthday cards, the lot. I still have many of them here. I recently got one from Yoko as well.

GEOFFREY: What year were you writing to John? Towards the end of his life?

NORMAN: It was a little bit after Harrie died. After 1973.

GEOFFREY: Let me ask you about your current situation with Yoko as regards this house.

NORMAN: Well, in the first place, John bought the place years ago, primarily so his sisters, Jacqui and Julia, would have a decent place to be brought up. I mean, our other place was fine, but when my wife and I moved here with David and the girls, not only did John buy the house, but [he] instructed the Beatles' office to underwrite any renovations and decorating expenses. John was always very generous. Even as a little boy, he would always be the first to share his sweets. This house was always meant as our home. First for the girls and then, when they left, for my wife, Harrie, and me. Suddenly, one day, out of the blue, I get this letter from Yoko's barrister telling me to sod off. I'm getting on now, you know, and of course, John's dying was so terrible for everyone in the family. But my God, I read that Yoko was left with several hundred million dollars. What could possibly be her motivation for needing the few thousand pounds extra this place would bring?

GEOFFREY: Greed, possibly? Do you think?

NORMAN: Well, I wouldn't really like to say. I don't pretend to know what's going on with the woman. Our old home was fine—I only ever sold it because John insisted. I suppose he figured he was moving up the ladder a bit, so why shouldn't we? I mean, look at cousin Stanley—he bought him his own garage. John enjoyed doing what he could for his family. After all, he had it rather rough as a boy, and I think he wanted us to be proud of him—which, of course, we were. I mean, the lad did all right for himself, didn't he?

GEOFFREY: Yes, he did. So John meant for you to have this house as your own?

NORMAN: He certainly did. He reaffirmed that several times over the years. The place was ours. Technically, however, I've come to find the deed was never transferred to our name. Now, when John was alive, of course, that was no problem, but after he died, I can only guess Yoko saw it as an opportunity to make some extra money, and being a businesswoman, she took it.

GEOFFREY: Of course, you realize for years now she's tried to cultivate this image of being Mrs. Peace and Love. On the face of it, it seems a bit hypocritical, doesn't it?

NORMAN: Well, it is, obviously. One has to question the woman's sincerity. My family and I have lived here practically all of our lives, and now this! I have no savings anymore. I did have, but when I sold the house, John encouraged me to spend it on the family. As long as John was alive, none of us had to worry. With Yoko at the helm, however, everything has somehow turned very sinister.

GEOFFREY: Do you hold it against John that he never transferred the property?

NORMAN: I should think he was rather too busy to be concerned or aware of such things. I blame myself more than anyone for not looking after it. It just never occurred to any of us that this would ever happen.

GEOFFREY: So what did you do when you received the letter from Yoko's hired gun?*

NORMAN: Well, I wrote her back, didn't I? To see what she was on about.

GEOFFREY: You wrote her or her solicitors?

NORMAN: Her, at home in New York. What's it called—the Dakota? I wrote her several times, but my letters were always returned unopened. The ironic thing was that every Christmas since John's death, she's always sent me cards and presents, odd records. It's strange, really.

GEOFFREY: What will you ever do if you have to leave here?

NORMAN: Sleep in the park—die, perhaps. If it wasn't so terrible, you could almost laugh. Where is this great compassion she is supposed to have for people? How can she live with herself?

GEOFFREY: What do you think people would say if they knew about this?

---

* New York show biz attorney David Warmflash.

NORMAN: From what I've read, the purchase price of this house wouldn't even cover one of her many fur coats. When the little boy there was five—what's his name?

GEOFFREY: Sean?

NORMAN: Sean, that's it. He apparently had his own private plane with a pilot on call, in case he wanted to go for a spin somewhere. John once told me on the phone he sometimes spent £500 a week on Polaroid film. Does it sound to you like they need the money?

GEOFFREY: What do you think John would say if he were here?

NORMAN: Oh, well, I think he'd say the same as when John and Yoko were here in my home and didn't like something she said. I think he'd tell her off. It wouldn't have happened if John were here.

GEOFFREY: But if he could come back . . .

NORMAN: Oh, don't be so silly. You Americans love hypothetical questions, don't you? If he came back, he'd probably box her ears and hang her out on the line to dry for being so naughty. I raised my children here, you know, John's sisters. My wife passed away here. This is my home, I have memories. Even if she succeeds in taking the place off me, she won't get those. I'll carry the happy memories to my grave.

Angela and Ruth McCartney*
INTERVIEW
•••••••••
Lockport, New York, 1994

GEOFFREY: As Paul McCartney's stepmom, you obviously had quite a lot of inter-action with John over the years. What was he like?

ANGELA McCARTNEY: John had a very rough exterior, but it was a glass wall. It was all bravado, only painted on. Life had been very tricky with him, with his mother dying so young and all. He was so artistic. He was a genius, there is no doubt about it. John had a very abrasive sense of humor and liked to mock people if there was something wrong with them. He used to make fun of cripples and people with impediments. I remember one time Paul called from the motorway to say he was driving up from London and he had John with him. It was a Monday, and every Monday Auntie Millie and Uncle Bertie came over. Millie would come over to do Jim's† laundry and help with the household chores. Bertie, her husband, would come straight from his job at the same cotton broker as Jim. Dinner was a ritual, and they would usually stay the night. So Jim says to me, "Paul just called and John is with him—they're on their way home. Better get Auntie Millie and Uncle Bertie out of here. You never know what kind of mood John might be in." And I thought, "Oh, dear, this is your home, and your son's coming home with a friend—what's the big deal?" Anyway, I took Bert and Millie home and dropped them off. When I got back, Paul and John had just arrived, and it was, "Hey, I'm starving—what have you got?" They were both fine. I dug something out of the freezer, made supper, then we all sat around chatting and drinking tea. John eventually went to bed in Michael's room, because he was away. The next morning Brian Epstein called and said, "Could you please go and wake John? We're number one in the charts." I had just been squeezing oranges and had a glass of juice in my hand. Jim said, "Well, just tap and leave it outside John's door, but don't, for God's sake, go in." There was a general fear of John I couldn't quite understand. I thought, "He's a friend of Paul's and a guest in the house. He's more than welcome. He's been taken care of. Why walk on eggshells?" But people did that sort of thing around John, which probably only made him that much worse. But I didn't, because I just couldn't see the relevance. I thought he was a tough kid, very talented, but I saw real warmth in him. There was no problem. I remember going up and tapping

---

* Angela McCartney is Paul's stepmother. Ruth is Paul's adopted sister. They no longer have any contact with Paul and Linda.

† Jim McCartney was Paul's father. He died from complications of severe arthritis in the late seventies.

on the door and saying, "Hey John, are you decent? I've got some orange juice for you, can I come in?" And he just sort of leaned over and fished for his glasses. I said, "I've got Brian on the phone downstairs, and he's got some good news for you. Do you want to pick up the phone?" It's just a little thing, but it's an incident that proves that people were, "Shhh, John's coming, he might be in a bad mood!" When you treat people like that, yes, they are going to be in a bad mood. Years later, Cynthia said to me, "You're the only person John is a little in awe of." I said, *"Me?"* She said, "Yeah, because you tell it like it is and you don't take any shit." He'd say, "Tea," and I'd say, *"Please!"*

Ruth McCartney: If you let John give you the runaround he'd give you the runaround! He was really good at it. But if you told him to sod off, he'd just wink and smile. That was his *job* as a Beatle—being the great, witty, inimitable John Lennon! Don't forget that when the boys would come home, George had parents, Ringo had parents, and so did Paul, but Auntie Mimi lived way down in Dorset. So on the occasions John would come home to Liverpool, he'd always stay at our house.

Angela: I remember a time when John was staying at Rembrandt* and the boys decided to take the bus to Chester, which is about fourteen miles from where we lived. They borrowed two old raincoats of Jim's, two trilby hats, and tucked their hair down the back of their collars and caught the bus down to Chester. They were gone for several hours. When they returned, Paul said, "There will be a van coming soon. We bought all sorts of stuff." There was a van, all right!

Ruth: Why didn't they hitch a ride back in the van?

Angela: They were out on an adventure. Two lads out on a skiff. They'd been to a pub, had a meat pie and a glass of beer. They were very thrilled about that—nothing like a meat pie and a glass of beer! So this van arrived with several huge Bibles. They bought brass crucifixes, picture frames, several old dusty books, which I'm sure neither of them would ever read. These things were littered all over the house, and poor Jim, like me, was fanatical about tidiness. Eventually, I had to hire another truck and send it down to London. It all went to Cavendish Avenue† so it must have been later than 1965. They were all just trinkets, but they probably shelled out a hell of a lot of money.

Geoffrey: Ruth, being Paul's stepsister,‡ you were always fairly close to Julian over the years. What can you recall about his early life?

---

* The name of Paul McCartney's suburban Liverpool family home on Baskerville Road, the Wirral, a home that he still owns.

† Cavendish Avenue, St. John's Wood, was then and is now Paul McCartney's London home. These days, his daughters Mary and Stella use it more than even Paul.

‡ Jim McCartney formally adopted Ruth after his marriage to Angela, so, legally, she is actually a full sibling. Today, she is a talented singer/composer and business woman.

RUTH: I remember Julian hadn't heard from John in years and years. He was about ten years old, and John must have had a sudden attack of guilt, like, "Oh my God, I've got a kid on the other side of the Atlantic! I'd better shower him with expensive gifts." Forgetting his child was just ten, he sent him a Suzuki motorbike, which the poor kid couldn't even drive!

GEOFFREY: Did old Jim really like John Lennon?

ANGELA: No, he didn't like John at all, because he had this tendency to mock the afflicted. John was always mocking cripples and people with speech impediments. He used to pull famous funny faces, very silly, which was definitely a facet of John's character. It would take the experts to analyze, but Jim didn't like it.

GEOFFREY: Did he do that around Jim?

ANGELA: He made one or two little cracks. He made one remark about Aunt Millie once, which Jim really resented. But rather than speak up and say, "That's not nice talk in my house, son" or something like that, Jim just bottled it up.

Harry Nilsson*
INTERVIEW
• • • • • • • • • •
New York, February 17, 1984

GEOFFREY: Why do you do these Beatle conventions?

HARRY NILSSON: To raise money to end handgun violence.

GEOFFREY: Can we assume that the initial impetus for your interest in ending handgun violence was instituted by the sad events of December 1980?

HARRY: You can assume that, yes.

GEOFFREY: Is it true?

HARRY: No. I was involved seven years before that, when a friend named Steve Wolf was shot for some unbelievably stupid reason. This guy broke into his kitchen and killed him, and it wasn't for the food. I got involved then as a tokenist, and then I became an activist after John was killed, because I had to hold Ringo's hand for a week. Do you know what that's like? It's like saying, "Listen, man, if I could take it from you I would, you know, but I *can't*. If I could, I would. There's nothing I can do, but let's do something about it, maybe. Let's put an end to some of the stupidity."

GEOFFREY: So what would you say to all these National Rifle Association boys with their "right to bear arms" bullshit?

HARRY: Well, I call them "jerks," and I think they have no intelligent arguments to offer anyone. I know what the Second Amendment of the Constitution says, and I challenge them to meet me on *my* ground. Let's be intelligent, let's be human and stop killing each other with stupid toy guns! Don't you realize in 1963–73 there were forty-six thousand U.S. Americans killed on foreign soil? During the same period of time, guess how many Americans were killed *in* America with handguns: eighty-four thousand. More people were killed by handguns in America than were killed in Korea. More people were killed by handguns in America than were killed in Vietnam. Get the picture? You're six times more likely to be killed by a handgun trying to protect yourself. Guess who the bad guys get their handguns from? They steal them from guys like us, the "good guys." You buy a handgun to protect yourself, and you hide it cleverly right next to the Christmas gifts, which the children have already found. And

---

* Harry Nilsson, a successful singer/songwrtier in his own right, was one of John Lennon's closest friends. He died of a heart attack in his sleep in the early nineties.

then some people are even so clever, they put the bullets in another place. That's how cool *they* are, you know? Meanwhile, somebody comes in, kills them, takes the bullets and the gun, and runs away and kills somebody else. I've never heard an intelligent argument for continuing handgun violence. Have you?

GEOFFREY: You're friends with Yoko. How is she feeling about gun control?

HARRY: Well, she's against violence, you know. I'll tell you something about Yoko: I know why John fell in love with her. She is one of the most ingratiating people in the world. She's one of the kindest, nicest, honest, and most pursued people on the planet. Who's the most famous Jap—Hirohito or Yoko? I don't want to turn this into some kind of epitaph, but look: she's wonderful. We clash a little bit about how to deal with handguns, but it's fine. She'd rather not know about violence, and I don't blame her. I personally have taken a stance, and I am involved. We're presently seated across from Terry Southern, one of the world's greatest cinema authors, probably *the* greatest. Terry wrote *Candy, Magic Christian, Dr. Strangelove, The Loved One, The Cincinnati Kid,* etc., etc., you know. And Terry is a nonviolent man. He believes in, "Let's talk sex, and let's not talk guns and violence." I prefer that stance. I'd rather be with Terry than any jerk with a handgun. I beg you to think about it and *don't buy one,* for openers. If they want to kill you, they'll kill you anyway. If you have one, they'll probably kill you with your own gun. I beg you to think about the issue, and if begging isn't enough, I don't know what else to say. Twenty-two thousand lives a year from stupid handguns. Hey, if you add it up, how many years will it take to make Hiroshima?

GEOFFREY: How many years does it take to clean it up?

HARRY: Well, that's a big question. But there *is* hope, and there are lots of good people out there. Some are fighting for registration, but registration isn't that great a deal. You register a gun, he steals it from you and kills him, so what have you accomplished?

GEOFFREY: Mark David Chapman had a registered gun!

HARRY: That's quite right, and it came in parts, by the way. It was assembled from parts from someplace else. We want to stop that influx of parts. So what I'm saying is, it's much easier just to have a good time than consider the fear that you have to live with when you even own one of them.

GEOFFREY: How come the good die young?

HARRY: It's not necessarily true. Bertrand Russell died late, I thought. Methuselah lived nine hundred years. I don't really know if the good die young. Herod killed a lot of bad kids, I'm sure. I have no idea what I'm talking about.

GEOFFREY: How did your relationship with John get started?

HARRY: He called me and said, "Harry, you're fucking great, man," and I said the same about him, then we became friends, and over the years we hung out, like Terry and I are hanging out now.

GEOFFREY: How do you remember John?

HARRY: It's not how I remember him, it's just that I miss his wit. We were preparing to go back to finish up Ringo's album—we were in Nassau. Ringo and I were sharpening our wit to get ready to go into action with John, because he was one of the wittiest men, you know. He'd always beat you to the punch—very fast—just a wonderful guy who liked show business. I do occasionally think about things we did, but I prefer to think of it this way: Damn it! No more jokes from John. That bothers me a bit—doesn't it bother you a little bit?

GEOFFREY: Makes me cry.

HARRY: Well, okay, that's good, cry. I only cry at basketball games.

GEOFFREY: How did the album *Pussy Cats** come about?

HARRY: We were bored . . .

GEOFFREY: And the *Lost Weekend*?

HARRY: Oh, the *Lost Weekend's* history. We were bored at a Joni Mitchell session, peeing in ashtrays, that sort of thing . . .

GEOFFREY: Jumping out of cars?

HARRY: No, we never did that, as far as I remember.

GEOFFREY: Spitting up blood?

HARRY: There was a little bit of that, yeah. But John announced to the room, "I'm gonna produce Harry Nilsson!" I didn't know whether we were drunk or not, you know, and so a couple of days later, he says, "What do you think?" He woke up earlier—he was shining his shoes at the time. John's a man who'd shine his own shoes, you know what I mean? I said, "If you're serious, man, you bet."

GEOFFREY: It's a great album.

HARRY: It's a raspy album, but it is a very good album. We could have gone back in the studio and cleaned up some of the shit, but we thought it unnecessary because it had that raw, "This is what happens in the studio when you're there and you're that way." And it was very good, I thought. There were three great cuts on it.

---

* An album of songs by Harry Nilsson produced by John Lennon.

GEOFFREY: I like "Mucho Mungo/Mt. Elga." You and John wrote that together, didn't you?

HARRY: Yes. But I prefer "Many Rivers to Cross." John was a crazy galoot. What's it like in Canada?

GEOFFREY: Cold. Getting nicer. Not bad.

HARRY: Lenny Bruce said, "You people in Canada, take care of those Plymouths."

GEOFFREY: What was it like living in that house with Keith Moon, Ringo, and John? Was it a big party twenty-four hours a day?

HARRY: Of course not, you can't do that. We lived a normal, reasonable life. We'd wake up in the morning—well, about one o'clock—and we'd eat food prepared by this couple we had serving us. At first we were very polite: "Would you mind passing the—oh, thank you very much," "Sugar, please—oh, thank you," and then after a while it was, "Keith, get your nose out of the emyl." You know, like that. Klaus Voorman went out for a swim in the ocean; my wife, Una, used to take walks on the beach; John and May would sleep late; I'd sleep late; and at six o'clock the limos would show up and we'd drive to Warner Brothers and record. We'd finish about two o'clock, come home, open up the brandy and listen to the takes very loudly, get drunk, and tell each other how good we were. So that's relatively normal, it's what people do when they go to nine-to-fives: "Oh, you should have seen what I did today at the office." "How were things at . . . " "Oh sugar, I'm home." You know.

GEOFFREY: What about the Phil Spector sessions for *Rock 'n' Roll*?

HARRY: That was pretty madness. Phil is a genius and a dear friend as well. Some of the sessions . . . there was one when John got too loaded, and Cher was there and she and I sang this song, because at the time, the union rules required if you had a band, you had to have a singer. And John had passed out or something, so he says, "I got it: Harry and Cher." I said, "You mean Nilssonny and Cher." He went, "Nilssonny and Cher!"

GEOFFREY: Do you have anything in the can you did with John that won't come out?

HARRY: That's a rather personal question.

GEOFFREY: I mean in the recording can, dear boy.

HARRY: Oh, is that how your mind works? There was something we did, a couple of tunes we started writing. Years ago we wrote a song called "You Are Here."

Geoffrey: That was on *Mind Games.**

Harry: Well, I don't know. I never actually listen to *Mind Games*, frankly.

Harry: This is something we started to write years ago. I never heard the final product. We used to send tapes to each other, and postcards and things, and we used to sign them "You are here." I miss him very much. I'd like to say I was a very close friend. I *wasn't* a very close friend. No one was a very close friend to John, other than the Beatles.

Geoffrey: Did he miss the Beatles?

Harry: Someone told me a few minutes ago they saw John walking on the street once wearing a button saying, "I Love Paul." And this girl said she asked him, "Why are you wearing a button that says, 'I Love Paul'?" He said, "Because I love Paul." I always thought Ringo and John were the Beatles. John once said, "Harry, look man, I was always the Beatles, you know that. Me and Ring . . . well, let's put it this way: Everybody, just like me, we all fell for Paul's looks. George knew more chords, Ringo's Ringo, and I'm just it. Just John, you know. I *am* the fucking walrus, you know." And I mean, he had that honesty, he loved show business, he was a wonderful man. And if there's any message to be said by Harry Nilsson to your audience, it's simply this: the sickness which attends handgun violence must be stopped. Until we have a means of curing that illness, we must at least take away access to the machine which allows us to act out our illnesses.

Geoffrey: Could John have forgiven this fellow who did what he did?

Harry: Well, I wouldn't. I'd say, "Shame on you."

Geoffrey: Do you think all this worship of the Beatles twenty years after their advent is healthy?

Harry: Yeah.

Geoffrey: It's not living in the past?

Harry: No, it's not. Welcome to the eighties.

Geoffrey: Beatles music has a statement for the eighties, then?

Harry: Sure. So does George Washington.

Geoffrey: How's your relationship with the rest of the Beatles?

Harry: I thought you were gonna say George Washington. Ringo and I speak a couple of times a week—we're very, very dear friends. "Goodnight, Ringo?" He's

---

* A solo album by John issued on Apple Records on November 16, 1973.

my pal. He was best man at our wedding, he's one of the dearest friends you can have in life, he's godfather to our children, and I hope I'm his best friend in life, you know. George and I are also very good friends. Paul is just Paul—I don't really know Paul. I've known him over the years, but I don't know him like Ringo or George. I know John a lot more than Paul. Macca is an amazing guy—smokes his joints and whistles his way through life. God bless him, too.

GEOFFREY: He shouldn't take it to the airport, though.

HARRY: Well, I think they should change the laws. I think it's stupid. How about when Yoko went over to England—they searched her cold cream, for Christ's sake. Let's talk reality, man. First of all, she's not a drug taker; she's the most beautiful fifty-one-year-old woman in the world. I read in a magazine the other day she was taught not to smile in public because shopkeepers smile in public in order to ingratiate themselves. That's a heavy thing to think about. Yoko's one of the most beautiful, fascinating women I've ever met in my life.

GEOFFREY: What about Sean?

HARRY: Sean is one of the brightest children I've ever seen. I have two or three bright children, but Sean is incredibly loose, open, and bright. He's fragile, he's aware, and he says things that are so accurate. He's very honest and admirable. He's just a wonderful, wonderful little boy.

GEOFFREY: How do you see his future?

HARRY: Well he's sort of locked into a bit of it, isn't he, being a "Son of." But he's so bright, he can handle it. He's very soft, and he's very bright.

GEOFFREY: Is he a lot like John?

HARRY: Well, yeah, and he's very much like Yoko. When Yoko smiles, everybody smiles with her. It's a genuine smile—you can't fake that. Sean does nice things—he'll write you notes saying "Happy Valentine's Day" or "Here, Harry" and draw arrows and things, or "Menu for Harry," with brandy and this and that. He's just one of the most joyful children. And he's got a lot to carry on his plate.

Frederic Seaman*
INTERVIEW
• • • • • • • • • •
Lockport, New York, November 1995

GEOFFREY: In the time that you knew John Lennon, what were his good feelings about his tenure with the Beatles?

FREDERIC SEAMAN: I was hired as John's assistant in 1979. Yoko basically conducted a perfunctory job interview, because she had already decided to hire me. She knew my birthday was the day after John's, and my uncle was an old friend of hers. She just told me very vaguely that I would be doing some shopping as well as helping John cook brown rice and answering phones. Eventually, I ended up running her office and traveling with John to Bermuda, Palm Beach, and Long Island. It was an all-consuming job, sometimes twenty-four hours a day. John talked about the Beatles on occasion when we'd be driving around and a Beatles song came on the radio. He would just talk about the recording session, whatever came to mind. He was very conflicted about the Beatles. He had a lot of good memories, but there was some lingering bitterness. Overall, John knew he had probably done some of his best work as a musician with the Beatles. There was no getting away from it, and he was proud of it. He was highly critical of his work—he was his harshest critic. Some songs people consider great he would dismiss as garbage. That was always surprising to me. But he had a lot of fondness for the individual Beatles. He liked Ringo the best—he was always closest to Ringo. Ringo was never a threat to him as a musician. They remained friends until the very end. George, he had some problems with. There was some fighting going all the way back to the Bangladesh concert, when Yoko wanted to be a part of it and George wouldn't let her, so that caused a lot of friction. He once told me that he loved Paul like a brother but he didn't like him. He had a lot of problems with Paul particularly, because of the in-laws. The Eastmans were sort of between them, but there was a lot of affection. Overall, I would say he was kind of detached from that whole period.

GEOFFREY: What was it like to be with John after so long in retirement or semi-seclusion, and he suddenly popped back and started to compose *Double Fantasy*? Talk about that period.

FREDERIC: It was surprising to me he was able to get back into action as a musician, because for the year I'd been with him he was virtually inactive, so I was

---

* Frederic Seaman was Lennon's final personal assistant, from 1979 until his death. He is today a noted author and lecturer.

very surprised when he decided to do the album. Once he actually got working on it, I saw what I like to think of as the real John Lennon. Someone who was extremely creative, almost obsessively devoted to his work, composing day and night. He would generally compose on the piano until he got the chords right, and then he would do another set of demos on the guitar, add a rhythm track. He had a rhythm box. I saw him at his best, when he was really doing what he loved. I was constantly astonished, because I would hear the demos in a very rudimentary form and then I would hear a later version with the rhythm track, and I was blown away, because I could see he knew exactly what he was doing. In his head, he basically heard the completed song. I was lucky enough to be with him in New York's Hit Factory and Record Plant when he did the album. He knew exactly what he wanted and he knew how to get it, and the final versions of those songs are amazing. The sad part is only a handful of songs were really honest: "Watching the Wheels," "Losing You," and "Face It," which wasn't even on *Double Fantasy*. It was released on *Milk and Honey*, the album Yoko put out posthumously in 1983. Those were real songs. A lot of the others—like "Woman," which is a beautiful, great-sounding piece, but it's a propaganda song. "Starting Over" was certainly designed to capture the market. As John told me, he crafted it along a certain formula, using bits of Elvis, Roy Orbison, and others, to write a familiar-sounding song people would find catchy. So the album itself was a compromise for John, and he was aware of it, but he knew that it would be a big hit—it couldn't miss. I mean, John Lennon's first album in five years! People were very anxious to hear it, but on the other hand, he was a little self-conscious, because he knew it wasn't an entirely honest album. Still, he was proud of it, because there was a handful of really great songs on there he knew would stand the test of time. He was proud of it, and he worked his ass off.

GEOFFREY: How did he feel about the Lennon and McCartney songwriting partnership, both personally and professionally?

FREDERIC: Well, he admired Paul, because he was a real craftsman. He had a better understanding of music theory, and Paul certainly was a better instrumentalist. Paul could play several instruments—he was a virtuoso bassist. But on the other hand, John was rather dismissive about Paul's songwriting skills. He thought Paul was a consummate hack who had no taste, who would basically put together songs designed for the teenybopper market. He thought that Paul didn't have much pride as a musician, and he saw his great contribution to Paul's music as that of an editor. When Paul went off the deep end, as John would put it, John would be there to tell him, "Hey, man, this is bullshit. Lets fix it up. There's a seed of something really great here—let's flesh it out." And that's what John would do. He would work on the material with Paul and make them into better songs. But on the other hand, the thing Paul did for John was to edit John's songs and give them a polish and a professional veneer, which would take

John's raw stuff and convert them into gems. So they were a great—perhaps the greatest—songwriting partners in history, because they really did complement each other in a very symbiotic way, and together they were able to fashion a body of work that ultimately would be regarded as some of the greatest songs in history.

GEOFFREY: In many ways, you'll have to be the spokesman for John Lennon's innermost feelings. You were probably closer to John than just about anybody— certainly towards the end of his life—so you're in a unique position to comment on what *he* thought about certain periods of his life. You tell me what you can remember about John's thoughts and feelings during those periods. First of all, playing with the Beatles at the Cavern.

FREDERIC: Those were some of John's fondest memories. Because to John, the early Beatles, the Cavern Club—and even before that, the various visits to Hamburg—that, to John, was the highlight of his life. In fact, he once told me the feelings he experienced in 1980, when he was working on *Double Fantasy*, were similar to those he experienced in 1960–61, when he was working in Hamburg and when he knew he was going to make it big. He knew at that point the Beatles had something special going and nothing could stop them. Sooner or later they would become very, very successful, and he was intoxicated with that feeling and knowledge. He felt very strong. He felt great all the time, and he savored that feeling from 1960 and '61, and he savored it in 1980. The Cavern Club was certainly a stepping-stone to the mass success that he achieved in 1963–64. Those gigs they played at the Cavern were certainly some of the greatest gigs the Beatles did. By the time the Beatles had mass fame and were touring the world, they were basically useless. John knew at the time Beatlemania hit it didn't matter how good they were, it didn't matter what they played, it didn't even matter if they played. They could've been up there lip syncing, and the fans would have gotten hysterical anyway, because the whole point was mass hysteria. It was Beatlemania—it had nothing to do with the music. It was just an excuse for millions of teenagers to go crazy and have orgasms. John knew that, and he was bitter about it and somewhat disappointed.

GEOFFREY: What were his feelings after the Beatles broke up and retreated back to the sanctity of the studio to try and perfect their work on a more intelligent level?

FREDERIC: John knew the Beatles had taken the art of rock in the studio to unprecedented heights, and he was justifiably proud of that. He actually had a lot to do with it, because he would ask impossible demands of George Martin and the other Beatles, considering they were working with 1940s technology. And he was proud of the kind of songs that they did under those conditions. The kinds of sounds they achieved by running tapes backwards and including all sorts of sound effects. It was he who dared go beyond the established boundaries, and it found a market. People loved it. John, for a while, tapped into a collective subconscious and expanded rock into areas no one else knew existed. He was very proud of it. He was also very aware of the others who were imitating it. For instance, he once told me the Electric Light Orchestra, their entire sound and repertoire, was based on "I Am the Walrus." He was aware of the innovations the Beatles achieved in the studio, and he knew it was due largely to his insisting on trying new things. Experimenting—he was really the great experimenter in the Beatles. Paul generally liked to play it safe, and the others went along. It was really John and his imagination that was responsible for the Beatles' sound.

GEOFFREY: What did he say about taking acid? How did it affect him as a person, and his work?

FREDERIC: John said acid transformed his personality. He told me that basically, deep down, he was a very angry, violent man and that acid mellowed out all of those feelings. It took the violent edge off of him while he was on acid. He spent most of 1967, some of 1966, on acid. He got into a very loving vibe. He would go to clubs, and instead of getting confrontational with someone who gave him a hard time, he would be loving. He felt acid had a positive effect. It transformed his personality in a positive way, but because he overdid it, it eventually came back to haunt him. There were times he went off the deep end. He talked about that period in 1968 when he had a kind of psychotic breakdown and thought he was Jesus. He talked about literally crawling around on all fours, feeling he was Jesus and demanding that Apple put out a press release announcing that John Lennon was Jesus reincarnated! He was very upset when people were skeptical about his religious conversion, but later he was able to look back on that with a sense of detachment and even amusement. For John Lennon, acid was a profoundly transformative experience, and it helped shape his persona, certainly in the late sixties and into the 1970s.

GEOFFREY: What good things did he feel came out of his search for spiritualism in India?

FREDERIC: John was always looking for gurus, and the Maharishi was the first great guru John met, and he really was a very faithful follower. He learned a lot from the Maharishi about acceptance—certainly when Brian Epstein died. The Maharishi helped John cope with his grief, considering the fact that Brian was the one man that John was closest to. In fact, he said in interviews he was closer to Epstein than any of the women in his life, including his wives, Cynthia and Yoko. So I think the Maharishi had a very crucial impact on John's life at a very crucial period. Unfortunately, John lost faith in the Maharishi when Magic Alex was able to convince him the Maharishi was not a good guy after all. So ultimately, John turned out to be disillusioned. But for a while there, John was really very devoted to following the Maharishi.

GEOFFREY: You saw Ringo and John together. What was that relationship like?

FREDERIC: Well, John and Ringo were very close friends. They understood each other. They had gone through a lot together, and there was a certain mutual respect. In front of Ringo, John didn't have to put on any airs—he could just be himself. When I saw the two of them together, it was a bad period for Ringo. He had just had surgery—he looked pretty bad. He wasn't feeling all that great, and John tried to cheer him up, acting like an older brother, even though I think Ringo was actually older than John. You could sense there was a great deal of mutual respect and affection. They were like old warriors who had gone through a lot of wild and crazy times together. They were survivors—there was that sense of them being survivors. They had shared a lot of good times together.

GEOFFREY: What did John say about the breakup of the Beatles?

FREDERIC: Well, John blamed it on Paul. Not really Paul, actually—on the Eastmans. John felt that if it hadn't been for Linda Eastman getting involved with Paul and bringing in Lee and John Eastman, the Beatles might have survived. He was also honest in the sense that he admitted he himself was looking for an alternative to the Beatles. By 1969, the Beatles knew they were really finished, musically. There were no real frontiers left to explore. Personally, they were all at each other's throats, and Yoko entering the picture certainly was a catalyst for the breakup. Yoko gave John an excuse to leave the Beatles. John always needed an alter ego, somebody that he could be involved with in a symbiotic way. Once John and Paul became estranged, around 1966–67, he was always looking for someone to take him away from the Beatles, and Yoko was that person. So it was probably really Yoko who broke up the Beatles, but John didn't want to admit it. He blamed Paul and Linda Eastman, which I suppose was a rationalization for him. Probably the truth is somewhere in between. It was really a combination of Yoko and the Eastmans entering the picture that broke up the Beatles.

GEOFFREY: Is it true they were going to get together for a reunion after Kurt Waldheim asked them?

FREDERIC: Well, John was sitting on the fence. His feeling was that if Paul and the other Beatles wanted to get together, he would come in as the last one and say, "Okay, let's do it." But the problem was, it wasn't really his decision—it was Yoko's decision. And what really happened there, and I know this because I was there at the time, was that Yoko fueled the speculation about the reunion. In fact, at the height of the whole hysteria surrounding the possible reunion, she came in and pulled the plug. She did it with great gusto. John was really an innocent bystander. That was the first time—I think this was in the fall of 1979—that I really became aware of who had the power in the relationship. Yoko was running the show, and John couldn't do anything without her approval.

GEOFFREY: Did he treat you like a slave, or were you equal partners? What was your relationship with him?

FREDERIC: John treated me like a friend most of the time. When he was under a lot of stress he treated me like a slave and later apologized for it. He would say things like, "I'm sorry, I got snappy or overbearing, but I wasn't feeling so well. I was frustrated." I accepted that and forgave him. Most of the time, he was gracious and friendly. He was a fun person to be with, because he was amusing and entertaining. He was also very knowledgeable and was interested in sharing his knowledge. He would lecture, and I learned a lot from him. He knew I was paying attention, and he appreciated it. It was worth it for me to put up with his bad side, because his good side really outweighed the bad.

GEOFFREY: What kind of man was he, really, in the final analysis?

FREDERIC: He was very tortured. He was somebody who was so divided, he really didn't know who he was. He didn't know what he wanted, and the way he dealt with it was by abdicating responsibility for his life and turning it over to Yoko, lock, stock, and barrel. He paid a very heavy price, as he said in the song "Woman": "My life is in your hands." He really believed that Yoko would take care of him, and he trusted her completely. He had blind faith, and I think he paid a very heavy price for that.

May Pang*
PRESS RELEASE INTERVIEW
• •
New York

QUESTION: How did your love affair with John begin?

MAY PANG: I remember the conversation with Yoko, in which she told me, "John and I are not getting along. We've been arguing. We're growing apart. John will probably start going out with other people. Who knows who he'll go out with?" Yoko smiled and said, "May, I know he likes you a lot." I couldn't believe what I was hearing. I did not want Yoko to think I had anything to do with her problems, and almost as if she could read my mind, she said, "May, it's okay. I know he likes you. If he should ask you to go out with him, you should go."

By then, I knew that Yoko's suggestions were, in fact, orders, and this one seemed insane. The more I argued, "I can't go out with John. He's married. He's my employer," the more Yoko said, "It's okay. I still think you should go. Wouldn't you like a boyfriend? You don't have time to find one. Wouldn't this be easier? You would be better off if you went out with John. Don't you like John? Do you want to see him hurt? It will make him happy. Tonight when you go to the studio would be a good time for you to begin. Don't worry, I'll take care of everything."

From everything I knew of John and Yoko together, Yoko had the uncanny ability to make him do anything she wanted. Yoko's coolness shocked me. I was hurt by the ease with which she was trying to hand over her husband, a man respected and loved by so many people. I felt trapped and sick. I didn't begin going out with John that night. I fought his advances and my feelings until the inevitable happened. As strange or incredible as it may sound, Yoko had arranged a relationship for me, a relationship that was making me happier than I ever would have believed.

QUESTION: During the eighteen-month "Lost Weekend,"† what was living alone with John like?

MAY: We had a lot of good times. There were some bad times, but there were the good ones, too. John had a chance to record more songs. He was so creative after *Mind Games*. He didn't give up. He was more social, and mixed with his music friends, like Ringo, George, Elton, Bowie, and Jagger. They all came to our house. He saw all of his friends. I never shut him off from his friends, and

---

* May Pang was John's lover during his infamous "Lost Weekend" in the mid-seventies.
† The term "Lost Weekend" refers to Lennon's wild period in Los Angelas in the mid-seventies.

encouraged him to see them. He became reunited with his son, Julian. And he experienced a lot of normal things in life. I got John walking through Central Park and out to movies. He was always driven in limos and was rather sedentary. When he was with me, we went out and did a lot of things. Though he was rich at that time, he had no money. It was all tied up, so we had to be creative. We would go out walking and have breakfasts for under two dollars at the International House of Pancakes or other musician hangouts. He was more relaxed and free to be himself.

QUESTION: What was the real John Lennon like?

MAY: John was as nervous as the next person when he was going to record. At the Dakota apartment, when he met strangers, John would dazzle them with his wit. Invariably, they found him brilliant and extremely funny. That was the John of *A Hard Day's Night*, the John they expected to meet. It was a role he could play to the hilt. People often mistook his public performance for self-assurance, never realizing that John's wit masked a deeply seated discomfort. John mistrusted most people. Did they want to know him because he had been a Beatle? Were they only after his money? It took him a long time to trust someone enough to let down his guard and show his gentler, more sensitive side. At his core, John was a frightened man. He dealt with his fear of women by allowing himself to be manipulated. He dealt with his fear of men by manipulating them.

QUESTION: What control did Yoko have over John?

MAY: Yoko had gone through primal therapy with John, and she knew where his weak spots were. It appeared that Yoko had the power to speak directly to the deepest, most insecure part of John, and it was essential for him to do what she said, to defend her against criticism, and to believe her if she criticized him. That connection defied all logic, and it was a truth I had to accept, even though it saddened and threatened me. I wanted to do everything I could to help John trust himself. Then he would not have to turn to anyone to be told what to do.

Ritchie Yorke
INTERVIEW
• • • • • • • • • •
Toronto, 1984

QUESTION: How did you first become associated with John?

RITCHIE YORKE: Well, in 1968 he was starting to move away from the Beatles and doing things by himself, like the Plastic Ono Band. I was working for the *Globe and Mail* in Toronto in those days, so I wanted to interview John and find out about his various activities.

QUESTION: Let me ask you about Apple. What kind of place was it?

RITCHIE: It was chaos. It was a great *idea*, very groovy, you know, but in a practical sense it was absurd. A lot of the employees were just milking it dry. It was a giant game. Swinging London was at its height, and the ultimate thing to do was to work at Apple.

QUESTION: You were around the Beatles when they were beginning to realize that Apple was never going to work, is that right?

RITCHIE: Yeah, it was starting to go a bit sour. There were some very unpleasant meetings with everyone shouting and screaming at each other. John was trying to get Allen Klein in as their manager, and Paul wanted his father-in-law, Lee Eastman, running things. It was a very dodgy scene.

QUESTION: How did John relate to you his feelings about the Beatles?

RITCHIE: The Beatles were over as far as John was concerned. Phil Spector was remixing *Let It Be*, and none of them even showed up at any of the sessions because no one really liked the album. John just didn't want to be a part of it anymore. And of course they couldn't be bothered doing the sort of things he wanted to do. They were always off on holiday somewhere, it seemed. I mean, the drive of the group had almost completely gone by late 1968. *Abbey Road* was basically done with each of the guys in the studio separately. It wasn't a group effort anymore. As a matter of fact Paul put together that whole medley on side two almost entirely on his own.

QUESTION: How were John and Paul interacting at this point?

RITCHIE: It was bitter, very bitter. John wouldn't go near Paul. John always sent Ringo to do any dirty work with Paul.

QUESTION: Surely Yoko was a catalyst in the breakup, wasn't she?

RITCHIE: Not really. That's not to say, however, that John didn't impose her presence on them. He certainly did. During the filming of *Let It Be*, for instance, John would never have been there if Yoko wasn't included, and that, of course, helped to build up the Beatles' resentment against her. It wasn't Yoko's idea to try and snuggle up to the Beatles or anyone. John wanted to demonstrate his independence from the Beatles in a very practical way. He was basically saying, "Hey, I do what I like, boys, and you do what you like." That was his attitude.

QUESTION: How did you go from interviewing a guy to becoming one of his closest associates?

RITCHIE: We just happened to hit it off, I guess. Actually, I realized that John wanted to make some serious statements with his music in the face of everything that was happening in the late sixties, and I just wanted to lend a hand if I could.

QUESTION: So give me a typical day in the life of John Lennon during the final days of the Apple kingdom.

RITCHIE: Well, they'd drive in from Tittenhurst Park and arrive at the office at around eleven o'clock in the morning. Then they'd usually just stay for the afternoon and see people, generally people they felt were important to the youth movement. For example, Tom Donahue, the guy who started underground radio, came by a few times, as did Ken Kesey and the poet Richard Brautigan. I mean, everyone would be trying to hit on them in those days. Remember, John and Yoko were the world's most famous couple. They also had a few friends from the media who dropped in occasionally, like Ray Connolly from the *Evening Standard*. Believe me, it was a real zoo. Very often some kid with an idea would get John's ear—if he happened to be there when the phones had stopped ringing— and John would invariably give him his shot.

QUESTION: John and Yoko traveled to Denmark in 1970. Did you accompany them on that trip?

RITCHIE: Yeah, and quite a "trip" it was. They went to Denmark to meet with Yoko's ex-husband, Anthony Cox, and see Yoko's little daughter, Kyoko. We all stayed at his farmhouse in the middle of this great snowy expanse in the Jutland region of Denmark. Cox made the two of them go through a kind of purification process before he'd allow them to see Kyoko. So they fasted for a few days, meditated, and some guy named Dr. Don Hamrik, who fancied himself a warlock, tried to hypnotize them into giving up smoking. John and I had to sneak outside whenever we wanted a smoke! And last but not least, Cox somehow managed to talk them into getting their hair chopped off in celebration of the new decade. So I arranged for this lady barber called Aase Hankrogh to come out from the hotel in Aalborg and do the job. The next morning every paper in the world carried the story in banner headlines!

QUESTION: What were John's spiritual beliefs at that time?

RITCHIE: He was into peace and human beings. A very intense humanist.

QUESTION: Tell me about the bed-in in Montreal. What did they hope to accomplish with that?

RITCHIE: Publicity for peace. Remember, they couldn't get into the States, but they wanted to get their message across to the nerve centers of the world. In England they were considered a bad joke by the media, so they couldn't very well do it there. They did a bed-in in Amsterdam originally, but the idea was always to get the attention of America. They flew down to the Bahamas, but it was too hot there to stay in bed for a week, and still a bit too far removed from the American press corps, so they settled for Montreal. It was about as close as they could get.

QUESTION: You traveled on your own quite a bit for John during the campaign, right?

RITCHIE: Ronnie Hawkins and I both went around the world spreading John's peace message. The idea was to try and set up John and Yoko centers everywhere so that we could produce their events internationally. We planned on using Telstar at one point in order to syndicate things like the peace festival. Anyway, in Hong Kong someone at a press conference said, "Okay, it's fine telling us all this, we think peace is great, but why don't you go and tell the Red Chinese!" So we said "Sure" and had one of the locals paint up a couple of "War Is Over" signs for us. So we climbed into an old beat-up Volkswagen with a local reporter named Sybil Wong and a couple of photographers and drove down to the first border checkpoint at Lokmachau. Somehow or other we managed to convince the guards to let us pass, and we just drove right up to the top of this hill, which was the Chinese no-man's land. Anyway, we held up the signs facing China, and of course immediately all the guards rushed out and were going to arrest us. Well, we talked our way out of that one, but the strange thing was, the next day the CIA confiscated all of our films, as they somehow thought that this little peace protest might escalate into an international incident. Incidentally, a week later someone was shot simply for standing in the same area!

QUESTION: Were you aware of that possibility before you went in?

RITCHIE: Oh yes. I didn't care, but Ronnie was a little worried about it. Remember, this was long before anyone from the West had gone into China, not even the ping-pong players!

QUESTION: How did John react?

RITCHIE: He thought it was the greatest thing that happened on the entire trip!

QUESTION: Tell me about the infamous Mosport Park John and Yoko Peace Festival.

RITCHIE: Well, the original idea was to hold the biggest music festival of all time.

QUESTION: Of course all the Beatles were going to be there.

RITCHIE: Yes, George was agreed, Ringo certainly would have done it, and Paul was yet to be confirmed, but John was very hopeful about it. The intention was to get every major rock star in the world there. Even Elvis was going to do it!

QUESTION: Was it to be a free festival, or were people expecting to get paid?

RITCHIE: Well, John wanted everyone to get some money. He figured that no one should be working for nothing, but they were certainly free to donate some of it back into a big peace fund if they wanted to. The main problem with the festival was the total lack of any real organization. It was such a mammoth undertaking that eventually it was buried under the strain of its own weight.

QUESTION: Whose idea was it to hold the festival?

RITCHIE: Mainly mine, but the whole thing was being handled by the Brower and Walker Agency out of Toronto. I went for the idea because after the incredible success of Woodstock, a beautiful sequel devoted to world peace was absolutely the right thing to be doing. Eventually, I took off with Ronnie on this global peace tour, and by the time we got back, John and Yoko were becoming pretty disenchanted with the whole thing.

QUESTION: Tell me about John and Yoko's meeting with Canadian Prime Minister Pierre Trudeau. Did you arrange it all?

RITCHIE: Yes, we talked to Ottawa from the Bag office quite a few times in order to sound them out.

QUESTION: Could John get through to anyone in the world he wanted to?

RITCHIE: Yes, but until that time no political leader had ever met with him. In England John and Yoko were generally regarded as a big joke. Somehow they managed to antagonize the old establishment something terrible. He had to get through to a prominent politician to lend credibility to his movement, and of course we were hoping to try and wrangle an endorsement. Trudeau was willing to meet them as long as there was no advance publicity, so we did it and then announced it afterward.

QUESTION: Beyond the publicity, what was the meeting all about?

RITCHIE: Just to talk about peace and music.

QUESTION: How was Trudeau disposed toward John and Yoko?

RITCHIE: Very, very friendly. He thought the whole thing was great, and even offered the use of the Canadian army for security! John was extremely nervous, having never actually met a world leader on a one-to-one basis before. But afterwards he felt fantastic.

QUESTION: What do you think John would have to say about the nature of his own death?

RITCHIE: I think he expected it, in a way. There was always the chance it would happen. John was a very misunderstood guy and a sincere, dedicated man as well as a great humanitarian. He believed that things didn't really have to be the way they are. Things could be different if people really set their minds to it. And all any of us can do now is to try and keep John's spirit alive.

Ronnie Hawkins*
INTERVIEW
● ● ● ● ● ● ● ● ● ●
Toronto, January 1985

GEOFFREY: So tell me, Ronnie, how did John and Yoko come to live with you back in 1969?

RONNIE HAWKINS: Well, I got a phone call from England one day from John's right-hand man, Anthony Fawcett, who asked me if they could stay at my house, as they'd just been through the bed-in and wanted some privacy.

GEOFFREY: You never knew John before he rang?

RONNIE: I'd met him when the Beatles played Maple Leaf Gardens in Toronto. I didn't really know him, though—just enough to say hello. When I met the Beatles at the Gardens, they were familiar with some of my old tunes I had out in the fifties, because I'd been to England long before they'd even gotten into music. I'd done a couple of TV shows over there, and if you watched TV at all you had to see me, because the BBC has only one or two channels, and that's it.

GEOFFREY: So what did you say to Fawcett?

RONNIE: I said it would be fine, because I lived out in Mississauga on a farm, so it wasn't very crowded. They wanted to be out in the country, but someplace where they could still get into town for business. Anthony said it would mean a lot of good publicity for us, and there was also their peace festival, which I'd heard quite a lot about, so there was a lot happening. Then there was that damn phone bill affair. It wasn't really John's fault I got stuck with it, you know. It ended up being about sixteen thousand dollars and change, I think!

GEOFFREY: What happened?

RONNIE: Well, the peace festival just went bankrupt, so I was stuck with all the bills. I learned a good lesson from that one, all right!

GEOFFREY: There's a story about John and Yoko taking a bath at your house.

RONNIE: Yeah, they went upstairs to run the water, went to sleep, and simply forgot all about the tub. I finally said, "Anthony, the ceiling is coming in," so he went up and knocked on the door, but nobody ever wanted to disturb them. Anthony was the one in between them and everybody else, because they certainly couldn't talk to everybody. It was very embarrassing for them at times, I

---

* Ronnie Hawkins is a well-known rockabilly singer who resides in Toronto.

think. John had an awful lot of fun, though. I had some Skidoos out back, and evidently he'd never done any of that, because I was told later he ordered three or four of them and had them sent over to his home in England. I saw that John was being bugged quite enough by everybody else, so all I did was show him where the bedroom was and then stayed completely clear. If they said hello in the morning I'd say hello, and that was about it.

GEOFFREY: How did you get involved with the "War Is Over" poster campaign? You were at your house in Mississauga one minute, and the next thing we know, you're in Red China protesting for John!

RONNIE: They just took a liking to me, I guess, especially John. At that time we were talking about the "Land of Bag." I don't know whether you've heard about that or not. The Land of Bag was a conceptual country that Yoko tried to have become a member of the United Nations! It's imaginary, of course, but it was to be a place with all the right laws and rules. No guns at all, and everybody would always be happy and helping one another out.

GEOFFREY: And you were an ambassador?

RONNIE: No, John wanted me to be the first knight—"Sir Ronald the Good Knight," he called me. So I got down on my knees and went through the whole thing, just like it was really ancient England.

GEOFFREY: So you got caught up in his vision, then?

RONNIE: Oh, yeah. He said to me, "It's just a dream, you know, but it could be reality. All people would have to do is stop being so greedy. Just stop the fighting, and the world would be an unbelievable place. There's no reason for anyone to ever steal or hurt anyone in Bag Land, because people would already have everything they ever wanted."

GEOFFREY: So tell me, Sir Ronald, about when John sent you on your first international mission to preach the gospel of Bag.

RONNIE: Well, at that time Ritchie Yorke was one of the top writers for *Rolling Stone* magazine, and they were behind it all, so we went right around the globe together. I was promoting my new album, and Ritchie was organizing the peace conference to help spread John and Yoko's philosophy. John asked me to do all this stuff for them, and they called a few people in Japan for us, so it was just unreal. The connections Yoko had all over the world were absolutely unbelievable. I don't think anybody since World War Two had been treated as well as I was in Japan! Yoko put out the front grease for me, right? I saw things that very few people have ever seen, I'm sure. The underground movement in Japan was very highly organized. I mean, they were five hundred thousand strong and could be mobilized and out on the streets in about an hour!

GEOFFREY: After you did the Chinese border protest, Ritchie said you phoned John at home and told him about it.

RONNIE: Well, actually, it hit the front page of every paper in Hong Kong. I was a little nervous, because I knew my room had been searched many times by several different international agencies. The only thing that separates Hong Kong from mainland China is a barrier in the road, you know.

GEOFFREY: How do you remember John?

RONNIE: I remember John as being exactly the opposite of what I had expected.

GEOFFREY: [You would have expected him to be] cynical, mean, and egotistical?

RONNIE: That's what you'd expect from somebody who was such a superhero, and I was really very surprised he handled things the way he did, after I saw everything he had to go through just to keep from making people mad at him. No wonder they hid out in their room every night. I wouldn't want to see anybody I didn't have to, either.

GEOFFREY: What about Yoko?

RONNIE: Well, Yoko was very different. She was so educated, she was very much above and beyond me. She could speak, read, and write about eight different languages.

GEOFFREY: Could you understand the attraction between John and Yoko?

RONNIE: I couldn't really, no, because when I look at John, the leader of the Beatles, I know he could have had fifteen or twenty of the most glamorous movie stars in the world swarming all over him.

GEOFFREY: He got tired of it, though, Ronnie, I'm sure.

RONNIE: Yeah, he probably did. He probably wanted someone as intelligent as Yoko, who had some highly creative ideas of her own.

GEOFFREY: Anything else you'd like to say about John?

RONNIE: Just that to me he was so damn sensible. Really more like a humble English country boy than a big rock star. Yoko was more business-minded, it seemed to me. She talked straight-ahead business, whereas John worried about people's feelings much more than Yoko did. If Yoko didn't like somebody, she would just say, "We don't want anything to do with you," because she could see right through people. John could see through people too, I think, but he didn't ever want to hurt anybody's feelings.

Francie Schwartz*
QUOTE
. . . .
New York, 1972

FRANCIE SCHWARTZ: Yoko and John moved in with us while their story was still something to hide. As the two of us cooked breakfast, she'd rap with a kind of new feminine wisdom about how hard it was to make them happy. She was fighting her own battle staying sane amidst racist attacks from the Apple cock-and-cunt garden. She was also opening up her wealth of strength and determination to John . . .

John, Yoko, and I would watch the telly evenings when Paul was out raving . . . The three of us felt young, weird, and relaxed, and talked about how we could save Apple if only it could change direction, motivation. I was amazed John never said a bad word about Paul's management capabilities. Especially when Paul put thumbs down on *Two Virgins*.

Yoko made opium cookies one night. The three of us sat staring at each other, waiting for something to happen. It never did, but that was one time John read through my giggle to the sadness of waiting up for Paul.

If there had been something John and Yoko could do to help me get Paul's head straightened out, they surely would have done it. I asked John why Paul didn't do a solo album. It would've seemed the logical outlet for all the ego crap he was laying down at the studio. John half laughed and said, "We thought of it a long time ago. It was going to be called *Paul McCartney Goes Too Far*. But he wouldn't do it. He's too hung up about us being Beatles, you know."

---

* Francie Schwartz was Paul McCartney's girlfriend just prior to his becoming attached to Linda Eastman. She is today a successful author and businessperson.

223

Dr. Timothy Leary*
INTERVIEW
* * * * * * * * * *
Los Angeles, 1996

GEOFFREY: You had quite a bit of association with John Lennon over the years, didn't you?

TIMOTHY LEARY: Sure. John and I go way back to the "Give Peace a Chance" session at the Queen Elizabeth Hotel in Montreal, during the Bed-in. I was in the chorus, so I guess that makes me a founding member of the Plastic Ono Band. Several years later, when I was hiding out from the FBI, he shuttled me five thousand dollars for expenses via the Black Panthers. It's not his fault if I never got it.

GEOFFREY: What, in philosophical terms, was acid [LSD]?

TIMOTHY: Well, it's just one of many compounds one can use to expand the perimeters of one's consciousness. Have you taken it?

GEOFFREY: Yeah, many times, in years gone by.

TIMOTHY: For thousands of years people have taken these compounds to activate new services to the brain, or, as we now say, "boot up" the right-brain circuits, which are usually kept censored by the left, more focused, literal side of the mind. These chemicals are used by every generation around the world. We are now able to understand how it all works because of the massive advances in neurology and computer science.

GEOFFREY: For many of us who went on that adventure, we saw it as a kind of spiritual awakening. How do you reckon that?

TIMOTHY: You're making speeches and giving me twelve ideas in one question . . .

GEOFFREY: Spoken like a true professor.

TIMOTHY: No, not like a true professor. It's about two human beings trying to communicate. You're rambling! Do you want to know if LSD is spiritual?

GEOFFREY: Yes.

---

* Dr. Timothy Leary, the former Harvard professor with two Ph.D.'s whose name became linked with the popular use of psychedelic drugs in the 1960s and '70s, died in May of 1996, just weeks after this interview was conducted.

TIMOTHY: The term "spiritual" is used by brain-carrying human beings to refer to something they cannot explain scientifically and objectively. Yes, the soul *is* located in the brain, and the spiritual side is accessed by activating circuits in the brain. I'm not saying the soul is the brain, but you're never going to get to the soul unless you use your brain as a tool.

GEOFFREY: Why, then, the resistance to exploring in this way?

TIMOTHY: Every totalitarian fundamentalist says they have "the way," and the last thing they want is a movement, or science, that allows individuals to activate and operate their own soul. That puts rabbis, ministers, and priests out of a job! It's clear in human history, individuals who have talked about *personal divinity* have gotten into trouble with authority. You can't argue that.

GEOFFREY: How do you see your place in all of this, historically? I've heard many people joke about your contributions and others discussing you in almost sacrosanct terms.

TIMOTHY: My words are just now coming to fruition, because everything I've done in the past dealt with the power of the individual to access their brain in order to think more clearly. [Back] then we used the ancient method of psyche-delic sacraments, but now I'm working full time creating multimedia electronic techniques with computers, to activate the brain the way psychedelic drugs do and be able to communicate it to other people, so you can have a group vision using multimedia screens. My work is really only just beginning. It's all been practice up till now.

GEOFFREY: You say that every time a fundamentalist government gets involved with personal divinity there's problems. We won't have any problems with computers, will we?

TIMOTHY: Well, yes, they used to be illegal in the Soviet Union. Computers and home video players are the number one enemies of religion. That's why right-wing fundamentalists don't want us to have that—that's why they are so busy censoring everyone. Right now the mass media controls the screens, but we're developing methods of liberating individuals, and I don't think they can stop it.

GEOFFREY: Talk to me about what you think the Beatles and John Lennon were all about.

TIMOTHY: Well, in the 1960s, the ancient methods of virtual, visionary explo-ration became a global phenomenon because of electronic communication. The British rock 'n' rollers, the Beatles and the Rolling Stones, did what bards and singers have done throughout history, but instead of simply using a harp or flute to be heard by, say, a hundred people, it was millions. So the Beatles and the other psychedelic rock 'n' rollers really created a global movement for the first time. It's still going on. It's going on in Europe. When the Berlin wall went down, everyone knew it was rock 'n' roll that did it. And it's still happening today, with people like Pink Floyd.

GEOFFREY: But the new music doesn't quite have the same innate power, does it?

TIMOTHY: The new music is more global, in the sense you have mixtures of reggae, the Mambo Kings are back, and there's David Byrne. The message is still going on, it's still being carried by music, but it's not as obviously revolutionary, because everything has loosened up. The new breed of young people around the world right now have been created by rock 'n' roll. There are new things called "raves," which I'm very involved with. In San Francisco tomorrow I'll be at a rave.

Peter Tork*

INTERVIEW
● ● ● ● ● ● ● ● ● ●
New York, 1995

PETER TORK: When I met John Lennon, I went and stayed with him at his home in Weybridge. He was really powerful. George was an easy guy to get to be friends with. Ringo was the most natural. It was just, there he was. Personally, I found Paul hard to get to know. He's in his own space and didn't seem to be very open and involved. But John was the most powerful, in a sense, and he was the one I got to know.

QUESTION: What were you doing when you found out about Lennon's death?

PETER: I was watching the football game. A lot of us were. It was a playoff game, wasn't it? And there is Howard Cosell, and he says, "It's only a game, you know." Then he says, "Former Beatle shot." It took me about a day and a half for it to hit me. Somebody once said he was killed because he offered hope, which McCartney didn't. McCartney would write and sing songs, and so does George, and Ringo is an actor, but John had a lot of ideas, a lot of hope, and he struggled with his own life. It takes a special kind of a guy to do that. When you get famous, it's awful easy to find the company of people who will not tell you what you don't want to hear. I think this happened to Elvis. He didn't want to hear that you can't live this way, that we love you too much to let this to happen you. He arranged to be surrounded by people that would tell him exactly what he wanted to hear and no more. When that happens, you start to feed on your own mind. And that's not how humans are built to live. You're built to feed on each other's minds. We're built to communicate, and if you withdraw and surround yourself with a wall, you don't communicate any longer, and you become inbred. Life is a pain sometimes, and Lennon truly embraced the pain of his living. He struggled with his own political understanding and strove to reach his own Lennonity. He worked like hell and gave it all he had. That's awful rare, and that's what made him so special.

---

* Former Monkees guitarist Peter Tork hung out with the Beatles in the mid-sixties.

Les Anthony*
INTERVIEW
. . . .
London, May 1968

QUESTION: Tell me how John came to frequent the Indica Gallery, where he first met Yoko. Was he a great patron there?

LES ANTHONY: John wanted to buy some daft exhibit consisting of a couple of wires taken from an army tank that lit up at each end. He paid £600. He also paid £200 for a magnet swinging in the middle of a bit of plastic.

Question: After John and Yoko first met that night at the gallery, what propelled the relationship forward? Who made the first real move?

LES: She came tripping out after him into St. James's and begged to come along to the studios where we were going to record. A few days later she turned up at Abbey Road Studio and was let in. John groaned about what a pest she was.

QUESTION: I assume you were around that infamous night when John and Yoko first slept together and recorded *Two Virgins*. Tell me about that.

LES: One day, Cynthia went up north. Yoko arrived at their home to talk to John about him sponsoring some art exhibition. It was supposed to be a business meeting. But she didn't go back until the morning, and after that, John couldn't leave her alone.

QUESTION: I understand you had a hand in making some of the very involved arrangements for John and Yoko's wedding. Didn't at one point they wanted to get married on a boat?

LES: I went to Southampton and talked to the skipper, who decided they couldn't, since marriages are no longer performed aboard ferries. He said they could marry on a Cunard ocean liner and that there was a round-the-world cruise departing that very day. I rang up John. But he had second thoughts

---

* Les Anthony was John Lennon's chauffeur in the mid- to late-sixties.

Emperor Gate/ Beatlespeak

JOHN ON JOHN, ETC.

It started, somehow, at the end of '73, going to do this *Rock 'n' Roll* album [with Phil Spector]. It had quite a lot to do with Yoko and I, whether I knew it or not, and then suddenly I was out on me own. The next thing, I'd be waking up drunk in strange places, or reading about meself in the paper doing extraordinary things, half of which I'd done and half of which I hadn't. And finding meself sort of in a mad dream for a year. I'd been in many mad dreams, but this was pretty wild. Meanwhile, life was going on, the Beatles' settlement was going on, and it wouldn't let you sit with your hangover, in whatever form that took. It was like something, probably meself, kept hitting me while I was trying to do something. I was still trying to carry on a normal life, and the whip never let up, for eight months. You can put it down to which night with which bottle or which night in which town. And it was just probably fear, and being out on me own, and gettin' old, and "Are you gonna make it in the charts? Are you not gonna make it?" All the garbage you really know is not the be-all and end-all of life, but if other things are going funny, that's gonna hit you. If you're gonna feel sorry for yourself, you're gonna feel sorry for everything. So it was a year that manifested itself in a most peculiar fashion. But I'm through it and it's 1975 and I feel better, and I'm sitting here and not lying in some weird place with a hangover.

• • •

I feel I want to be them all: painter, writer, actor, singer, player, musician. I want to try them all, and I'm lucky enough to be able to. I want to see which one turns me on. I want to see what I'll be like when I've done it.

• • •

The class thing is just as snobby as it ever was. People like us can break through a little, but only a little. Once, we went into this restaurant and nearly got thrown out for looking like we looked, until they saw who it was. "What do you want?" the headwaiter said. "We've come to bloody eat, that's what we want," we said. Then the owner spotted us and said, "Ah, a table, sir, over here, sir." It just took me back to when I was nineteen, and I couldn't get anywhere without being stared at or remarked about. It's only since I've been a Beatle that people have said, "Oh, wonderful, come in, come in," and I've forgotten a bit about what they're really thinking. They see the shining star, but when there's no glow about you, they only see the clothes and the haircut again.

We weren't as open and truthful when we didn't have the power to be. We had to take it easy. We had to shorten our hair to leave Liverpool and get jobs in London. We had to wear suits to get on TV. We had to compromise. We had to get hooked, as well, to get in, and then sort of get a bit of power and say, "This is what we're like." We had to falsify a bit, even if we didn't realize it at the time.

• • •

I'm not a cynic. They're getting my character out of some of the things I write or say. They can't do that. I hate tags. I'm slightly cynical, but I'm not a cynic. One can be wry one day and cynical the next and ironic the next. I'm a cynic about most things that are taken for granted. I'm cynical about society, politics, newspapers, government. But I'm not cynical about life, love, goodness, death. That's why I really don't want to be labeled a cynic.

• • •

I believe Jesus was right, Buddha was right, and all of those people are right. They're all saying the same thing, and I believe it. I believe what Jesus actually said, the basic things he laid down about love and goodness, and not what people claim he said.

• • •

If Jesus being more popular means more control, I don't want that. I'd sooner they'd all follow us, even if it's just to dance and sing for the rest of their lives. If they took more interest in what Jesus, or any of them, said, if they did that, we'd all be there with them.

• • •

If being religious meant being "concerned," as Paul Tillich, the late Protestant theologian, once put it, well, I am, then. I'm concerned, all right. I'm concerned with people.

• • •

People often ask me how I write. I do it in all kinds of ways—with piano, guitar, any combination you can think of, in fact. It isn't easy—it's torture. Well, mainly torture. Yoko says the writing is easy compared with the recording. That's when I go through hell. When I've finished an album, I think, "Screw it!" for a bit. I think I won't write any more songs, because I don't have to be panicked into it. Then when I haven't done any for a few months, I get all paranoid, thinking, "Oh, Christ, I can't write. I'll have to do some more."

Musicals? Stage musicals? I'll never do that. I hate musicals. I've always loathed them, since my cousin made me sit through one years ago. They bore me stiff, and they're always lousy music.

When I was fifteen, my ambition was to write *Alice in Wonderland* and be bigger than Elvis. In our family, the radio was hardly ever on, so I got to pop later—not like Paul and George, who'd been groomed in pop music coming over the radio all the time. We never had it in the house, and I only heard it at other people's homes. This fellow I knew called Don Beatty showed me the name Elvis Presley in the charts in the *New Musical Express* and said he was great. It was "Heartbreak Hotel." And I thought it sounded a bit phony, you know, "Heartbreak Hotel." But then when I heard it, it was the end for me. I think I heard it on Radio Luxembourg first.

When I wrote "I Want to Hold Your Hand," I was writing in a very objective way, thinking to myself,

"This is how Goffin and King write, so this is how rock 'n' roll is written." Like artists who start off derivatively painting, I was writing separately from myself, and I wasn't too much personally concerned. That lasted for a bit, until it got embarrassing, and then it just changed, and I began writing about whatever happened to me.

Admittedly, "I Am the Walrus" didn't mean anything—the melody came from hearing a wailing police-car siren—but a lot of others were straight diaries. "Strawberry Fields Forever" meant a lot. It was about me, and I was having a hard time. "Help" was about me, although it was a bit poetic. In "Help" I was in a hell of a state. I say in the song that when I was younger I was doing all right but then things got more difficult. "In My Life" was pretty truthful. And I suppose "I'm a Loser" was more of a mood than anything.

But normally, when I was younger I used to hide my real emotions in gobbledegook, like in the book *In His Own Write*. When I wrote teenage poems I wrote in gobbledegook, because I was always hiding my real emotions or whatever from Mimi. I'm now writing about me completely.

• • •

After Brian [Epstein] died, we collapsed. Paul took over and supposedly led us. But what is leading us when we went round in circles? We broke up then. That was the disintegration.

1970

• • •

The Beatles' *White Album*. Listen, all you experts: none of you can hear. Every track is an individual track—there isn't any Beatle music on it. I just say, listen to the *White Album*. It was John and the band, Paul and the band, George and the band, like that. What I did was sort of say, "Fuck the band. I'll make John, I'll do it with Yoko," or whatever. I put four albums out last year, and I didn't say a fucking word about quitting.

1970

• • •

When we read all this shit [about the breakup] in the paper, Yoko and I were laughing, because the cartoon is this: Four guys on a stage with a spotlight on them. Second picture, three guys onstage, breezing out of the spotlight. Third picture, one guy standing there, shouting, "I'm leaving." We were all out of it.

1970

• • •

I don't believe in the Beatles, that's all. I don't believe in the Beatles myth. There is no other way of saying it, is there? I don't believe in them, whatever they were supposed to be in everybody's head, including our own heads for a period. It was a dream. I don't believe in the dream anymore.

1970

• • •

I always felt bad George and Ringo didn't get a piece of the publishing. When the opportunity came to give them five percent each of Maclen, it was because of me they got it. It was not because of Klein or Paul, but because of me.

1980

● ● ●

What would you suggest I do? Give everything away and walk the streets? The Buddha says, "Get rid of the possessions of the mind." Walking away from all the money would not accomplish that.

SEPTEMBER 1980

● ● ●

I didn't really enjoy writing third-person songs about people who live in concrete flats and things like that. I like first-person music. But because of my hang-ups and many other things, I would only now and then specifically write about me. Now I write all about me, and that's why I like it. It's me, and nobody else! So I like it. It's about me, and I don't know about anything else, really.

1970

● ● ●

Sometimes you wonder—I mean, really wonder. I know we make our own reality and we always have a choice, but how much is preordained? Is there always a fork in the road, and are there two paths equally preordained? There could be hundreds of paths, where one could go this way or that way. There's a choice, and it's very strange sometimes.

DECEMBER 5, 1980

● ● ●

Whereas actually, the first time I performed without the Beatles for years was the Rock 'n' Roll Circus, and it was great to be onstage with Eric [Clapton] and Keith Richard and a different noise coming out behind me, even though I was still singing and playing the same style. It was just a great experience. I thought, "Wow, it's fun with other people!"

DECEMBER 6, 1980

● ● ●

There is nothing conceptually better than rock 'n' roll. No group, be it Beatles, Dylan, or Stones, has ever improved on "A Whole Lotta Shakin'," for my money. Or maybe I'm like our parents—you know, that's my period and I dig it, and I'll never leave it . . . It will never be as new, and it will never do what it did then.

1970

● ● ●

It's real—it's not perverted or thought about, it's not a concept. It is a chair—not a design for a chair, or a better chair, or a bigger chair, or a chair with leather or with design. It is the first chair. It is a chair for sitting on, not chairs for looking at or being appreciated. You sit on that music.

1970

● ● ●

It was around before. It's harder when you're on the make to be generous, because you're all competing. But once you're sort of up there, wherever it is, the rock papers love to write about jet-setting rock stars, and they did it, and we dig it in a way. The fact is that, yeah, I see Mick, I see Paul, I see Elton, they're all my contemporaries, and I've known the other Beatles, of course, for years, and Mick for ten years, and we've been hangin' around since *Rock Dreams*. And suddenly it's written up that we're trying to form a club. But we always were a club. We always knew each other. It just so happens it looks more dramatic in the paper.

JUNE 1975

• • •

Heroin? It was not too much fun. I never injected it or anything. Yoko and I sniffed a little when we were in real pain. I mean we just couldn't . . . people were giving us such a hard time.

1970

• • •

I was a hitter. I couldn't express myself, and I hit. I fought men and I hit women. That is why I am always on about peace, you see. It is the most violent people who go for love and peace. I will have to be a lot older before I can face in public how I treated women as a youngster.

SEPTEMBER 1980

• • •

In Yoko's and my pleas for peace I refuse to be a leader, and I'll always show my genitals or do something which prevents me from being Martin Luther King or Gandhi and getting

killed. Because that's what happens to leaders.

1970

• • •

Language and song is, to me, apart from being pure vibrations, like trying to describe a dream. And because we don't have telepathy, we try and describe our dreams to each other. To verify to each other what we know, what we believe is inside each other. And the stuttering is right, because we can't say it. No matter how you say it, it's never how you want to say it.

As soon as you find the pattern, you break it. Otherwise it gets boring. The Beatles' pattern is one that has to be scrapped. If it remains the same, it's a monument or a museum, and one thing this age is about is no museums. The Beatles turned into a museum, so they have to be scrapped, deformed, or changed.

We are moving towards complete freedom and nonexpectation from audience, musician, or performer. And then, when we've had that for a few hundred years, then we can talk about playing around with patterns, bars, and music again. We must get away from the patterns we've had for these thousands of years.

JUNE 1970

• • •

What Yoko was saying is true— woman is still the nigger. There's only one. You can talk about blacks, you can talk about Jews, you can talk about the Third World, you can talk about everything, but under the whole crust of it is the women, and beneath them the children. As Dick Gregory said to us in 1969 in Denmark, "Children's liberation is the next movement," because they have no rights whatsoever—absolutely none. Women have a certain amount but children is the next thing—"children power"—but the women will liberate the children.

1980

• • •

Watching the wheels? The whole universe is a wheel, right? Wheels go round and round. They're my own wheels, mainly. But watching myself is like watching everybody else. And I watch myself through my child, too. Then, in a way, nothing is real, if you break the word down. As the Hindus or Buddhists say, it's an illusion, meaning all matter is floating atoms, right? We all see it, but the agreed-upon illusion is what we live. The hardest thing is facing yourself. It's easier to shout "Revolution" and "Power to the people" than to look at yourself and try to find out what's real inside you and what isn't, when you're pulling the wool over your own eyes. That's the hardest one.

I used to think the world was doing it to me and that the world owed me something, and that either the conservatives or the socialists or the fascists or the Communists or the Christians or the Jews were doing something to me, and when you're a teenybopper, that's what you think. I'm forty now. I

don't think that anymore, because I found out it doesn't fucking work! The thing goes on, anyway, and all you're doing is jacking off, screaming about what your mommy or daddy or society did, but one has to go through that. Most assholes just accept what is and get on with it, right, but for the few of us who did question what was going on I have found out personally—not for the whole world—that *I* am responsible for it, as well as them. I am part of them. There's no separation—we're all one. So in that respect, I look at it all and think, "Ah, well, I have to deal with me again in that way. What is real? What is the illusion I'm living or not living?" And I have to deal with it every day. The layers of the onion. That is what it's all about.

DECEMBER 5, 1980

• • •

It's a big, wonderful world out there. And Yoko and I are going to explore it until we die.

1975

• • •

Because of my attitude, all the other boys' parents, including Paul's father, would say, "Keep away from him." The parents instinctively recognized what I was, which was a troublemaker, meaning I did not conform and I would influence their kids, which I did. I did my best to disrupt every friend's home I had.

SEPTEMBER 1980

• • •

My marriage to Cyn was not unhappy. But it was just a normal marital state where nothing happened, and which we continued to sustain. You sustain it until you meet someone who suddenly sets you alight.

1973

• • •

As I said in an interview, with Julian I would come home and there'd be a twelve-year-old-boy there who I had no relationship with whatsoever. Now he's seventeen, I'm getting a relationship now, because we can talk about music and girlfriends and that kind of stuff. I'd come back from Australia, and he'd be a different size. I wouldn't even recognize how he looked half the time.

December 6, 1980

• • •

It's handy to fuck your best friend. That's what it is. And once I resolved the fact that it was a woman as well, it's all right. We go through the trauma of life and death every day, so it's not much of a worry about what sex we are any more. I'm living with an artist who's inspiring me to work. And, you know, Yoko is the world's most famous unknown artist. Everyone knows her name, but nobody knows what she does.

March 1971

• • •

We never decided to give up our private life. We decided that if we were going to do anything like get married, or like this film we are going to make now, that we would dedicate it to peace and the concept of peace. Peace is still important, and my life is dedicated to living. Just surviving is what it's about, really, from day to day.

1970

• • •

We have basically decided, without any great decision, to be with our baby as much as we can until we feel we can take time off to indulge ourselves in creating things outside the family.

October 1977

• • •

An incredible thing happened to me today . . . I baked my first loaf of bread, and you can't believe how perfectly it rose, and I've taken a Polaroid picture of it, and I think I can get it out to you [in L.A.] by messenger tonight.

1977

• • •

I'm often afraid, and I'm not afraid. But it's more painful to try not to be yourself. People spend a lot of time trying to be somebody else, and I think it leads to terrible diseases. I think it has something to do with constantly living or getting trapped in an image or an illusion of themselves, suppressing some part of themselves, whether it's the feminine side or the fearful side.

December 5, 1980

• • •

You don't have to be trained in rock 'n' roll to be a singer. I didn't have to be trained as a singer—I can sing. Singing is singing to people who enjoy what you're singing—not being able to hold notes. I don't have to be in rock 'n' roll to create. When I'm an old man, [Yoko and I] will make wallpaper together, but just to have the same depth and impact. The message is the medium.

1970

• • •

I was emperor, I had millions of chicks, drugs, drink, power, and everybody saying how great I was. How could I get out of it? It was just like being in a fuckin' train. I couldn't get out.

I couldn't create, either. I created a little, it came out, but I was in the party, and you don't get out of things like that. It was fantastic! I came out of the sticks, I didn't hear about anything—Van Gogh was the most far-out thing I'd ever heard of. Even London was something we used to dream of, and London's nothing. I came out of the fuckin' sticks to take over the world, it seemed to me. I was enjoying it, and I was trapped in it, too. I couldn't do anything about it—I was just going along for the ride. I was hooked, like a junkie.

1970

• • •

[My music] became journalism and not poetry. And I basically feel that I'm a poet. I'm not a formalized poet. I have no education, so I have to write in the simplest forms, usually . . . I realized that we were poets, but we were really folk poets, and rock 'n' roll was folk music.

JUNE 1975

• • •

George hasn't done his best work yet. His talents have developed over the years. He was working with two fucking brilliant songwriters, and he learned a lot from us. I wouldn't have minded being George, the invisible man, and learning what he learned. Maybe it was hard for him sometimes, because Paul and I are such egomaniacs, but that's the game.

1970

• • •

George's relationship [with me] was one of young follower and older guy. He's three or four years younger than me. It's a love-hate relationship, and I think George still bears resentment toward me for being a daddy who left home. I don't want to be that egomaniacal, but he was like a disciple of mine when we started.

1980

• • •

When we were all together, there was periods when the Beatles were in, the Beatles were out, whatever opinion people hold. There's a sort of illusion about it. But the actual fact was, the Beatles were in for eight months, the Beatles were out for eight months. The public, including the media, are sometimes a bit sheep-like, and if the ball starts rolling, well, it's just that somebody's in, some-body's out. George is out for the moment. And I think it didn't matter what he did on tour.

JUNE *1975*

• • •

Band on the Run is a great album. Wings is almost as conceptual a group as Plastic Ono Band. Plastic Ono was a conceptual group, mean-ing that whoever was playing was the band. And Wings keeps changing all the time. It's conceptual—I mean, they're backup men for Paul. It does-n't matter who's playing. You can call them Wings, but it's Paul McCartney music. And it's good stuff. It's good Paul music.

JUNE *1975*

• • •

Going back to the Beatles would be like going back to school. I was never one for reunions. It's all over.

1971

• • •

PAUL ON JOHN, ETC.

I can't remember, I can't express, I can't believe it! It was crazy, it was anger, it was fear. It was madness, it was the world coming to an end. Will it happen to me next? I was very terri-fied right after John's death, because it was such a horror. I talked it over with Yoko, and she says people don't like me because when John was killed

I was asked for a quote and I said, "It's a drag." Thinking back on it, I was just stunned. I couldn't think of anything else to say. I could have tried to put it all into words, but I *couldn't*. "Blub-blub" would have made about as much sense as "It's a drag." But that, put in cold print, "Paul in his reaction today said, 'It's a drag,' and then he got into his car and zoomed off," and that's the terrible thing about all of that.

1984

• • •

"Wedding Bells" is what it was: "Wedding bells are breaking up that old gang of mine." The Beatles used to sing that song. It was like an army song and for us the Beatles became the army. We always knew one day "Wedding Bells" would come true, and it did.

OCTOBER *1986*

• • •

Somebody once said to me, "But the Beatles were antimaterialistic." That's a huge myth. John and I literally used to sit down and say, "Now let's write a swimming pool." We said it out of innocence, out of normal fucking working-class glee that we were *able* to write a swimming pool. For the first time in our lives, we could actually do something and earn money.

FEBRUARY *1990*

• • •

I really didn't like that [John's using heroin]. Unfortunately, he was driftin' away from us at that point, so none of us actually knew. He never told us, but we heard rumors and we were very sad. But he'd embarked on a new course, which really involved anything and everything. Because John was that kind of guy—he wanted to live life to the full as he saw it.

JANUARY 1986

• • •

Looking back on it with John, you know, he was a really great guy. I always idolized him. We always did, the group. I don't know if the others will tell you that, but he was our idol.

NOVEMBER 1987

• • •

People keep saying, "When are you getting back together again?" They don't realize *I can't.* There was a play on in the West End called *John, Paul, George, Ringo & Bert* which made out that all the others wanted to keep it going. It set me down in history as the one who broke the group up. The opposite is true. Ringo left first, because he didn't think he was drumming well enough, and we persuaded him he was the best. Then George left during *Let It Be.* They had all left.

1984

• • •

[Harry Nilsson's] *Pussy Cats.* They jammed together, and I think it was John who said to me, "Man, it was great, we're a great band." Because that's the great thing about the Beatles: we really were a great band.

I know now from playing with other people that it's not always you can sit down and actually get in a groove. With the Beatles, it nearly always was . . . and that is something you cannot buy.

NOVEMBER 1987

• • •

GEORGE ON JOHN, ETC.

There was a certain amount of relief after that Candlestick Park concert. Before one of the last numbers, we actually set up this camera—I think it had a fisheye, a very wide-angle lens. We set it up on the amplifier and Ringo came off the drums, and we stood with our backs to the audience and posed for a photograph, because we knew that was the last show.

Then we spent what seemed like fifty years going in and out of each other's houses, writing tunes and going into the studio for *Sgt. Pepper* and the *White Album.* But for me, I think for all of us, it was just too much. The novelty had worn off. Everybody was getting married and leaving home. I think it was inevitable, really.

NOVEMBER 1987

• • •

Is it really a priority to go around being a rock 'n' roll star? There's no time to lose, really. There are lots of times I've been heavily into it, and other times I come right back out of it. There are a lot of people in this business I love, friends, who are really great but who don't have any desire for knowledge or realization. It's good to boogie once in a while, but when you boogie your life away, it's a waste of a life and of what we've been given.

1975

• • •

The very first time we took LSD, John and I were together. And that experience and a lot of other things which happened after that, both on LSD and on the meditation trip in Rishikesh, we saw beyond each other's physical bodies, you know. That's there permanently, whether he's in a physical body or not. I mean, this is the goal anyway: to realize the spiritual side. If you can't feel the spirit of some friend who's been that close, then what chance have you got of feeling the spirit of Christ, Buddha, or whoever else you may be

interested in? "If your memory serves you well, we're going to meet again." I very much believe that.

November 1987

• • •

RINGO ON JOHN, ETC.

I won't go to funerals, because I don't believe in them. I totally believe your soul has gone by the time you get into the limo. She or he's up there, or wherever it is. I can't wait to go, half the time.

1980

• • •

Yoko's taken a lot of shit, her and Linda, but the Beatles' breakup wasn't really their fault. It was just that suddenly we were all thirty and married and changed. We couldn't carry on that life any more.

1981

Small Universe
Running

A Lennon Chronology

....

1855–1980

OCTOBER 26, 1855: John Lennon, Sr., John's paternal grandfather (known throughout his life as "Jack"), is born in Liverpool. He later becomes a founding member of the famous American traveling musical troupe "The Kentucky Minstrels."

AUGUST 22, 1874: George Ernest Stanley, stern patriarch of John's mother's family, is born at 120 Salisbury Street in Everton. He later spends many years at sea, then comes ashore to work as an insurance investigator for the Liverpool Salvage Company.

DECEMBER 14, 1912: Alfred ("Alf") Lennon, John's seafaring father, is born at 27 Copperfield Street, Toxteth Park, Liverpool. His mother, Mary Maguire, will bear two more sons, Charles and Stanley.

MARCH 12, 1914: Julia Stanley, mother of John Lennon, Victoria Stanley, and Julia and Jacqui Dykins, is born in Liverpool to Annie Millward and George Stanley.

1916: John Albert Dykins is born. He will become Julia Stanley Lennon's common-law husband and the father of their two girls, Julia and Jacqui.

AUGUST 1917: John Lennon, Sr., dies of a liver disease at the age of sixty-one, leaving his three sons in the custodial care of Liverpool's Bluecoat Orphanage.

FEBRUARY 18, 1933: Yoko Ono is born into the family of a wealthy Tokyo banker.

DECEMBER 3, 1938: Despite strong objections from the Stanleys, Alf Lennon marries the free-spirited young Julia at the Liverpool Register Office. Immediately after the austere civil ceremony, both return to their parents' homes. Three days later, Lennon signs on for a three-month tour of duty aboard a cargo ship bound for the West Indies.

SEPTEMBER 10, 1939: John's first wife, Cynthia Powell, is born in Blackpool.

JUNE 23, 1940: Future Beatles bassist Stuart Sutcliffe is born in Edinburgh.

JULY 7, 1940: Richard ("Ringo") Starkey is born to Richard and Elsie Starkey at 24 Admiral Grove, the Dingle, Liverpool.

OCTOBER 9, 1940: John Winston Lennon enters this world during a German air raid over Liverpool at 7 o'clock in the morning. Shortly after his birth, he is placed under his mother's sturdy iron bed at the Liverpool Maternity Hospital. He is called John after his grandfather and Winston in honor of the prime minister, Winston Churchill. Once again, his father, Alf, is away at sea.

NOVEMBER 24, 1941: Randolph Peter Best, the Beatles' first really professional drummer, is born in Madras, India.

JUNE 18, 1942: James Paul McCartney is born to Mary Patricia Mohin and James McCartney in Liverpool.

1942: Finally giving in to family pressure, Julia Lennon agrees to temporarily turn over care of her infant son to her sister Mimi and Mimi's husband, gentleman dairy farmer George Smith.

1942: Despairing of her globetrotting husband, Alf's, ever settling down, Julia finally ends their "on-again-off-again" relationship. She is soon to meet and fall in love with congenial barman John Albert Dykins. Together they take a small flat in the then tatty Gateacre district of Liverpool.

FEBRUARY 25, 1943: George Harold Harrison, the youngest child of Harry and Louise Harrison, is born at 12 Arnold Grove, Wavertree, Liverpool.

JUNE 19, 1945: Julia gives birth to her second child, Victoria Elizabeth, at the Salvation Army's Elmswood Infirmary in North Mossley Hill Road, Liverpool. The father is not listed on the birth certificate but was thought to be an army gunnery officer. The infant girl was subsequently adopted and is believed to have been taken by her new parents to Norway, where her fate remains a mystery.

SEPTEMBER 1945: Young John begins attending school at Dovedale Primary, just around the corner from his aunt Mimi's home at 251 Menlove Avenue in Woolton.

JULY 1946: Alf returns from sea unexpectedly and convinces Mimi to allow John to accompany him on an impromptu holiday trek to Blackpool, secretly intending to spirit the boy away to a new life together in New Zealand. Luckily, Julia locates the two and takes John back home to Liverpool.

MARCH 5, 1947: Julia Dykins, John Lennon's second sister and the first child of Julia Lennon and John Dykins, is born in Liverpool.

OCTOBER 26, 1949: Jacqui Gertrude Dykins is born in Liverpool.

SEPTEMBER 1950: Young John Lennon is awarded a beginner's swimming certificate by the Liverpool Association of Schoolmasters.

JULY 1952: John leaves Dovedale Primary.

SEPTEMBER 1952: John starts at Quarry Bank High School for Boys.

JUNE 5, 1955: George Smith, Mimi's husband, dies unexpectedly at home of an undisclosed liver ailment, aged 52.

JUNE 15, 1956: Paul McCartney meets John Lennon for the first time at a Saturday afternoon performance by Lennon's schoolboy skiffle group, the Quarrymen, at St. Paul's Parish fete, in Woolton. Shortly afterward, he is invited to join the group by Pete Shotton, a mutual friend of John and Paul's (as well as being the Quarrymen's erstwhile washtub player).

SEPTEMBER 1957: Cynthia Powell, aged 18, enrolls as a lettering student at the Liverpool Junior Art School. She soon transfers to Liverpool Art College, where she meets her future husband, fellow student John Lennon.

FEBRUARY 6, 1958: Crackerjack guitarist George Harrison joins the Quarrymen. The nucleus of what would later be known as the Beatles is now formed.

SPRING 1958: His Holiness the Maharishi Mahesh Yogi arrives in Hawaii to begin propagating his Transcendental Meditation Movement in the West.

JULY 15, 1958: Julia Lennon, John's mother, is knocked down and killed just outside Mimi's home on Menlove Avenue by an off-duty police officer suspected of drinking. John and his sisters are at home with John Dykins, playing outside. Julia's final words to Mimi just before the accident are, "Don't worry."

DECEMBER 1958: John and Paul perform a few gigs together as the Nurk Twins.

AUGUST 29, 1959: The Quarrymen are invited to play at the opening-night party of the Casbah, a teenage coffee club run by Mona Best, Pete's fun-loving mother.

NOVEMBER 15, 1959: Now renamed Johnny and the Moondogs, the band fails an audition for Carrol Levis at the Manchester Hippodrome.

MAY 5, 1960: The flagging group, renamed once again as the Silver Beatles, fails another big audition to back singer Billy Fury. They are, however, chosen to tour with another young crooner, Johnny Gentle, on an upcoming trek through Scotland.

AUGUST 1960: Paul McCartney invites Pete Best to join the Beatles as their regular drummer on their first trip to Germany.

AUTUMN 1960: The Beatles make their first professional recording with members of their rival Liverpool group, Rory Storm and the Hurricanes, at Akustik Studios in Hamburg.

DECEMBER 5, 1960: The Beatles' trek to Germany is interrupted after George is found to be underage by German immigration officials and is unceremoniously deported. The other Beatles soon follow and end up back in Liverpool, feeling beaten and dejected.

MARCH 21, 1961: The Beatles appear at the Cavern for the first time. Over the next two years, they will play there 292 times.

OCTOBER 1, 1961: John and Paul take off on a two-week hitchhiking trip to Paris.

NOVEMBER 9, 1961: Wealthy Liverpool record retailer Brian Epstein unexpectedly drops in to the Cavern to hear the Beatles after being deluged with requests for their first official record release, "My Bonnie" (a German Polydor import).

DECEMBER 3, 1961: Epstein invites the group to his office to discuss the possibility of taking over as their manager. They readily agree.

JANUARY 1, 1962: The Beatles travel down to London to audition for Decca Records. Despite a rousing performance by the Fabs, they are ultimately turned down by Decca bigwig Rick Rowe, who, ironically, tells Brian that groups with guitars are on the way out.

APRIL 10, 1962: Stuart Sutcliffe tragically dies of a brain hemorrhage in Hamburg. He is just twenty-one years old.

MAY 9, 1962: The Beatles are offered a recording contract with Parlophone Records, a tiny offshoot of the vast EMI entertainment empire. Their recording manager is the brilliant George Martin.

AUGUST 16, 1962: For reasons that remain a mystery to this day, drummer Pete Best is unceremoniously sacked from the group, and Ringo Starr is quickly brought in to fill the gap.

AUGUST 23, 1962: John Lennon marries Cynthia Powell in a civil ceremony at the Mount Pleasant Register Office in Liverpool. Fellow Beatles Harrison and McCartney attend.

OCTOBER 5, 1962: The single "Love Me Do" is released.

DECEMBER 31, 1962: The Beatles make their final club appearance in Hamburg.

MARCH 2, 1963: "Please Please Me" hits the coveted number one position on the *Melody Maker* chart.

APRIL 8, 1963: John Charles Julian Lennon is born to John and Cynthia at 6:50 A.M. at Sefton General Hospital in Liverpool.

FEBRUARY 1, 1964: "I Want to Hold Your Hand" is the number one record in America.

FEBRUARY 6, 1964: The Beatles appear on *The Ed Sullivan Show* in New York. During their performance, an estimated 73 million television viewers experience John, Paul, George, and Ringo for the first time. Across America, not a single crime is committed by a teenager.

MARCH 23, 1964: John Lennon's first book, *In His Own Write*, is published. Almost overnight, it becomes an international bestseller.

JULY 10, 1964: A civic reception is held in Liverpool to honor its most famous sons; over 100,000 people attend. Among them are John's sisters Julia and Jacqui as well as most of Lennon's family.

FEBRUARY 15, 1965: John Lennon finally passes his driving test (after driving illegally for years).

JUNE 12, 1965: Buckingham Palace announces that the Beatles will be awarded MBEs later that year.

JUNE 24, 1965: John's second book, *A Spaniard in the Works,* is published.

AUGUST 3, 1965: John buys his aunt Mimi a lovely seaside bungalow at 26 Panorama Road, in Poole, Dorset.

DECEMBER 31, 1965: Alf Lennon suddenly reappears on the scene, this time to release his one and only record, "That's My Life, My Love and My Home." Although initially it receives quite a lot of airplay, it is critically panned and sells poorly.

MARCH 4, 1966: During an interview with British journalist and Beatle crony Maureen Cleave, John makes his infamous remark about the Beatles' being more popular than Jesus Christ.

JULY 31, 1966: Radio stations across America join in an ad hoc ban on Beatle music as a direct result of John's controversial remarks on the decline of Christianity in the West. Over the next few weeks, there are reports of record burnings and other protests by groups ranging from the Ku Klux Klan to the Daughters of the American Revolution. In the midst of this furor, John is persuaded by Brian Epstein to publicly recant his remarks, in an effort to calm middle America's shattered faith in the Fabs.

AUGUST 29, 1966: The Beatles give their final American concert, at Candlestick Park in San Francisco.

NOVEMBER 9, 1966: John meets Yoko Ono for the first time at a special preview showing of her one-woman conceptual art show, *Unfinished Paintings and Objects,* at the Indica Gallery in London.

MAY 26, 1967: *Sgt. Pepper's Lonely Hearts Club Band* is released just in time to kick off the celebrated "summer of love."

AUGUST 24, 1967: The Beatles and an entourage of girlfriends, wives, and hangers-on attend an introductory lecture on transcendental meditation given by the Maharishi at the Hilton Hotel, London.

AUGUST 27, 1967: While attending a special weekend meditation seminar held in Bangor, Wales, the Beatles receive word that Brian Epstein has been found dead in his London townhouse from an unexplained overdose of drugs. The Maharishi attempts to comfort them by reminding them to try to "be happy" and "don't worry."

JANUARY 5, 1968: Alf Lennon and his nineteen-year-old fiancée, Pauline Jones, meet John to seek his blessing for their forthcoming marriage. John is not happy about this unexpected romance but reluctantly gives the two of them his support.

FEBRUARY 16, 1968: John, Cynthia, George, and his wife, Pattie, join the Maharishi in Rishikesh, India, for an intensive two-month instructor's course in transcendental meditation. The rest of the Beatles' entourage arrives fours days late.

APRIL 12, 1968: The Beatles leave the peaceful mountain ashram two weeks ahead of schedule after a nasty rumor circulates that the giggly Indian fakir attempted to compromise the virtue of fellow meditator Mia Farrow.

AUGUST 22, 1968: Cynthia Lennon sues John for divorce, citing his alleged adultery with Yoko Ono as the cause.

OCTOBER 18, 1968: John and Yoko are busted for possessing 219 grains of hashish at their flat at 34 Montague Square, London. A charge of obstructing justice is also brought against the couple, who, according to old Liverpool chum Pete Shotton, had been warned of the impending bust beforehand.

OCTOBER 25, 1968: Word leaks to the press that Yoko is pregnant. John Lennon is reportedly the father.

NOVEMBER 8, 1968: Cynthia Lennon is granted a divorce from John in an uncontested suit brought before magistrates in London.

NOVEMBER 21, 1968: Yoko suffers her first painful miscarriage. John remains constantly at her bedside at Queen Charlotte's Hospital in London, where he beds down next to her in a sleeping bag for several days.

NOVEMBER 28, 1968: John pleads guilty to unauthorized possession of cannabis at Marylebone Magistrates Court. A fine of £150 is imposed, as well as court costs of 20 guineas. The obstruction of justice charges are dropped against both him and Yoko.

NOVEMBER 29, 1968: John and Yoko's infamous *Unfinished Music No.1: Two Virgins* is released. The scandalous album cover depicts the free-spirited couple naked.

JANUARY 30, 1969: The Beatles play their last live public performance ever on the rooftop at Apple Studios. The impromptu gig is filmed for inclusion in the Beatles' eclectic cinematic swan song, *Let It Be.*

FEBRUARY 2, 1969: Yoko Ono is granted a divorce from her husband, Anthony Cox.

MARCH 20, 1969: John and Yoko are married in a quiet civil ceremony on the island of Gibraltar.

MAY 26, 1969: The Lennons fly to Montreal to hold an eight-day "Bed-in" for peace at the Queen Elizabeth Hotel. While there, they record the now famous counterculture anthem "Give Peace a Chance."

JULY 1, 1969: While visiting John's aunt Mater in Durness, Sutherland, Scotland, the Lennons and their children, Julian and Kyoko, are involved in a car accident in Golspie. Although no one is seriously injured, John requires seventeen stitches on his face and head. His son, Julian, is also treated for shock.

OCTOBER 12, 1969: Yoko miscarries yet another baby. This time, however, the pregnancy is sufficiently long for the child, a little boy, to be given the name John Ono Lennon; he is buried in a tiny white coffin somewhere outside London. Only John and Yoko attend the service.

APRIL 10, 1970: Paul McCartney publicly quits the Beatles.

DECEMBER 31, 1970: Paul brings suit against the other Beatles in an effort to legally dissolve the group.

SEPTEMBER 3, 1971: John and Yoko say goodbye to England forever and fly off to America to make their new home.

MARCH 16, 1972: The Lennons are served with a deportation notice from American immigration officials as a result of John's 1968 drug conviction in England.

SEPTEMBER 18, 1973: John and Yoko go their separate ways. John departs for Los

Angeles, while Yoko stays ensconced in their palatial seven-room Manhattan apartment. The couple have been married four years.

JANUARY 1975: John returns to New York and is reunited with Yoko. "The separation just didn't work out," he tells the press.

JUNE 19, 1975: John files suit against former attorney general John Mitchell for what his lawyers call "improper selective persecution" relating to the government's deportation proceedings.

SEPTEMBER 23, 1975: As Yoko is now pregnant once again, immigration officials temporarily halt their deportation proceedings against John on what they call "humanitarian grounds."

OCTOBER 7, 1975: The New York Supreme Court reverses the deportation order against Lennon by a two-to-one vote.

OCTOBER 9, 1975: Yoko gives birth to the Lennons' only child together, a seven-pound baby boy they name Sean Ono Taro Lennon, on John's thirty-fifth birthday.

JANUARY 5, 1976: The Beatles' former road manager and friend, Mal Evans, is shot dead by police in Los Angeles following an incident in which Evans allegedly pointed a gun at officers responding to a domestic disturbance call. John is said to be deeply disturbed by the tragedy.

APRIL 1, 1976: Alf Lennon, aged 63, dies of cancer at Brighton General Hospital.

JULY 27, 1976: John finally receives his green card at an immigration hearing in New York. John's only comment to the press is, "It's great to be legal again."

OCTOBER 9, 1976: John's self-imposed "retirement" from show business and so-called "househusband" period commences. "From now on," Lennon tells the press, "my chief responsibility is my family."

OCTOBER 15, 1979: John and Yoko contribute $1000 to the New York Police Department for the purchase of several bullet-proof vests for officers.

JULY 14, 1980: John and Sean set sail on the 63-foot sloop "Isis," bound for Bermuda and accompanied by a five-man crew. It is during this holiday that John finally begins composing again.

AUGUST 4, 1980: John and Yoko begin recording at the Hit Factory in New York for the first time in six years. The music culled from those sessions is later to form the albums *Double Fantasy* and *Milk and Honey.*

OCTOBER 9, 1980: John celebrates his fortieth birthday with his son Sean, who is five on the same day.

NOVEMBER 17, 1980: *Double Fantasy* is released worldwide.

DECEMBER 5, 1980: John and Yoko are interviewed on their "comeback" by *Rolling Stone* in New York.

DECEMBER 8, 1980: In the late afternoon, on his way out of the Dakota apartment building in Manhattan, John Lennon stops to give an autograph to a young man from Hawaii named Mark David Chapman. The two are photographed together. At 10:49 P.M., Chapman steps out of the shadows and guns down John Lennon as he returns home from a recording session accompanied by his wife, Yoko. The world mourns John's death.

John Lennon Discography

An asterisk (*) indicates information the author has been unable to verify.

TITLE	LABEL	COUNTRY	RELEASE DATE

The artists in this category includes both the Beatles and John Lennon as a member of the group and as a solo artist.

ALBUMS:

TITLE	LABEL	COUNTRY	RELEASE DATE
Introducing The Beatles	Vee Jay	United States	*
Please Please Me	Parlophone	United Kingdom	March 1963
With The Beatles	Parlophone	United Kingdom	November 1963
Twist and Shout	Capitol	Canada	January 1964
Meet The Beatles!	Capitol	United States	January 1964
The Beatles' Second Album	Capitol	United States	April 1964
A Hard Day's Night	Capitol	United States	June 1964
A Hard Day's Night	Parlophone	United Kingdom	July 1964
Something New	Capitol	United States	July 1964
The Beatles Verses The Four Seasons (Double Album Set)	Vee Jay	United States	October 1964
Songs, Pictures and Stories of the Fabulous Beatles	Vee Jay	United States	October 1964
The Beatles' Story (Double Record Set)	Capitol	United States	November 1964
Beatles For Sale	Parlophone	United Kingdom	December 1964
Beatles '65	Capitol	United States	December 1964
The Early Beatles	Capitol	United States	March 1965
Beatles VI	Capitol	United States	June 1965
Help! (Original Soundtrack Album)	Capitol	United States	August 1965
Rubber Soul	Parlophone	United Kingdom	December 1965
Rubber Soul	Capitol	United States	December 1965
Yesterday and Today	Capitol	United States	June 1966
Revolver	Capitol	United States	August 1966
A Collection of Beatles Oldies	Parlophone	United Kingdom	December 1966
Sgt. Pepper's Lonely Hearts Club Band	Capitol	United States	June 1967
Magical Mystery Tour	Capitol	United States	November 1967
Unfinished Music Number 1/Two Virgins	Apple	United States	November 1968
The Beatles (White Album)	Apple	United States	November 1968
Yellow Submarine	Apple	United States	January 1969
Unfinished Music Number 2/Life With The Lions	Apple	United States	May 1969
Abbey Road	Apple	United States	October 1969
Wedding Album	Apple	United States	October 1969
The Plastic Ono Band/Live Peace In Toronto	Apple	United States	December 1969
Let It Be	Apple	United States	May 1970
John Lennon/Plastic Ono Band	Apple	United States	December 1970
Imagine	Apple	United States	September 1971
Sometime In New York City	Apple	United States	June 1972
Mind Games	Apple	United States	November 1973
Walls and Bridges	Apple	United States	September 1974
John Lennon Sings The Great Rock & Roll Hits	Adam VIII, Ltd.	*	1975
Rock 'n' Roll	Apple	United States	February 1975
Shaved Fish	Shaved	United States	October 1975
Double Fantasy	Geffen Records	United States	November 1980
Milk and Honey	Geffen Records	United States	*
Heart Play—Unfinished Dialogue	PolyGram	Canada	1983
Milk And Honey	PolyGram	United States	1984

251

TITLE	LABEL	COUNTRY	RELEASE DATE
Includes Lennon with the Beatles and as a solo artist.			
SINGLES:			
MY BONNIE (LIES OVER THE OCEAN)/ THE SAINTS (WHEN THE SAINTS GO MARCHING IN)	Polydor	Germany	June 1961
MY BONNIE/CRY FOR A SHADOW	Polydor	United States	April 1962
LOVE ME DO (VERSION ONE)/ P.S. I LOVE YOU	Parlophone	United Kingdom	October 1962
PLEASE PLEASE ME/ASK ME WHY	Capitol	United States	January 1963
FROM ME TO YOU/THANK YOU GIRL	Capitol	United States	April 1963
SHE LOVES YOU/I'LL GET YOU	Swan	United States	August 1963
I WANT TO HOLD YOUR HAND/THIS BOY	Parlophone	United Kingdom	November 1963
THE BEATLES CHRISTMAS RECORD	Fan Club	United States	December 1963
ROLL OVER BEETHOVEN/ PLEASE MR. POSTMAN	Capitol	Canadian	December 1963
I WANT TO HOLD YOUR HAND/ I SAW HER STANDING THERE	Capitol	United States	January 1964
PLEASE PLEASE ME/FROM ME TO YOU	Vee Jay	United States	January 1964
TWIST AND SHOUT/THERE'S A PLACE	Tollie	United States	March 1964
KOMM, GIB MIR DEINE HAND/ SIE LIEBT DITCH	*	Germany	March 1964
CAN'T BUY ME LOVE/YOU CAN'T DO THAT	Capitol	United States	March 1964
DO YOU WANT TO KNOW A SECRET/ THANK YOU GIRL	Vee Jay	United States	March 1964
LOVE ME DO/P.S. I LOVE YOU	Capitol	United States	April 1964
SIE LIEBT DICH/I'LL GET YOU	Capitol	United States	May 1964
A HARD DAY'S NIGHT/THINGS WE SAID TODAY	Capitol	United States	July 1964
A HARD DAY'S NIGHT/ I SHOULD HAVE KNOWN BETTER	Capitol	United States	July 1964
AND I LOVE HER/IF I FELL	Capitol	United States	July 1964
I'LL CRY INSTEAD/ I'M HAPPY JUST TO DANCE WITH YOU	Capitol	United States	July 1964
DO YOU WANT TO KNOW A SECRET/ THANK YOU GIRL	Capitol	United States	August 1964
SLOW DOWN/MATCHBOX	Capitol	United States	August 1964
I FEEL FINE/SHE'S A WOMAN	Capitol	United States	November 1964
ANOTHER BEATLES CHRISTMAS RECORD	Fan Club	United States	December 1964
EIGHT DAYS A WEEK/ I DON'T WANT TO SPOIL THE PARTY	Capitol	United States	February 1965
TICKET TO RIDE/YES IT IS	Capitol	United States	April 1965
HELP!/I'M DOWN	Capitol	United States	July 1965
YESTERDAY/ACT NATURALLY	Capitol	United States	September 1965
ROLL OVER BEETHOVEN/MISERY	Capitol	United States	October 1965
BOYS/MEDLEY: (KANSAS CITY/ HEY-HEY-HEY-HEY!)	Capitol	United States	October 1965
WE CAN WORK IT OUT/DAY TRIPPER	Capitol	United States	December 1965
THE BEATLES THIRD CHRISTMAS RECORD	Fan Club	United States	December 1965
NOWHERE MAN/WHAT GOES ON	Capitol	United States	February 1966
PAPERBACK WRITER/RAIN	Capitol	United States	April 1966
YELLOW SUBMARINE/ELEANOR RIGBY	Capitol	United States	August 1966
THE BEATLES FOURTH CHRISTMAS RECORD	Fan Club	United States	November 1966
PENNY LANE/STRAWBERRY FIELDS FOREVER	Capitol	United States	February 1967
ALL YOU NEED IS LOVE/ BABY, YOU'RE A RICH MAN	Capitol	United States	July 1967
HOW I WON THE WAR/AFTERMATH (BY MUSKETEER GRIPWOOD AND THE THIRD TROOP)	*	United Kingdom	October 1967

TITLE	LABEL	COUNTRY	RELEASE DATE
Includes Lennon with the Beatles and as a solo artist.			

SINGLES: (continued)

TITLE	LABEL	COUNTRY	RELEASE DATE
HELLO GOODBYE/I AM THE WALRUS	Capitol	United States	November 1967
CHRISTMAS TIME IS HERE AGAIN	Fan Club	United States	December 1967
LADY MADONNA/THE INNER LIGHT	Capitol	United States	March 1968
HEY JUDE/REVOLUTION	Apple	United States	August 1968
1968 CHRISTMAS RECORD	Fan Club	United States	December 1968
GET BACK/DON'T LET ME DOWN	Apple	United States	April 1969
THE BALLAD OF JOHN AND YOKO/ OLD BROWN SHOE	Apple	United States	June 1969
GIVE PEACE A CHANCE/REMEMBER LOVE	Apple	United States	July 1969
SOMETHING/COME TOGETHER	Apple	United States	October 1969
COLD TURKEY/DON'T WORRY KYOKO (Mummy's Only Looking For A Hand In The Snow)	Apple	United States	October 1969
THE BEATLES SEVENTH CHRISTMAS RECORD	Fan Club	United States	December 1969
INSTANT KARMA (We All Shine On)/ WHO HAS SEEN THE WIND	Apple	United States	February 1970
HEY JUDE	Apple	United States	February 1970
LET IT BE/YOU KNOW MY NAME (LOOK UP THE NUMBER)		United States	March 1970
THE LONG AND WINDING ROAD/ FOR YOU BLUE	Apple	United States	May 1970
MOTHER/WHY?	Apple	United States	December 1970
POWER TO THE PEOPLE/OPEN YOUR BOX	Apple	United Kingdom	March 1971
POWER TO THE PEOPLE/TOUCH ME	Apple	United States	March 1971
IMAGINE/IT'S SO HARD	Apple	United States	October 1971
HAPPY XMAS (WAR IS OVER)/ LISTEN, THE SNOW IS FALLING	Apple	United States	December 1971
WOMAN IS THE NIGGER OF THE WORLD/ SISTERS, O SISTERS	Apple	United States	April 1973
MIND GAMES/MEAT CITY	Apple	United States	October 1973
WHATEVER GETS YOU THRU THE NIGHT/ BEEF JERKY	Apple	*	*
NO. 9 DREAM/WHAT YOU GOT	Apple	United States	December 1974
STAND BY ME/MOVE OVER MS. L.	Apple	United States	March 1975
IMAGINE/WORKING CLASS HERO	Apple	United States	October 1975
(JUST LIKE) STARTING OVER	Geffen Records	United States	October 1980
NOBODY TOLD ME	Geffen Records	United States	*

TITLE	LABEL	COUNTRY	RELEASE DATE
EPs (EXTENDED PLAY):			
Twist and Shout	Parlophone	United Kingdom	July 1963
TWIST AND SHOUT/A TASTE OF HONEY/ DO YOU WANT TO KNOW A SECRET/THERE'S A PLACE			
The Beatles' Hits	Parlophone	United Kingdom	September 1963
FROM ME TO YOU/THANK YOU GIRL/PLEASE PLEASE ME/LOVE ME DO			
The Beatles (No.1)	Parlophone	United Kingdom	November 1963
I SAW HER STANDING THERE/MISERY/ANNA (GO TO HIM)/CHAINS			
All My Loving	Parlophone	United Kingdom	February 1964
ALL MY LOVING/ASK ME WHY/MONEY (THAT'S WHAT I WANT)/P.S. I LOVE YOU			
The Beatles	Capitol	United States	March 1964
MISERY/A TASTE OF HONEY/ASK ME WHY/ANNA (GO TO HIM)			
Four By The Beatles	Capitol	United States	May 1964
ROLL OVER BEETHOVEN/ALL MY LOVING/THIS BOY/PLEASE MR. POSTMAN			
Long Tall Sally	Parlophone	United Kingdom	June 1964
LONG TALL SALLY/I CALL YOUR NAME/SLOW DOWN/MATCHBOX			

TITLE	LABEL	COUNTRY	RELEASE DATE
EPs (EXTENDED PLAY): (continued)			
4 By The Beatles	Capitol	United States	February 1965
HONEY DON'T/I'M A LOSER/MR. MOONLIGHT/EVERYBODY'S TRYING TO BE MY BABY			
Beatles For Sale (No.2)	Parlophone	United Kingdom	June 1965
I'LL FOLLOW THE SUN/BABY'S IN BLACK/WORDS OF LOVE/I DON'T WANT TO SPOIL THE PARTY			
The Beatles' Million Sellers	Parlophone	United Kingdom	December 1965
SHE LOVES YOU/I WANT TO HOLD YOUR HAND/CAN'T BUY ME LOVE/I FEEL FINE			
Yesterday	Parlophone	United Kingdom	March 1966
YESTERDAY/ACT NATURALLY/YOU LIKE ME TOO MUCH/IT'S ONLY LOVE			
Nowhere Man	Parlophone	United Kingdom	July 1966
NOWHERE MAN/DRIVE MY CAT/MICHELLE/YOU WON'T SEE ME			

TITLE	LABEL	COUNTRY	RELEASE DATE
12 INCH MAXI SINGLES:			
GIVE PEACE A CHANCE/REMEMBER LOVE	Apple	*	*
Plastic Ono Band			
Elton John Band	Metronome Musik	Germany	*
FUNERAL FOR A FRIEND/LOVE LIES BLEEDING/	GMBH		
ROCKET MAN/BENNY AND THE JETS/TAKE ME TO THE PILOT/			
WHATEVER GETS YOU THROUGH THE NIGHT/			
LUCY IN THE SKY WITH DIAMONDS/I SAW HER STANDING THERE			
John Lennon & The Muscle Shoals Horns			
Elton John Band	Metronome Musik	Germany	*
I SAW HER STANDING THERE/WHATEVER GETS YOU	GMBH		
THROUGH THE NIGHT/LUCY IN THE SKY WITH DIAMONDS			
John Lennon & The Muscle Shoals Horns			
John Lennon Imagine	Apple	*	*
IMAGINE/IT'S SO HARD			
Plastic Ono Band			
John Lennon IMAGINE/WORKING CLASS HERO	Apple	*	*
John Lennon/Yoko Ono	Geffen Records	*	1980
(JUST LIKE) STARTING OVER/KISS KISS KISS			
John Lennon Borrowed Time	PolyGram	*	1982
(Limited Edition)			
YOU'RE THE ONE/NEVER SAY GOODBYE			
John Lennon Borrowed Time	PolyGram	*	1984
YOUR HANDS/NEVER SAY GOODBYE			
John Lennon I'm Stepping Out	PolyGram	*	1984
SLEEPLESS NIGHT/LONELINESS			

Lennon Family Tree

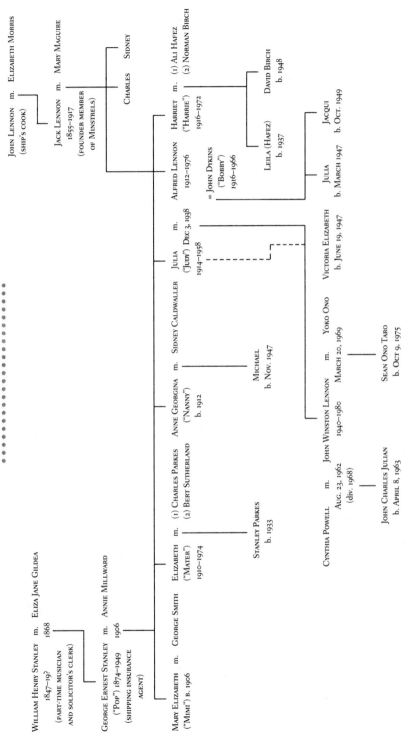

JOHN LENNON m. ELIZABETH MORRIS
(SHIP'S COOK)

JACK LENNON m. MARY MAGUIRE
1855–1917
(FOUNDER MEMBER
OF MINSTRELS)

CHARLES   SIDNEY

ALFRED LENNON   HARRIET m. (1) ALI HAFEZ
1912–1976   ("HARRIE")   (2) NORMAN BIRCH
                1916–1972

= JOHN DYKINS   DAVID BIRCH
  ("BOBBY")   b. 1948
  1916–1966

              LEILA (HAFEZ)
              b. 1937

JULIA m.   JULIA   JACQUI
("JUDY") DEC 3, 1938   b. MARCH 1947 b. OCT. 1949
1914–1958

                    VICTORIA ELIZABETH
                    b. JUNE 19, 1947

WILLIAM HENRY STANLEY m. ELIZA JANE GILDEA
1847–19?   1868
(PART-TIME MUSICIAN
AND SOLICITOR'S CLERK)

GEORGE ERNEST STANLEY m. ANNIE MILLWARD
("POP") 1874–1949   1906
(SHIPPING INSURANCE
AGENT)

MARY ELIZABETH m. GEORGE SMITH   ELIZABETH m. (1) CHARLES PARKES   ANNE GEORGINA m. SIDNEY CALDWALLER
("MIMI") B. 1906   ("MATER")   (2) BERT SUTHERLAND   ("NANNY")
                                      1910–1974   b. 1912

                                      STANLEY PARKES   MICHAEL
                                      b. 1933   b. NOV. 1947

CYNTHIA POWELL m.   JOHN WINSTON LENNON m. YOKO ONO
               AUG. 23, 1962   1940–1980   MARCH 20, 1969
               (div. 1968)

                                                  SEAN ONO TARO
                                                  b. OCT 9, 1975

JOHN CHARLES JULIAN
b. APRIL 8, 1963

Index

About the Authors

GEOFFREY GIULIANO is a top international biographer and popular culture authority whose previous books include *The Beatles: A Celebration; John Lennon: My Brother* (written with Lennon's sister, Julia Baird); *Dark Horse: The Private Life of George Harrison; Blackbird: The Unauthorized Biography of Paul McCartney; The Beatles Album: Thirty Years of Music and Memorabilia; Rod Stewart: Vagabond Heart; The Rolling Stones Album: Thirty Years of Music and Memorabilia; The Illustrated Series; Paint It Black: The Murder of Brian Jones; The Lost Beatles Interviews;* and *Behind Blue Eyes: A Life of Pete Townshend.*

In addition, Giuliano can be heard regularly on the Westwood One Radio Network, and has created a line of audio rocumentaries for Durkin Hayes Publishing, as well as a series of biographical CD boxed sets and video documentaries on various popular musicians for Laserlight Digital.

BRENDA GIULIANO is co-author of *Not Fade Away: The Rolling Stones Collection; The Illustrated Series;* and *The Lost Beatles Interviews.*